The Impact of Norms in International Society

The
IMPACT OF NORMS
in International Society

THE LATIN AMERICAN EXPERIENCE,
1881–2001

Arie M. Kacowicz

UNIVERSITY OF NOTRE DAME PRESS
NOTRE DAME, INDIANA

Copyright © 2005 by University of Notre Dame
Notre Dame, Indiana 46556
www.undpress.nd.edu
All Rights Reserved

Manufactured in the United States of America

Library of Congress Cataloging-in-Publication Data

Kacowicz, Arie Marcelo.
    The impact of norms in international society : the Latin American
experience, 1881–2001 / Arie Marcelo Kacowicz.
        p. cm.
    "From the Helen Kellogg Institute for International Studies."
    Includes bibliographical references and index.
    ISBN 0-268-03306-4 (cloth : alk. paper)
    ISBN 0-268-03307-2 (pbk. : alk. paper)
    1. Latin America—Foreign relations.   2. Pacific settlement of international
disputes.   3. Normativity (Ethics)   4. Social norms.   5. International
relations—Moral and ethical aspects.   I. Helen Kellogg Institute for International
Studies.   II. Title.
JZ1519.K33   2005
327.8'009'04—dc22

                                                              2005004878

∞ *This book is printed on acid-free paper.*

This book was written under the auspices of

The Leonard Davis Institute for International Relations,
Hebrew University of Jerusalem

The Helen Kellogg Institute for International Studies,
University of Notre Dame

and

The Joan Kroc Institute of International Peace Studies,
University of Notre Dame

To the memory of
Tzvika Golombek and Moshe (Mesh) Yedid-Levi

CONTENTS

TABLES

A FEW YEARS AGO, IN MY BOOK *ZONES OF PEACE IN THE THIRD WORLD*, I presented nine alternative explanations for the maintenance of peace in two regions of the developing world: South America since 1883 and West Africa since the early 1960s. Among those explanations, a common cultural framework and normative consensus on conflict management encompassed a Grotian approach by assuming the existence of an international society with common norms, rules, and institutions. In this book I focus on that particular explanation (a regional normative framework) and its relevance to understanding the reality of Latin American international politics.

Back in April 1994 I had a thrilling conversation with Professor Emanuel Adler in a coffee shop in Madison, Wisconsin. Both Emanuel (a native of Montevideo, Uruguay) and I (a *porteño*, a native of Buenos Aires, Argentina) felt very proud about the illustrious record of the Latin American region in general, and South America in particular, in dealing with territorial disputes and international conflicts in a peaceful fashion. Perhaps there was "something" particular, unique, and peculiar about Latin America? Something worthy of a serious study, against the background of less fortunate regions like the Middle East?

So, after completing *Zones of Peace* and co-editing, about four years ago, a volume on stable peace in international relations, I began in earnest to research the Latin American case, within a more general framework of the normative dimension of international relations. The result is this book, which addresses the problems of identifying international norms and their relevance and impact upon the behavior of states in the international society in a regional context. The research traces several norms of peace and security and examines their impact in Latin America over the last 120 years (1881–2001). By suggesting a synthesis between positivist and constructivist approaches, I identify those norms through their formal development in terms of international law and their "translation" into actual state behavior and regional institutionalization in Latin America.

During 1997–1998 I was very fortunate to spend my sabbatical year at the University of Notre Dame, affiliated simultaneously with the Kroc Institute of International Peace Studies, the Kellogg Institute for International Studies, and the Department of Government. Inspired by a setting that combined Latin American and peace studies, I started my research and writing at Notre Dame, benefiting from the comments and suggestions of many students as well as faculty fellows and friends, including first and foremost Alan Dowty, Michael Francis, Robert Johansen, George Lopez, Scott Mainwaring, Raimo Väyrynen, Ithai Stern, Guillermo O'Donnell, George Lopez, Robert Fischman, Jorge Vargas-Cullell, Miguel Gutierrez-Saxe, Marcia Stephenson, and Gustavo Gallón. The staff of the Kellogg Institute in particular helped me to gather primary sources, through the expert hands of Vonda Polega and Scott J. Van Jacob, and with the help of Martha Sue Abbott and Judy Bartlett.

Several friends and colleagues from the Department of International Relations and the Faculty of Social Science at the Hebrew University suggested useful comments and insights, including especially Yael Krispin and Shlomo Griner, who read the entire manuscript and offered me invaluable comments; Emanuel Adler, who has always been a model and a source of inspiration; and Galia Bar-Nathan, Eitan Barak, Orit Gal, Moshe Abalo, Edy Kaufman, Luis Roniger, Mario Schnajder, Micha Bar, Korina Kagan, Moshe Hirsch, Noam Kochavi, Avraham Sela, and Oded Lowenheim. In addition, I want to thank other colleagues and friends, including Micha Bar, Gabriel Elad, Nicholas Onuf, Patrick James, Gordon Mace, Rut Diamint, Kjell Goldmann, Michael Doyle, Kathryn Sikkink, Michael Barnett, Carlos Moneta, José Paradiso, and Jeanne Hey. During my last sabbatical year at Georgetown University I was fortunate to present parts of the manuscript at the Center for Latin American Studies, the Center for Peace and Security Studies, and the Department of Government, so I want to express my gratitude to Robert Lieber, Arthuro Valenzuela, Michael Brown, and Salomon Bergman. In addition, I am grateful to many other students and faculty who criticized some of my arguments in papers presented at the Department of International Relations in Jerusalem, my Fall seminars about the International Relations of Latin America, and at the ISA and the APSA Annual Meetings. I am particularly thankful to the Leonard Davis Institute for International Relations for its support and sponsorship from the inception to the production of the book, especially its former directors Dr. Sasson Sofer and Professor Yaacov Bar-Siman-Tov, as well as its unique staff, especially Sharon Yakin-Mazar, the staff of the Harry S Truman Institute Library, and the precious research assistance of Lea Gedalia and of Michal Lewin-Epstein, who helped me to compile the difficult tables for chapter 6. As always, my wife Orly has been critical and pointed in making this work more readable and consistent. As for our three children, Itai encouraged me to write and complete this book, while Ela, whose age overlaps with that of this project, seems to be very happy that I am done with it. Elior's recent arrival coincided with the last stages of the revision of the book and its production, bringing the joy of a new baby and overruling that of a new book. The transformation of the manuscript into a book has been possible under the auspices of the University of Notre Dame Press and the warm support and encouragement of its former associate director, Jeffrey Gainey; Barbara Hanrahan, the current director; Rebecca DeBoer, the managing editor; and Nancy Dziedzic, the precious book editor.

As with the intriguing (and more thrilling) book by Julio Cortázar, *Rayuela* (1979), the potential reader can find here three paths for his or her reading. The book can be read from chapter 1 through chapter 6, in the usual way. Alternatively, those interested in the theoretical and general aspects of international norms can read chapters 1 and 2, browse chapter 3, and get quickly to chapter 6. Finally, students of Latin American issues will probably focus on chapters 3 through 5 and find there a wealth of empirical material. Parts of chapter 3 have been previously published in my article "Latin America as an International Society," which appeared in *International Politics* in June 2000 (vol. 37, no. 2), copyright © Palgrave Macmillan. I am grateful to the publishers for allowing me to use the material for this book.

The writing of the manuscript was completed in the last three years, since the fatidic date of September 11, 2001. Parts of the book were redacted and typed at my home in Gilo, an Israeli neighborhood in Southern Jerusalem a half mile away from Palestinian Bet-Lehem, in the academic year 2001–2002. Exposed to the sporadic shots of Palestinian snipers, I experienced my own surrealistic "normative dissonance" between the general optimistic tone and morale of this book dealing with peace and security in Latin America and the absurd and tragic reality of the Israeli-Palestinian conflict. Furthermore, I dedicate this book to the memory of two Israeli youngsters who were killed in two different terrorist attacks in Jerusalem in August and December 2001. Tzvika Golombek was a former senior student of mine in the seminar on Latin American international relations. Captivated by the Latin American magic, he wanted to explore the civil war of Colombia, not being aware that *la violencia* could reach him at a pizzeria in Jerusalem. Moshe

Yedid-Levi was my nineteen-year-old neighbor from the apartment below us, a serious and diligent young man, a real *mentch* who stood out in our neighborhood for his joy and politeness. I hope that this book will honor their memory and somehow contribute to make norms more relevant for the study and practice of international relations. Perhaps we can learn from the Latin American experience and extrapolate from it in our search to find a rational and moral solution to the virulent conflict in the Middle East.

A. K., Jerusalem, Summer 2004

The Normative Dimension of International Relations

THIS BOOK EXPLORES THE STUDY OF INTERNATIONAL NORMS BY SUGGESTING several different perspectives and foundations for a much-needed dialogue on the normative dimension of international politics. In this book I examine alternative approaches to international relations that partially overlap with constructivism and might be equally effective in the *empirical* study of international norms, such as international law and the Grotian approach to international relations (the so-called English school of international relations). I suggest that while the definition of international norms presupposes a shared or intersubjective social reality, one does not have to be an *explicit* constructivist scholar in order to study and examine international norms.

This book addresses the problem of identifying international norms and assessing their impact on the behavior of states in the international society within a regional context. My general assumption is that norms do indeed matter, by registering the "oughts" of society and by reflecting what people do or want to do (Legro 1997, 31; Barkun 1964, 128–29). The research traces several international norms of peace and security and their impact in Latin America in the last 120 years. I identify international norms through their formal development in terms of international law, and their translation into actual state behavior and regional institutionalization in Latin America, including the interaction among states and other nonstate international actors.

A vast body of literature in the social sciences in general and in political science and international relations in particular addresses the subject of social norms. It includes the war convention; the democratic peace; the long peace; alliance dynamics; and international regimes (Raymond 1997, 208–13). However, this literature is disparate and not sufficiently systematic. To rearrange this literature in a logical sequence, two distinctions are warranted, philosophical and epistemological.

Philosophical distinctions. Norms can be considered moral (ethical) artifacts, stressing their deontological character; or social and legal conventions, emphasizing their utilitarian character. In other words, norms may or may not emphasize an ethical condition.[1]

Epistemological distinctions. According to a rationalist or positivist logic, international norms are social institutions subordinated to the actors' interests, as in the case of international regimes. Positivists share a clear disadvantage in studying international norms, since it is difficult (though not impossible) to be a positivist and at the same time to study social facts such as norms, since they rely heavily on methodological individualism.[2] Norms are rules, identifiable as such on linguistic grounds. If you cannot state it, it is not a norm. Thus, mental states and cognitive dispositions are not necessarily norms. If norms are considered elusive and invisible as opposed to material facts, it is because they are informal.[3] Alternatively, international norms can be *understood* according to a constructivist approach, positing a more interactive, intersubjective relationship among norms, actors, and interests. For the purposes of this book, I will refer equally to both positivist and post-positivist approaches to the study of norms, in order to avoid the "excessive epistemologism" that has infected the discipline in the last decade. One should get about explaining, with all the tools and perspectives that can fit, actual regularities in as rigorous a way as possible, and then prescribe as systematically and persuasively as we can, without paying too much attention to the different "isms" and the futile metatheoretical and epistemological debates.[4]

Despite the existence of a booming industry in international relations that has established empirical and even causal links between specific norms and international behavior (such as "democratic peace"), this literature is underdeveloped with respect to theoretical formulations of international norms (How do they originate and why? How do they evolve and why?), and even more in the empirical testing of their impact and evolution. Only a few exceptions can be mentioned.

Gary Goertz (1994), for example, in an intriguing study on contexts of international politics, has elaborated a "pre-theory" of international norms and tested it in the context of decolonization. Similarly, Judith Goldstein and Robert O. Keohane (1993) edited a stimulating volume on the role of ideas in the framing of foreign policy, geared more toward the empirical evidence than toward a strict theoretical formulation (in which ideas and norms are close relatives, but not twins). In the last decade several scholars in the constructivist school addressed theoretical issues regarding the origins and influence of norms in the international society, including Audie Klotz (1995), Martha Finnemore (1996), Emanuel Adler (1997), John Ruggie (1998), and the edited volumes by Peter Katzenstein on the culture of national security (1996) and Emanuel Adler and Michael Barnett (1998) on security communities. Moreover, there is an important legalist/constructivist tradition to the study of norms in international relations, initiated by Kratochwil (1989) and Onuf (1989), which transcend the English school because of the latter's limitation to norms in the international society and the lack of reference to agents as actors.

Yet there is a further need in this literature to build bridges between the philosophical, legal, and theoretical discussion of the role of international norms and the empirical evidence of their actual impact on the international society. We should focus on more practical, or empirically oriented, approaches to the study of international norms: international ethics, international law, and, in more general terms, the Grotian approach to international relations. From a neo-Grotian perspective, a plausible synthesis between positivism and constructivism can be elaborated, one that focuses upon international law and the empirical evidence on the impact of norms and institutions upon the behavior of states. This neo-Grotian model assesses and traces the origins and impact of norms of peace in the Latin American context, as one of the alternative explanations for the relative lack of international wars in South America after 1885 (Kacowicz 1998).

In empirical terms, one of the major problems we face in the study of international norms is identifying their effects on the behavior of states in international society in general and in a regional context in particular. I contend in this book that international norms can be recognized as a distinctive phenomenon in international relations separated from the actors' self-interests. Furthermore, norms do make a difference to the quality of life in the international society, and this impact can be empirically assessed.

The Argument and the Evidence

The main argument of this book is that norms can be considered as an independent and dynamic factor that affects the quality of international society. This thesis stems from three basic assumptions: (1) The existence and persistence of international norms assumes the reality of an international (or regional) society (Waalkes 1997, 2); (2) These international norms are expressed, empirically, through social practices and institutions, such as instruments of international law; and (3) International norms of peace and security do make a difference in the foreign and domestic policies of the member-states of that society.

Accordingly, the three research questions formulated in the book are: (1) Where do international norms come from? (2) Under what conditions can regional norms impact or influence the political behavior of states? and (3) What is the impact of norms on the domestic and foreign behavior of states in any given region? I will emphasize particularly the second and third questions, generalizing on the basis of the Latin American diplomatic history of the 120 years to the rest of the world.

To pursue the research questions and to prove the claims stated above, the empirical chapters of the book refer to several basic norms of peace and security that have affected the action of the Latin American international society in the years under study. These norms include *uti possidetis* (the recognition of former colonial borders); peaceful settlement of international disputes; respect for sovereignty and territorial integrity; nonintervention; self-determination; *convivencia* (peaceful coexistence); *concertación* (consensus-seeking); arms control and disarmament; nonproliferation and CBMs (confidence-building measures). In the domestic realm, one could add political democracy and the respect for human rights as well-recognized (if not always followed-upon) norms. This cluster of regional norms has affected the politics of the region, both domestically and internationally, in several distinctive ways. It is clear that the very existence of norms having to do with restraining or avoiding war and sustaining peace might be prima facie evidence for a regional predisposition toward achieving these very ends, as articulated, expressed, and translated into instruments of international law. For instance, the "long South American peace" since 1883, the attempts of economic and political regional integration and coordination, the focus on domestic conflicts and civil wars, the rigidity of international borders, the plurality of political regimes (until the 1980s), the lack of claims of self-determination, the persistence of international disputes without escalation to war, and the reduction of international conflicts can all be linked directly or indirectly to those international norms of peace and security. Similarly, the "transitional" character of former authoritarian regimes (until the 1980s), the "deepening" of regional peace in the 1990s, the schemes of integration, cooperation, and the contagion or "domino effect" (in Spanish, *la moda*) of democratization can be also attributed to the formal norms of legalism, political liberalism, democratization, and respect for human rights in the region. The impact of international norms on Latin American politics is summarized in Table 1.1.

This normative impact has been uneven and indeterminate across a large set of interstate cases of territorial disputes in Latin America that have ranged

Table 1.1. The Impact of International Norms on Latin American Politics

International Norms of Peace and Security	Impact on International Society and Domestic Politics
peaceful settlement *convivencia* *concertación* *uti possidetis* sovereignty and nonintervention territorial integrity	long South American peace attempts at regional integration focus on domestic conflicts focus on civil wars rigidity of international borders plurality of political regimes no claims of self-determination persistence of international disputes, without escalation to war attempts at regional coordination
arms control and disarmament confidence-building measures (CBMs) nonproliferation collective security comprehensive, mutual security	reduction of international conflicts long South American peace focus on domestic conflicts
legalism political liberalism democratization	transitional nature of authoritarianism deepening of regional peace schemes of integration political (regional) cooperation "domino effect" of democratization concern and respect for human rights

from "successes" (peaceful resolutions of interstate conflicts) through "mixed cases" (peaceful settlements following long-deadlocked and armed conflicts) up to "failures" (wars). The two major empirical chapters of the book (chapters 4 and 5) cover such a range of eleven cases from 1881 to the present (see Table 1.2 for the list of cases).

Table 1.2. Case Studies

Case	Parties	Norms	Result
Misiones (1858–1898)	Argentina/Brazil	peaceful settlement arbitration *uti possidetis*	success (peaceful outcome)
Tacna-Arica (1883–1929)	Chile/Peru arbitration (failed)	peaceful settlement sovereignty self-determination territorial integrity	eventual success (mixed results)
Chaco Boreal (1906–1938)	Bolivia/ Paraguay	peaceful settlement sovereignty *uti possidetis* mediation territorial integrity	failure (war)
Leticia dispute (1932–1934)	Colombia/ Peru	peaceful settlement sovereignty *uti possidetis* territorial integrity nonintervention	eventual success (no escalation to war); mixed results
Oriente/Mainas (1828–1998)	Peru/ Ecuador	peaceful settlement sovereignty *uti possidetis* territorial integrity	failure (successive rounds of war: 1941, 1981, 1995); negotiations and finally success (peace) in 1998
Beagle Channel (1847–1984)	Argentina/ Chile	peaceful settlement arbitration (failed) *uti possidetis* sovereignty territorial integrity	failure (rejection of arbitration), followed by military crisis, mediation, and negotiations; peace in 1984
demilitarization of Magellan Strait (1881)	Argentina/ Chile	peaceful settlement arms control	success

Table 1.2. Case Studies (*cont.*)

Case	Parties	Norms	Result
Mayo Pacts (1902)	Argentina/ Chile	peaceful settlement arms control disarmament	success (but ephemeral, only five years)
Tlatelolco Treaty (since 1967)	almost all Latin American states	arms control disarmament nonproliferation	eventual success
nuclear cooperation (since 1979)	Argentina/ Brazil	arms control disarmament nonproliferation democratization	eventual success
Contadora/ Esquipulas (since 1984)	Central American states, "Group of Eight," and Rio Group	peaceful settlement mediation nonintervention sovereignty *concertación* arms control CBMs disarmament democratization mutual security	initial failure, but eventual success in the early 1990s

Although there is an emerging consensus about the importance of norms in leading to different and alternative outcomes, it is not clear what their *relative* impact is and *under what conditions* they do impact. For example, we should recognize that the outbreak of war (or the maintenance of peace) ought not to be directly related to international norms; war (or peace) can be achieved by a host of other reasons and alternative explanations (Johnson 1991, 303). However, norms are an important part of the "story" to be told in this book, though their effects are difficult to gauge empirically and should be studied alongside other economic, political, and international factors, usually collapsed under the rubric of "interests." Yet this distinction between "norms" and "interests" is analytical rather than substantial; in the "real world" those two are blurred and interconnected. Hence, we should change our focus of inquiry from metatheoretical debates back to problem-oriented and real-life issues, recognizing that *both* norms and interests impinge upon and affect international behavior. By demonstrating that norms of peace and security are independent, rather than intervening, variables, I claim that norms sustain substantial policy relevance for the formulation and implementation of foreign policies in the contemporary international system.

The Ubiquitousness of Norms in International Relations

Norms are everywhere, but nowhere in the material sense. They are complicated and ambiguous to study due to their ubiquitousness in terms of international law, international ethics, and "normal" practices and behavior. Under the rubric of "the normative dimension of international relations" we mean the *normative* (i.e., ethical, moral) considerations of what ought to be the prescriptive guiding rules for a peaceful and better international order. At the same time, we also mean the *positive* (or *positivist*) description and analysis of how norms originate, develop, impact, and decay, for instance, in terms of positive international law (Tannenwald 1992, 9). It is not easy to reconcile and link those two different, sometimes contrasting, categories.

What is the nature of the complex relationship between international rules and morality? What moral quality, if any, imbues international norms and rules? A partial answer to these complicated questions can be obtained through the analysis of the mutual relationship between international law and international ethics. First, international law can be a source as well as an object of ethical judgments. Second, international morality might determine the general direction for the development of international law, though that is not always the case. Third, portions of modern international law are strongly concerned with the ethical aspects ("oughts") of the international system (see Nardin 1992, 19; Kelsen 1942, 38; Jones 1992, 58). Hence, there is an inextricable and mutual relationship between the two, as pillars of international society and as different and complementary authoritative practices that constrain the pursuit of different purposes (Nardin 1983, ix).

Normative issues in international relations include questions relating to the causes and conduct of war, nuclear weapons, use of force, international terrorism, intervention, self-determination, refugees, secession, distributive justice, ecology, international organizations, supranational authorities, and human rights (among other subjects) (see Frost 1996, 76–77).

An initial list or inventory of basic or constitutive legal principles of international society might include the following norms: the sovereign equality of states, the territorial integrity and political independence of states, nonintervention in the affairs of other states, good faith (which includes the principle of *pacta sunt servanda,* respect for treaties), the self-determination of peoples, prohibition on the threat or use of force, peaceful settlement of disputes, respect for human rights, and international cooperation (Kocs 1994, 539). Similarly, Dorothy Jones (1989) ennumerates a "code of peace," a series of agreed-upon norms in international society that includes all those norms mentioned above, in addition to the most recent norms of distributive justice, including the commitment to economic development and protection of the environment (see also Jones 1992, 44–45). A common theme running through these norms is that relations between states in the international community ought to be *peaceful.* Peace is the desired norm. States are not to use or threaten to use force, and they are supposed to settle disputes peacefully (Jones 1992, 47; see also Franck 1995, 135). This code of peace represents an evolving consensus on ethical principles that serve as the normative foundation of international relations, at the convergence between international law and international ethics. This is particularly relevant for the international relations among democracies (i.e., "democratic peace"), which fit into the category of "stable peace" or a "pluralistic security community," according to which states not only do not fight each other, but do not expect or significantly prepare to fight each other (see Russett 1993, 42; Kacowicz and Bar-Siman-Tov 2000, 15–17; Risse-Kappen 1995, 492).

The list of international norms does not end here. There are many other norms that can be catalogued as well, such as decolonization (Jackson 1993); the preservation of the society of states; anti-imperialism; balance of power; patriotism; protecting the interests of a state's citizens; collective security; democratization; free trade; and abolition of slavery (Frost 1996, 111–12; Nadelman 1990). Moreover, not all the norms enumerated have to be necessarily "good" or desirable ones. Thus, social norms can prescribe ethically reprehensible behavior—such as slavery or violence—as well as charity and kindness (Finnemore 1996, 32). Paradoxically, despite this impressive list of items, the normative dimension of international relations, especially in its ethical applications, has tended to be neglected as subject matter for research. Even the renewed attention to the study of international norms in the last decade, brought about by constructivist scholars in their attempt to separate the concept of norms from its practical institutionalization in formal organizations, has usually overlooked the ethical aspects of norms. In the next sections

I explain in general terms the characteristics of Latin America as an international society, indicate the eclectic methodology chosen for this study, and briefly present the contents of the book.

The Latin American Experience, 1881–2001

To illustrate the impact of international norms in a regional setting, the empirical research focuses on the example of the Latin American international society. Kalevi Holsti (1993, 19) argues that the Latin American countries, through a long historical and learning process, have managed to establish a unique normative system of a Latin "diplomatic culture" that has helped their governments to resolve many of their international conflicts short of war. Since gaining independence in the early nineteenth century, the Latin American countries have gradually built up a sophisticated and highly developed system of regional international law and institutions, including a series of regional norms that have regulated their international and domestic behavior. The Latin American nations, especially in South America, have succeeded in developing a theory and practice of Latin American exceptionalism regarding their recourse to international law—through arbitration of disputes, mediation, bilateral negotiations, and other techniques for the peaceful settlement of international disputes, rather than the use of force. It should be pointed out, however, that this normative and legal reluctance to engage in war against fellow Latin American nations never implied the lack of serious interstate disputes throughout the entire region. Moreover, the contrast between great internal violence and instability in Latin American politics and its relatively benign and civilized international relations discloses a puzzling paradox that has to be addressed as well.

The norms and principles of international law adopted by this regional society since independence include sovereignty, equality of states, and nonintervention; *uti possidetis* (recognition of the former colonial borders) and territorial integrity; peaceful settlement of international disputes, including the principles of peaceful international coexistence (*convivencia*) and consensus-seeking (*concertación*); arms control, disarmament, and collective security; and political legalism and commitment to democracy and the protection of human rights.[5]

It is clear that these norms have been interrelated both logically and in historical terms. The core of the Latin American legalist tradition has been a very formalistic and sophisticated corpus of legal norms enhancing the norm of sovereignty and the principle of nonintervention. From that core derived a series of norms regarding international (intraregional) relations in the areas of peace and security, such as *convivencia,* peaceful settlement of international disputes, *uti possidetis,* and the prohibition of nuclear weapons and nonproliferation. In addition, a social/economic norm of *desarrollismo* ("developmentalism," or right to develop) derived from the will to shape a real content to the formal concept of sovereignty. Finally, the norm of commitment to political democracy and democratization is part and parcel of the same very long tradition of political legalism and preference for the rule of law, at least at the formal level, despite the relatively long periods of bureaucratic-authoritarian regimes in the Southern Cone of Latin America (e.g., Argentina, 1966–1973 and 1976–1983; Brazil, 1964–1984; Chile, 1973–1989; and Uruguay, 1973–1983).

In more specific terms, three clear influences can be traced from these common norms on the international relations of the region: (1) Regional norms and institutions have contributed to the maintenance of the "long peace" in South America since 1883; (2) They have reshaped the definition of state interests in terms of their foreign relations; (3) In some cases they have moved and "upgraded" already existing peaceful relations in Latin America in the direction of a pluralistic security community. There are several examples of the impact of this normative framework:

- Between 1851 and 1922 at least fourteen peaceful cessions and exchanges of territory related to territorial disputes took place in South America. Eight of these cases were resolved following arbitration and the rest through direct negotiations, good offices, and mediation. Moreover, the Latin American nations seem to have preferred the continuation of the status quo, even if it led to continuing tensions, rather than escalating their disputes into full-scale wars.
- Norms of peaceful settlement and *convivencia* have had a restraining effect in the direction of de-escalation and resolution of international conflicts and civil wars. This has been evident in the cases of the Leticia dispute in 1932–1934 (between Peru and Colombia); the resolution of the Beagle Channel crisis of 1978 and the subsequent negotiations between Argentina and Chile (1979–1984); the regional initiatives of Contadora (1983–1986) and Esquipulas (1987) to peacefully resolve the civil wars in El Salvador and Nicaragua; and, more recently, the final and peaceful resolution of the long conflict between Peru and Ecuador in October 1998.
- In the Southern Cone of South America the return to democracy in Argentina (1983), Brazil (1985), and Chile (1989) has clearly affected and

"upgraded" the quality of the peace among these three countries and the level of *rapprochement* and security cooperation between Argentina and Brazil since 1985, and between Argentina and Chile since 1990.

In sum, the effects of these regional norms on Latin American politics can be considered both constitutive and regulative, both shaping interests and identities and reflecting them. Moreover, the effects have had a "double" or combined impact, both domestic and international, or what might be called *intermestic.* The norms themselves have also an intermestic origin and impact, deriving from both the domestic and the international arenas. After all, it is only through their (domestic) internalization within the different Latin American states, and their institutionalization at bilateral and multilateral levels, that these norms have become effective, if at all.

Considering the fact that most of the time most of the Latin American political regimes *have not* been democratic (with the exceptions of Chile, Uruguay, and Costa Rica), it is quite striking to observe that norms of peace and security have flourished in a regional system characterized by authoritarian regimes (until the 1980s). In other words, the Latin American experience has proved that nondemocratic states can share some of the normative perspectives and institutional restraints that characterize democracies. In this sense, Latin American international regional society has been a successful Grotian laboratory to test the presence, effect, and impact of regional norms.

Methodology and Preview of the Book

How Should We Study International Norms?

Assuming that norms are a dynamic and elusive phenomena, which have a certain, though undetermined, effect and impact on foreign policy and international relations, how should we study them? What is the empirical evidence for the impact of norms? How do we know that norms are not an ideal or idealistic personification of egoistic interests?

Sometimes we have only circumstantial evidence for the existence of a given norm. For instance, if we find a regulative norm, somewhere there should also be the "parent" constitutive, formative norm.[6] Where should we look for the latter? My suggestion is to shy away from the methodological/ formal traps of an obscure post-positivist language (or "discourse"), while accepting many of its metatheoretical and epistemological claims regarding the importance of norms and identity, which actually derive and overlap with the older English school of international relations. Hence, adopting a Grotian (or so-called neo-Grotian) approach for the study of international norms implies accepting the basic framework of international law, a recognition of the existence of ethics in international affairs, and a positivist and empiricist focus on the practical, real, down-to-earth manifestations of this normative dimension.

The preliminary answer(s) to the question "How do we recognize a relevant international norm when we actually see one?" reads, then, as follows:

1. *Through written recognition,* such as reading documents of international law.
2. *Norms are embedded in formal institutions.* Norms become institutionalized through multilateral mechanisms of cooperation involving states and other actors in the international society.
3. *Norms are part of customs and practices,* as evidenced formally in international law and in the formation of several international regimes, and practically in the behavior and practices of states. That behavior relates, refutes, or corroborates the prescribed norm(s).

The three methodological rules presented above lead us to focus the research on international norms upon their empirical evidence, through the analysis of international law and practices. This is a demanding and challenging theoretical and methodological exercise, since we should beware of counterfactual claims here. It is very difficult to assess and measure norms when they are working "normally." We usually do not look at the norm-conforming behavior, but rather at the exceptional cases of disruption of "normal" normative behavior. Yet no single counterfactual occurrence necessarily refutes the existence of any given norm. Thus, even when a norm is violated, that does not mean it is insignificant, or that it does not have any political effect at all. In that case, we still need the insights of a more sociological/interpretative approach, whether this is found in a neo-Grotian perspective or in more recent constructivist explorations. In any case, we cannot study empirically international norms without knowing the relevant context, including the specific instruments of international law, and at least being aware of its ethical ("normative") dimension.

Methodology

Three complementary research methods (or methodologies) are used in this book, in order to test the impact of international norms in a regional perspective:

First, I employ an interpretative method, based upon an intersubjective analysis of the social reality by the actors themselves, involved in a certain, specific, historical context. This discourse can be traced through documents, statements, treaties, and autobiographies.

Second, I use a qualitative content analysis of the international norms that have been "translated" into legal instruments of international law and into formal institutions and organizations in a regional context (here, the Latin American institutions).

Third, I provide a historical analysis of the political behavior (essentially, foreign policy) of several states in a certain region of the world (here, Latin America) throughout a long period of time, according to certain norms of peace and security.

These three methods are logically intertwined and applied simultaneously through a comparative approach of several international norms throughout the perusal of eleven cases of interstate (and, in the case of Central America, also intrastate) interactions, mainly territorial disputes. The cases cover the period from the neutralization of the Magellan Strait in 1881 to the more recent incorporation of Argentina, Chile, and Brazil into the Tlatelolco regime of a nuclear-weapons-free zone in 1994 and the nuclear cooperation between Argentina and Brazil in the 1990s and into the twenty-first century. They range from "successes" (peaceful settlements) through "mixed successes" (peaceful settlement only after protracted and violent conflicts) through "failures" (war and/or stagnation).

Preview of the Book

Chapter 2 ("A Framework for the Study of International Norms") suggests a theoretical model (or framework) to study and understand the impact of international norms, both in general and in a regional perspective. I define and classify international norms and analyze their importance according to different philosophical approaches. I then examine the genealogy and evolution of international norms (Where do they come from? How do they evolve?). The bulk of the chapter focuses on the impact of international norms: Do norms have an impact on the quality of life in the international society? How do norms affect the foreign policies of individual countries in a given region, and the intraregional international relations? Under what conditions?

Chapter 3 ("Latin America as an International Society") presents the case of Latin America in general terms. After defining the main elements of any international society, I identify the historical background and the elements of

Latin American society in particular, tracing the movements of Bolivarianism versus Panamericanism and the role of the United States in defining the Latin American identity. This chapter introduces the regional international law and the relevant norms of peace and security. Furthermore, I answer the questions formulated in the theoretical framework: Where do norms come from in Latin America? How do they evolve over time? What has been the impact of international norms of peace and security on the domestic and foreign policies of the Latin American states?

Chapter 4 ("Norms of Peace") focuses on the norms of peaceful settlement and *uti possidetis*. It presents a general assessment of their impact in Latin America, especially at the international level. Most of the chapter deals with the following case studies: Misiones, 1858–1898 (between Argentina and Brazil); Tacna and Arica, 1883–1929 (between Peru and Chile); Chaco Boreal, 1906–1938 (between Bolivia and Paraguay); the Leticia dispute, 1932–1934 (between Colombia and Peru); the Oriente/Mainas dispute, 1828–1998 (between Peru and Ecuador); and the Beagle Channel dispute, 1847–1984 (between Argentina and Chile).

Chapter 5 ("Norms of Security") focuses on the norms of arms control and disarmament, demilitarization, neutralization, CBMs, collective security, and comprehensive and mutual security. The bulk of the chapter analyzes and compares five cases: the demilitarization of the Magellan Strait in 1881 (between Argentina and Chile); the Mayo Pacts of 1902 (between Argentina and Chile); the evolution of the nuclear nonproliferation regional regime of Tlatelolco (creation of a nuclear-weapons-free zone) since 1967; the security cooperation between Argentina and Brazil in the 1980s and 1990s; and the peace initiatives of Contadora (1983–1986) and Esquipulas (1987) to resolve the Central American civil wars.

Finally, chapter 6 ("Latin American Norms in a Comparative Perspective") infers patterns about the impact of international norms reflecting successes, failures, and "mixed cases" in the Latin American region. Did these norms make a difference for the international relations of the region, if at all? What has been their significance? I briefly compare the impact of norms in Latin America to other regions of the world, including North America, Western Europe, Africa, the Middle East, South Asia, Southeast Asia, and East Asia. On a theoretical level, I criticize both positivism (realism and neoliberalism) and constructivism, offering instead a plea for the adoption of a neo-Grotian approach to the study of international relations through international law. On a policy level, I recommend the transcendence of the (false) dichotomy between norms and interests.

CHAPTER TWO

A Framework for the Study
of International Norms

A GROWING BODY OF EVIDENCE UNDERSCORES THE IMPORTANCE AND
autonomy of norms in world politics, including the contribution of international law to the study of norms (Raymond 1997, 206). And yet we do not
know how, precisely, norms do affect the behavior of states. For instance, how
do we differentiate between norms and interests? How can we recognize a
norm when we see one?

Definition and Classification of International Norms

International norms (and norms in general) pose serious analytical problems
because of their elusive nature, in contrast to more clear concepts of rational
choice. In the first place, it is important to draw distinctions among ideas,
norms, and ideologies, and between norms and institutions. Norms are social
institutions by definition, while ideas and ideologies create or wish to create
norms. While ideas can be assessed on a subjective, personal basis, norms are
intersubjective by definition, to the extent that they are a *social,* collective phenomenon. In the second place, there is a myriad of definitions of norms and
of international norms, which converge according to different philosophical
traditions and theoretical approaches, as explained below.

From a *constructivist* perspective, norms are considered as *a set of collective
expectations regarding the proper behavior of states (and other actors), in a given context*

or identity. In this sense, norms are directly related to collective identities. They either define or constitute identities, prescribe or regulate behavior, or they do both (Katzenstein 1996, 5). The expectations expressed by international norms pertain to a proper action by states and other nonstate actors. In other words, norms communicate injunctions that prescribe certain actions but proscribe others (Kegley and Raymond 1990, 14).[1]

From a *positivist* perspective, norms are defined as *standards of behavior, defined in terms of rights and obligations* (Krasner 1982, 186). Norms act as rules, standards, or patterns for action, guiding us on what to do and how to do it, irrespective of moral considerations (Onuf 1998). In this sense, norms are general prescriptions of behavior, which regulate intentions and effects. They act as communication devices, expressing expectations about behavior that in turn reflect normative beliefs. In this way, they are guides that direct the expression of social behavior (see Thomson 1993, 74; Kratochwil 1989, 88; Kegley and Raymond 1986, 214).

From an *ethical* perspective, norms can be defined as *moral prescriptions*. In other words, theories of justice and rights express themselves through moral or ethical norms of behavior, assuming the possibility of moral choice. In this sense, deontological criteria define and justify norms and normative action. According to McElroy (1992, 31), a moral norm can be defined as "a behavioral prescription that is universal in the claims it makes and that involves a consideration of the effects of the actors' action on others, not from the point of view of the actors' own interest, but from the point of view of the others' interests." Thus, moral norms encompass prescribed guides for behavior and action that are recognized on a universal and altruistic basis, and entail a collective evaluation of behavior in terms of what ought to be done.[2]

From a *sociological* perspective, norms imply *normal practices in the international system:* what the normal, usual, and customary practices are. Whether these practices reflect normative beliefs, habit, fear, or acquiescence to leadership is a separate analytical issue (Thomson 1993, 67). According to this definition, a distinction can be drawn between the moral and nonmoral aspects of norms. Hence, whether norms reflect an ethical perspective or not, they always define for us what are considered to be "normal practices" or "standard behavior." Thus, practices may be considered "normal" simply because no one questions their utility, legitimacy, or morality.

From a *rational choice* perspective, norms act as a *sanction system*. According to Axelrod (1986, 1097), "a norm exists in a given social setting to the extent that individuals usually act in a certain way and are often punished when seen not to be acting in this way." According to this definition, the extent to which a given type of action is considered a norm depends on how often the action is taken and how often someone is punished for not taking it. The assumption here is that in social systems—such as the international society—violations of norms, rules, and customs are sanctioned. Interestingly, we can find here a convergence between the ethical perspective and a rational choice approach to norms.

Finally, in terms of *international law*, international norms *regulate the mutual behavior of states, as specific subjects of international law* (Kelsen 1942, 115). International law is considered law to the extent that it incorporates some form of a coercive order, by attaching certain coercive acts (sanctions) to certain facts. From this perspective, this definition encompasses many other aspects that were mentioned above, such as collective expectations, standards of behavior, moral prescriptions, normal practices, and a sanction system.

To sum up, different approaches and perspectives offer a variety of definitions of norms and international norms. They all include shared or collective notions, as "social facts," though they are not necessarily universal. Norms might be linked to a shared set of expectations, standards of behavior, rules, moral prescriptions, sanctions, and law. For the purposes of my research, all the definitions can be useful since they tend to converge and overlap, with my predilection for the positivist, sociological, and international law variants. Moreover, we should be aware of the different philosophical and methodological approaches that underlie these alternative definitions.

Classification of International Norms

This list of definitions conveys the need to classify norms so that we can identify different types of norms with different functions, according to competing and sometimes overlapping theoretical and philosophical approaches. First, we should differentiate between "moral" or prescriptive ("normative") norms, stemming from an international ethics position, and "nonnormative" or "nonmoral" norms, stemming mainly from positivist approaches, including international law (see Morgenthau 1934). "Moral" norms tend to be prescriptive regarding ethical arguments, with a clear sense of "rightness" attached to them (Tannenwald 1992, 5). Conversely, "nonmoral" norms are behavioral, regarding the dominant, standard, or "normal" behavior. Hence, not all norms necessarily entail moral commitments, though all norms define a certain accepted behavior within a given social environment. Only norms that can be considered as *evaluative* (of "good" and "bad," of right and wrong), as related to the possibility of moral choice, stress questions of morality and of moral commitment and fulfillment.

Second, in functional terms (according to the roles norms play), norms can be classified as *constitutive, regulative,* and *practical,* though the same norm can fulfill all three functions simultaneously.[3]

Constitutive Norms. These operate like rules that define the identity of an actor; hence, they define the essence of the game and the parameters of the possible interactions. For instance, in international relations the norm of sovereignty is considered to be the constitutive norm of the international society since the Treaty of Westphalia in 1648. The emergence of this constitutive norm of sovereignty is usually predicated on the previous existence of states with a defined territory, a stable population, and a suitable government. In the modern international society constitutive norms of sovereignty define ultimately what counts as statehood (see Sørensen 1998, 4–5; Raymond 1997, 214).

Regulative Norms. These operate as standards that specify the proper enactment of an already-defined identity. In other words, they establish the rules of the game in terms of rights and obligations. Most of the rules of peaceful coexistence, and even those of conflict interaction (such as the "rules of war"), are examples of regulative norms, which specify how sovereign states ought to conduct themselves in times of war and peace. Thus, a substantial part of international law is defined by these regulative norms.

Practical Norms. These focus on commonly accepted notions of "best solutions," as epitomized by custom and recurrent behavior. Over time, constitutive norms (such as the principle of sovereignty) and regulative norms (such as reciprocity) have become practical norms, as part and parcel of the practices and common interactions among states and other actors of the international society.

The Importance of International Norms

Several philosophical and methodological approaches define differently and confer various degrees of importance to norms in international relations. I refer here to realism and neorealism, neoliberalism, the Grotian approach to international relations, constructivism, and rational choice theory.

Realism and Neorealism

Realism has never been particularly good at showing how to distinguish the national interests from the realm of norms and the values underlying those norms, whether at the domestic or the international levels. Yet what are perceived to be interests derive many times from the normative values of the perceivers and the national decision makers themselves (Johnson 1991, 290). For instance, acting to preserve the balance of power and to maintain peace is based upon nonmoral norms such as prudence, a principle that has been emphasized by realists since Nicholas Machiavelli.

In general, realists have tended to downgrade the importance of norms, and regard them as epiphenoma, reflecting a given power structure and the underlying material forces. They regard norms as the powerless product of interests, reflecting a given power distribution. If norms matter at all, they do so at the discretion of the power structure (i.e., hegemony, or balance of power bipolar or multipolar). This view is rather deterministic: norms reflect the underlying material forces as dependent variables.

A realist conception of the international system would see states concluding treaties and formulating customary international legal rules as suited to their interests—usually the interests of the dominant states (Arend 1997, 10). For instance, the powerful democratic states export their democratic beliefs and impose human rights on their weaker neighbors as a function of the power distribution, usually in their favor. Similarly, the most powerful state or states in the international system might establish hegemonic norms, such as free trade, since for them there is a plausible convergence between norms and their national interest (Goertz and Diehl 1994, 106).

At the same time, even realists cannot live without norms, since the behavior they propose is presented and depicted as "normative." The most sophisticated among the realist writers recognize a certain role for international norms and rules, as an ancillary mechanism for the normal conduct of international relations. Thus, Robert Gilpin states explicitly: "In addition to the distribution of power and the hierarchy of prestige, the third component of the governance of an international system is a set of rights and rules that govern or at least influence the interactions among states. This need for rules and rights arises from the basic human condition of scarcity of material resources and the need for order and predictability in human affairs" (Gilpin 1981, 34). In other words, international norms and rules provide standards of behavior that regulate the "normal" action of states, in times of peace and war.

Another implicit recognition of the importance of the normative dimension comes from the discussion of reputation and prestige. Since even diehard realists recognize that sometimes the application of force is prohibitive, they turn to subtler uses of power, such as influence, persuasion, reputation, and prestige. Prestige, like successful deterrence or compellence, depends on the other party's expectations about the likelihood, scope, and domain of any retaliatory action. The more explicit this framework becomes, the more prestige becomes mediated by a normative order, defined as a certain set of rules of expected behavior (Kratochwil 1987, 143).

Two of the most important realist writers of the twentieth century, Hans Morgenthau and Edward H. Carr, recognized a certain role for international norms and standards of behavior in international politics. Morgenthau had a nostalgic view of the international normative order of the nineteenth century, which was based on a common moral and intellectual consensus. These common standards were destroyed by the forces of democratization and nationalism in the twentieth century, leading to a lack of moral consensus and want of international legislative bodies with the sufficient moral and physical authority to fulfill their functions (Morgenthau and Thompson 1985, 477–78; McElroy 1992, 22). Nowadays, moral norms have a distorted and dangerous role in international politics, as an ideological justification of the self-interested actions of states and the definition of their national interests.

Edward H. Carr had a more complicated, even convoluted, vision of the role of moral norms in international politics. On the one hand, he condemned the hypocritical position of the most powerful and wealthy states that advocated international norms, since they could afford to be "altruistic." As the forerunner of the hegemonic stability theory, Carr denounced the liberal values of Great Britain and France after World War I as a front for the crude realities of power distribution. But on the other hand, Carr was constantly searching to resolve the puzzle of peaceful change and to find the elusive equilibrium between power and morality. He highlighted the role of morality in political change as a "common feeling between nations," or a "common feeling of what is just and reasonable" (Carr 1964, 220). Thus, a spirit of give and take, collective sharing, and even self-sacrifice or self-abnegation should balance the crude adjustment to the changed relations of power. For Carr, the best possible world was one in which peaceful change could be achieved through a compromise "between the utopian conception of a common feeling of right" and "the realist conception of a mechanical adjustment to a changed equilibrium of forces" (Carr 1964, 223). Hence, moral norms are an essential ingredient of international politics, and, in fact, international legitimacy, morality, reputation, prestige, and public opinion become intangible but important components of state power. Yet norms do not supersede power politics; rather they complement and are subservient to it.

In sum, realism, except for its extreme or vulgar versions, does recognize the existence and importance of norms, both moral and nonmoral. Yet normative calculations are inferred first of all as a function of the power distribution and the rational calculation of national interests. Norms are largely the product of rational utility calculations on the part of state actors. This rationalist or positivist view makes neorealism a close relative (if not twin) of the neoliberal approach to international norms.

Neoliberalism

According to the neoliberal perspective, norms serve the egoistic interests of individual, rational actors. Based on a cost-benefit analysis, norms fulfill an intervening variable role between the underlying material forces and the possible outcomes. In this sense, norms may play an influential role in certain issue-areas, though they are still a superstructure built on a material basis (Checkel 1998, 327).

From this perspective, norms overlap with rational choice calculations and serve the egoistic interests of individual, rational actors. They serve as proxies or intervening variables for the actors' interests, being the epiphenomena or the formalization of a given, preexisting reality.

The importance of norms according to neoliberalism can be traced in the research on international regimes, as explicit injunctions with prescriptive status. The norms articulated in international regimes (in issue-areas such as trade, monetary affairs, the protection of Antarctica, or even nuclear nonproliferation) promote and regulate the common interests of the members of that particular regime. Over time, however, norms and regimes can acquire a "life of their own," shaping institutions and even the behavior of the actors that created them in the first place, by changing the costs and benefits associated with cooperation. States do create institutions and international regimes based on their selfish and rational calculations of costs and benefits. These international regimes encompass a series of principles, norms, rules, and decision-making procedures that pattern state expectations and behavior. The norms of the international regime help to strengthen cooperation among the participating actors based on the ideas of self-interest and reciprocal benefits. In this sense, norms fulfill a regulative function, helping actors with given interests to maximize their utility (see Arend 1997, 15; Raymond 1997, 213; Burley 1992, 183).

According to this rationalist approach, which is shared by both neorealism and neoliberalism, norms are exogenously determined coordinating mechanisms that enable actors to overcome problems of collective action. Norms arise and have impact when they are "needed" or are "functional," though the actors' preferences and their causal beliefs are given and predetermined (Goldstein and Keohane 1993, 4). Hence, norms introduce a modicum of predictability in world politics, such as their institutionalization through international regimes. In this view, norms remain epiphenomenal, though they might gain some autonomy through their institutionalization.

The Grotian Approach to International Relations

According to the "English school of international relations" (the Grotian approach), the international system is considered a "society" in which states, as members of that society, adhere to shared norms and rules in a variety of issue-areas. Material power matters, but its effects should be assessed within a framework of normative expectations, embedded in a set of public and customary international law, incorporating certain elements of international (but not necessarily world or global) morality.

In this international society, the sense of common interests about the elementary goals of social life (such as security, freedom, and peaceful coexistence) does not in itself provide a precise guidance as to what behavior should be consistent with these elementary goals. That is precisely the function of norms as rules. Hence, norms establish behavior, as they refer to international law, moral rules, custom, and established practice (see Bull 1977).

The existence and persistence of an international society is postulated on the following premises: a core of common norms—common standards and customs—having its partial embodiment in international law; an even distribution of power among the members of that society; and a common right of self-defense and coercion through collective security, which is most fully justified when it is undertaken by the members of the international society collectively (Wight 1966, 103–4).

The norms of the international society provide a clear guidance as to what behavior is consistent with the general goals of the society (such as life, liberty, and truth). These norms may have the status of international law, moral rules, custom, and established practices, or merely operational "rules of the game" (Bull 1977, 67). Their range is vast: from the constitutive principles of sovereignty, through the "rules of coexistence," which restrict the use of violence in international politics, to the norms that regulate cooperation among states. These norms, rules, and practices embody the common interests and values of states, reflecting a pluralistic society of sovereign states that recognize each other and are engaged in legal relations with each other (see Jackson and Zacher 1996, 25; Cutler 1991, 54–55).

According to the Grotian approach, the importance of international norms is paramount, since "normal" international relations can take place only within a framework of normative rules, which are essential for the maintenance of order (and, by extension, of justice). The existence and relevance of these norms make the collectivity of states a *society*, rather than a mere system (see Wilson 1989, 56; Brown 1995, 185–86).

Since norms act in an autonomous fashion, while international law and practices shape both behavior and interests, one can notice a great overlap between the (older) Grotian approach and the (more recent) constructivist approach. Both schools refer to international law much more than structural realists and rationalist (neoliberal) institutionalists do (Arend 1997, 25–26). International legal rules are socially constructed, they have intersubjective meaning, and they constitute the nonmaterial structure of the international system. For both Grotians and constructivists, international law and practices shape both the behavior and the interests of states. Yet the advantage of the Grotian approach in general, and of international law in particular, is that it can be *empirically tested*. Thus, one can take law very seriously, as both a crystallization of state expectations and as a vehicle for transforming state understandings and practices.

In sum, according to the Grotian approach, norms fulfill an independent role and are paramount to understanding international relations within the framework of an international society. At the same time, we should not conceive of norms as "independent variables" in the simple positivist fashion, but rather as reasons, motivations, justifications, and rationale for states and other actors to behave in a certain way.

Constructivism

The social constructivist approach regards norms as crucial elements of society and the social construction of reality. Norms shape both the goals of state actors—their perceptions of their interests—and the means they use to achieve these goals. Overall, norms help to determine the articulation of preferences by states and nonstate actors.

The term constructivism implies that "people and societies construct, or constitute, each other" (Onuf 1989, 36). Social structures and practices are intersubjective rather than material, and they can be conceived in terms of rule-following, language games, and the creation of institutions and collective ideas such as social norms (Dunne 1995, 372).

In the last decade or so, constructivists as social theorists have located themselves equidistant from both positivist and postmodernist approaches in their analysis of social reality in general and of international norms in particular.[4] Constructivists assume that the structure of the international system is a "social structure." As such, it can be studied only in a mediated fashion, through the "intersubjective meaning" attributed to and by the actors involved in that social structure. Since norms are inherently social, collective, and inter-subjective, it is evident that constructivists, almost by definition, will emphasize the impact of norms in the creation and re-creation of the social reality, as an integral part of that social structure. Norms reflect a certain collective identity, while at the same time they can affect and change the interests and the consequential behavior of states. In this sense, the interests of states are partly created and changed, by way of the interaction between the social structure and the actors, through the action of norms.

For constructivists, norms are *constitutive* components of both the international system and society, and of states' interests. Norms shape the identities of the state actors ("the agents") and partially define their interests, beyond merely constraining the state's behavior. International norms carry a specific social content, and they are often independent from any given power distribution. Norms constitute the states (as actors and agents), by providing them with an intrinsic understanding of their own interests, in terms of what is important or valuable and what are the effective and/or legitimate means to obtain these valued goods. In sum, while neoliberal institutionalists and regime theorists accord to norms only a limited role, the constructivists elevate norms (and identity) to the center of their research program.

Rational Choice Theory

There is a false dichotomy between normative research and rational choice theory. The two are interrelated: One cannot have a rational choice analysis without a previous normative framework, and vice versa. Thus, we have to think more clearly about the complex relationship between rationality and social construction, or between interests and norms.

According to Finnemore and Sikkink, rationality is not the issue that divides scholars in international relations. And yet scholars are divided about the role that choice plays in norm-based behavior, about what motivates choice, and about the role persuasion plays in normative processes and how to treat it (Finnemore and Sikkink 1998, 917).

Social norms and rational choice theories can mutually inform and enrich each other. For instance, game theory provides a rich source of insights as well as useful tools for the explanation of social norms (Ullmann-Margalit 1977, 16). Conversely, certain types of norms can suggest solutions to problems posed by certain interaction situations, like Prisoner's Dilemma (PD) and co-ordination situations (Ullmann-Margalit 1977, 9). Norms can then affect the substantive preferences' ordering of the actors against which the cost-benefit analysis applies. They can have an impact on the rational behavior of actors, and vice versa. Depending on the empirical question being asked, one could model the social (normative) context as a background to explain rational choice, or, conversely, how cost-benefit calculations lead to a normative choice (Finnemore and Sikkink 1998, 911). Hence, processes of social construction (i.e., normative creation) and strategic bargaining (rationality) are deeply inter-twined.

According to John Harsanyi, "People's behavior can be largely explained in terms of two dominant interests: economic gain and social acceptance" (quoted in Pettit 1990, 726). The economic gain is directly related to a cost-benefit analysis and to methodological individualism. However, the second interest reflects a concern with reputation and prestige (what others might think of you) that is congenial with both methodological individualism and with a normative, sociological framework. To demonstrate the degree of over-lap between social norms and rational choice, one can argue that either social norms are rational (to the extent of being efficient means to achieve individual or social welfare), or that what is rational conforms to social norms (Bicchieri 1990, 838).

The conclusion to be drawn from these observations is that from a rational choice perspective, norms can be very important, even if they are regarded as superfluous. That is, more often than we think, norms and self-interests tend to coincide rather than stand in opposition to each other. They usually move in the same direction, and they complement each other. Thus, interests might shape norms, but norms also shape interests (Tannenwald 1992, 24). In other words, we should recognize that self-interests and norms frequently coexist in a "parallelogram of forces that jointly determine behavior" (Elster 1989, 106; quoted in Raymond 1997, 232).

Genealogy and Evolution of International Norms

After assessing the importance of international norms according to different approaches, we should turn to the analysis of their dynamics: Where do norms come from? How do they evolve and change over time?

Where Do Norms Come From?

A critical question in understanding the dynamics of international norms refers to how they emerge in the first place. There are several possible answers: New norms are responses to critical changes in the international environment; they are the result of imitation or emulation; they are created through internal processes stimulated by subnational groups; they are the outcome of a given distribution of power within the state system; they derive from the prominence of a potential rule or from the coherence between that rule and the larger, pre-existing normative order; or they are the result of the action of "moral (normative) entrepreneurs."

There are multiple answers to this complicated question. In the first place, we should distinguish between rationalist (i.e., realist or liberal) and interpretative (i.e., constructivist or Grotian) claims. From a *rationalist perspective,* the origins of norms are a function of the anarchical system, the interactions among the actors, and the aggregation of individuals' preferences. Hence, norms are generated *de novo* (again) or *ex nihilo* (for the first time), in order to promote a certain political agenda. For instance, following their emphasis on material interests and coercion, neorealists such as Gilpin (1981) argue that norms reflect the hegemon's national interests or its domestic values. Alternatively, focusing more on external incentives than on coercion, neoliberals argue that norms are generated by the interactions among actors, under "cooperation under anarchy" (Klotz 1995, 21–22). Conversely, from an *interpretative viewpoint,* norms are embedded in already existing webs of metanorms. Thus, new norms emerge from within preexisting social institutions (Klotz 1995, 22–23).

A variety of mechanisms explain the origins and further evolution of international norms, including social practices, "ecological processes," social and internal processes, and historical evolution and evolutionary models. "Ecological processes" derive from the pattern of relations between actors and their environment. Social processes stem from the relations among the actors themselves. Finally, internal processes stem from the internal characteristics of the actors themselves (Kowert and Legro 1996, 470).

Social Practices

International norms are based on preexisting cultural knowledge and institutions, including other, previous norms. From a Grotian perspective, as well as from a constructivist viewpoint, norms can be embedded and derived from preexisting practices and customs (for instance, codification of international law based on custom and commonplace rules of behavior). In this sense, international norms are not deduced by teleological reasoning from some transcendental moral order. Their origin is much more mundane: they are the products of ordinary practice with a binding force that derives from consent (Raymond 1997, 228). There would be a greater impact for these social practices if existing powerful actors (such as the great powers in a given historical period) sustain and uphold them. This is true for both "normative" (ethical, moral) and "nonmoral" norms of behavior as well.

The relevant mechanisms here include imitation and social learning. Specifically, complex social learning takes place when identities and interests are learned in response to how actors are being treated by significant others in a strategic interaction context (Checkel 1998, 346; Bicchieri 1990, 839). In this sense, norms are "built" rather than "created," since they are based upon preexisting cultural knowledge and institutions. Thus, every norm has a "source" defined as such by other, previous norms. New norms stem from old ones by way of intervening practice, like the sources of international law (Onuf 1998, 25).

Ecological Processes

An ecological process implies an explicit interaction between actors and their environment. In this sense, norms can be the result of conscious promotion of actors (so-called moral entrepreneurs); they can also be negotiated among the different actors, or they can be imposed from an hegemonic position (as in the initial establishment of economic international regimes after World War II) (see Kowert and Legro 1996; Nadelman 1990). In all these cases, norms arise and have an impact whether they are "needed" or simply considered to be "functional."

Since international politics is a "two-level game," new norms must initially survive an initial domestic process of political selection within the confines of at least one state. Norms must win over the support of relevant policy experts (epistemic communities) and/or of "moral entrepreneurs," individuals, or organizations morally motivated to change the current discourse of foreign policy. Norm entrepreneurs act out of moral convictions, since they believe in the ideals and values embodied in the norms promoted, even though the pursuit of the norms may have no effect (or even a detrimental one) on their own well-being (Finnemore and Sikkink 1998, 898). These moral entrepreneurs act also on a transnational basis by creating networks of advocacy and constructing new cognitive frames that attempt to redefine the interests of other actors.

Social and Internal Processes

Similarly, the etiology and evolution of international norms are linked to social processes such as social diffusion, transgovernmental networks, epistemic communities, and transnational movements (which include moral entrepreneurs). Some of these processes are international and transnational (they spill over borders), while some are domestic (within the borders of a given state).

At the core of the social processes that explain the genesis of norms are the crucial mechanisms of dominance and reputation. As Axelrod (1986, 1108) points out, it is easier to get a norm started if it serves the interests of the powerful few. Once started, the powerful party supports the norms, since the norms support the strong (as in the case of hegemonic stability and the establishment of international regimes).

Yet the adoption of international norms remains at different stages an *internal* process, characterized by the *internalization* of the norm at the domestic (state) and individual (cognitive and psychological) levels (Checkel 1998, 332 and 339). For example, in terms of international law, international norms of behavior are adopted and implemented once they become *internalized* as national (domestic) laws, given the preeminence and supranational essence of international law.

How Do Norms Change over Time?

Norms constitute a dynamic phenomenon; they might evolve and change over time. To understand the dynamics of their evolution, we should pay attention to the historical context, including alternative historical narratives. Hence, there is a strong path-dependent character to the processes of normative evolution. For example, the legitimacy of a normative claim in international law is explicitly linked to the "fit" of that claim within a preexisting normative framework; the more legal arguments seem to be persuasive, the more they are rooted and grounded in legal precedents.

Social institutions in general, and norms governing social behavior in particular, are supposed to emerge and develop from an evolutionary process. Thus, "good" social norms are supposed to win out in an ongoing process of evolutionary competition, out of "moral" and/or "functional" reasoning (Ullmann-Margalit 1990, 764). There are alternative evolutionary models in this regard that complement each other. There is a model that posits an analogy between norms and genes; hence, norms are transmitted from one individual to another through similar processes of inheritance (see Florini 1996, 367; Patrick 1997). A second model, based on behavioralist explanations, stresses the importance of dominance, reputation, legitimation, conformity, and esteem (see Axelrod 1986; Finnemore and Sikkink 1998, 903). A third model, close to liberalism and constructivism, emphasizes learning and cognitive evolution (Adler 1997). The three models also posit a logic and an explanation for the origins and evolution of norms, as mentioned above.

Processes of Inheritance (Norms as Genes)

According to this model, norms are contested, transmitted, and selected for application in a way similar to the selection of genes. The basic assumption is that human choices about behavior are based far more on simple imitation, encoded in the form of a norm, than on deliberate weighting of well-considered and well-understood options (Florini 1996, 378). Norms evolve because they are subjected to selection and contestation, like genes, in a rather mechanistic or deterministic way. Yet to emerge as a "winner," unlike genes, a norm must be initially prominent, thanks to the action of a moral entrepreneur; coherent with other (preexisting) norms in the system; and must grow in a favorable international environment (Väyrynen 1997, 4; Florini 1996, 374).

Behavioralist Processes: The Importance of Dominance and Reputation

A second evolutionary model stresses the importance of dominance, reputation, and prestige. In terms of dominance, norms might evolve as the result of a hegemonic power that imposes norms as a means of systemic diffusion. Thus, norms change and evolve as a result of the change in the great powers' interest over time, so that a hegemonic power can fulfill the role of a moral entrepreneur. In terms of reputation and prestige, norms might evolve through an international or regional demonstration effect of "contagion," according to which states care about their self-image, so they conform and adapt to the "peer pressure" of their normative environment (see Finnemore and Sikkink 1998, 903).

Cognitive Processes: Cognitive Evolution as Learning

A third evolutionary model focuses on cognitive evolution as a framework for understanding the dynamics and evolution of international norms over time. Cognitive evolution could be considered as a theory of international learning, if by learning we understand the adoption by policy makers of new interpretations of reality. These new "social realities" are created and introduced to the political system by individuals and social actors (Adler 1997), both within and between states. In this sense, socialization, imitation, and social learning all derive from cognitive evolution.

In itself, cognitive evolution involves three interrelated processes: (a) *innovation:* the creation of new norms, as an outcome of new findings and understandings; (b) *selection:* political processes that determine which norms will be selected to be tested in politics in order to be perpetuated over time; and (c) *diffusion:* the dissemination of norms on an international and transnational basis (Adler 1991, 55–56).

In all the three models presented above, the evolution of international norms is the result of a process of selection, competition, and contestation, as well as of adaptation and socialization. In this sense, there is an important role for emulation: actors see others behaving in a certain way and copy those behaviors, bringing occasional changes in and of norms.

The Impact of Norms in International Relations

Do norms matter in international relations? Do they have an impact on the quality of life in international society? Assuming that the answers to these two questions are positive, how do norms matter? Under what conditions do they impact the foreign policy of individual states and international relations in general?

Do Norms Matter in International Relations?

It is not obvious that there is anything new or substantial to be said about the question of whether norms matter or not. After all, this was the question underlying the large body of scholarship that goes by the name of "regime theory." Moreover, for anyone who had doubts about whether regime theory fully answered the question, in recent years constructivists too have tackled this issue. In a way, only the most diehard neorealists would deny that norms have any significant impact on international relations. There seems to be an emerging consensus that norms do indeed matter, by registering the "oughts" of society and by reflecting what people do or want to do.

The general assumption of this book, which reflects the emerging consensus on the issue, is that norms do indeed matter in international relations. But then the problem, or the puzzle, becomes that of elucidating how norms do matter, and under what conditions. It is the question of which norms matter, when, and how much, that remains at the heart of a persistent debate among different philosophical schools of international relations. Although almost everyone agrees that norms might have some potential influence on the behavior of actors, there is a substantial variation in the enactment of, and compliance with, norms. This is true for both any single actor behaving across different situations and for different actors responding to similar situations (Steiner 1998, 5).

How and When Do Norms Matter in International Relations?

If norms can be considered as an independent, rather than an intervening variable, then they exercise a significant impact and policy relevance for the formulation and implementation of foreign policies in the contemporary international system. Due to the discrepancies in the study of norms in international relations, one can suggest alternative answers regarding the impact of norms, or what I call six "alternative paths of influence," as follows.

First, *the normative context (regional or global) affects international and domestic politics in direct or indirect ways, through the shaping of foreign and domestic policies, or at least its structural normative constraining.* Norms do constrain behavior, by affecting what one wants to do and what one may be able to persuade others to do or not to do (Russett 1993, 136). In more specific terms, norms can set the regional (or global) agenda for the relevant actors by "teaching" them how to behave under specific conditions, in both domestic and international politics. Thus, international norms can affect a nation's foreign policy because governmental and nongovernmental actors may promote them as a result of moral scruples, legal considerations, reputational concerns, or a desire to emulate others (Raymond 1997, 216).

For instance, without ruling out competing explanations of *Realpolitik* and self-interest, it is clear that norms of peaceful settlement have partly explained the maintenance of regional peace in different regional settings, such as South

America since 1883, West Africa since 1957, and Southeast Asia since 1967. Similarly, the phenomenon of decolonization in the aftermath of World War II was above all the result of an international change of normative ideas about legitimate and illegitimate rule, not just a change in the balance of power or the economic utilities of imperialism (Jackson 1993, 129).

Second, *international norms have an impact on the domestic political discourse and the domestic behavior of states*. Norms affect a country's policy choice by way of the actions of domestic political actors (such as leaders and interest groups). This happens when: (a) norms influence the beliefs and values of decision makers within the state; and/or (b) norms become part of the domestic law and the standard operational procedures (SOPs) of the existing bureaucratic agencies. The conditions that facilitate the impact of norms through domestic processes include: (1) a cultural match between the international norm and the local, preexisting culture (including ideas, values, and norms); (2) the salience, influence, and leverage of government officials such as authoritative national leaders who express their opinions regarding the norms (local entrepreneurs); (3) the role and salience of societal groups, including interest groups, epistemic communities, and local members of NGOs and transnational networks of advocacy; and (4) the role and salience of domestic institutions, which provide information regarding the extent to which the international norms' proscriptions and prescriptions have already become part of the domestic political discourse (Cortell and Davis 1997, 5–7; Checkel 1997, 476–77).

The impact of international norms is usually mediated through domestic (political and economic) structures (Cortell and Davis 1996, 451–53). International norms have important effects on state behavior via domestic political processes; they become internalized or "domesticated." The domestic empowerment of norms might occur as a result of nonstate actors and policy networks mobilizing and coercing decision makers to change their state policy (a "bottom-up" process). Alternatively, norms might become internalized by the decision makers themselves through a process of social learning, leading the political leaders to adopt prescriptions embodied in international norms (a "top-down" process) (Checkel 1999, 88).

Third, *international norms are exogenously coordinating mechanisms that enable actors to overcome problems of collective action*. From a rationalist perspective, norms arise and have an impact when they are "needed" or are "functional." Hence, they introduce a modicum of predictability in world politics, such as their institutionalization through international regimes.

In more specific terms, norms fulfill a series of essential functions for the "normal" proceedings of the international society. First, norms keep and promote international order. They delineate boundaries and communicate the scope of a state's entitlements, the extent of its obligations, and the range of its jurisdiction. Second, norms serve as signposts or heuristic mental aids to warn policy makers of the prearranged actions that might be taken by various states under certain circumstances, as in the case of international regimes. Third, norms routinize many aspects of international and transnational relations, offering a template for coordinating joint action. Norms thereby fulfill a function similar to that of standard operational procedures (SOPs). Fourth, international norms perform a tripwire function, warning about the potential transgressions in case widely accepted rules are being violated (see Raymond 1997, 214–15; Kegley and Raymond 1990, 16–19).

Fourth, *international norms shape state interests and state identities*. From a constructivist perspective, norms either define identities in the first place or prescribe or proscribe ("regulate") behaviors for already-constituted identities, generating expectations about how these identities will shape behaviors in varying circumstances (Jepperson et al. 1996, 54). The social nature of international politics creates normative understandings among actors that, in turn, coordinate values, expectations, and behavior. Hence international norms help to shape interests, and interests in turn shape actions, though neither link is necessarily deterministic or causal in the sense of independent and dependent variables. Norms provide states with a general sense of direction and goals for action, submitting a "logic of appropriateness" in contrast to the "logic of consequences." Norms constrain not only because of the expected (negative) consequences of their possible transgression, but mainly because they are embedded in social structures that partially demarcate communities of value. Therefore, while rationalist accounts of the constraining effects of norms are a good starting point for any plausible explanation, constructivists transcend rationalists by pointing the way toward the deeper constitutive effects of norms (Keck and Sikkink 1998, 34–35).

For instance, through a process of cognitive evolution (social learning), decision makers might learn new values and interests; hence, they might adopt the prescriptions embodied in international norms. Furthermore, norms may also constitute or shape the basic identities of states. Thus, diffuse normative structures such as sovereignty or even "civilizations" shape the particular identities of actors on the international stage, as well as the rules for enacting these identities (see Katzenstein 1996; Kowert and Legro 1996, 468).

Fifth, *international norms affect the foreign policy of individual countries in a given region and the intraregional international relations in general through their institutionalization in the regional international society, usually through multilateral instruments of international law.* Through the different institutions of the international society—the states themselves, international diplomacy, international law, mechanisms of balance of power, and even the wage and limitation of wars—international norms shape and affect individual foreign policies and regional international relations. Furthermore, legal rules provide relatively firm guidance not only with respect to ends, but also regarding the means adopted (Kratochwil 1984, 350). Norms of international law involve a process of legitimation for policy choice, signaling and shaping the "proper" or "acceptable" behavior. For instance, the norm of *pacta sunt servanda* has put a heavy burden on those who want to breach legally established regimes (Müller 1993, 385).

Sixth, *international legal norms and rules constitute the nonmaterial structure of the international system.* From the perspective of international law, norms fulfill a crucial role. They enshrine the doctrine of sovereignty, establish the criteria for membership in the international society, provide rules that determine when and whether other legal rules will be binding, establish a language for diplomacy, and give normative value (and justification) to actions and claims made by international actors (Arend 1997, 39).

The impact of international legal norms is effected in two parallel and interconnected ways. On the one hand, in a *direct* path, international norms affect the foreign policies of states since states are motivated by considerations of reputation and prestige in their international relations through processes of socialization and emulation. Thus, states comply with international law since they are concerned with their image and their legitimacy.[5] Within the international society, the United Nations embodies many of the most important constitutive norms, prescribing how modern sovereign states should behave. These norms might emerge from both a climate of fear, reflecting a concern for what might happen if these norms are not being followed, and by a spirit of hope, regarding how the international community ought to operate (see Jones 1992, 44–45; Barnett 1997, 542).

On the other hand, in an *indirect path,* international law affects foreign policy through the internalization of norms, which in turn affect foreign policy through domestic political processes. Once treaty obligations are translated into domestic legislation, those responsible for violations can thus be held responsible through domestic legal processes. In this way, those who wish to breach the norms actually violate the (domestic) laws of the land (Müller 1993, 385).

Charles Kegley and Gregory Raymond (1986) have shown persuasively that when states accept international norms such as *pacta sunt servanda* and alliance commitments, the incidence of war is reduced. Hence, the maintenance of peace is associated with periods in which the dominant tradition in international law considers alliance norms binding and the unilateral abrogation of international commitments and treaties as illegitimate (Vasquez 1994, 213). In the same vein, Peter Wallensteen (1984) refers to "norms of universalism" by which the major powers of a region or of the system as a whole have tried to stabilize the territorial status quo by enhancing their normative consensus regarding conflict management and resolution. Thus, if a mechanism of normative consensus to cope with international conflict is well established and entrenched, international norms that enable political decisions to take place might fulfill a function equivalent to that of war (see Vasquez 1992, 1993, and 1994).

As far as international moral norms are concerned, to the extent that we can distinguish them from mere legal norms, they might impact international relations through three different mechanisms, located at three levels of analysis: (1) the conscience of the national decision makers (first level); (2) the influence of domestic public opinion (second level); and (3) international reputational pressures (third level). These three mechanisms interact through considerations of reputation and extrapolation. In other words, by mobilizing around an international moral norm, states might create significant reputational pressure on a nonobservant state, thus leading the national decision makers to adopt a norm-observant course of action. It is plausible for the decision maker to change his or her mind because of some moral remorse (evidence for conscience?), domestic pressure, international pressure, or all of them. What is clear is that he or she is concerned about his or her prestige, being entrapped by extrapolation. After all, norms are shared "identity indicators" that signal to the members of the society what type of person one is. And in international relations, as in interpersonal relations, states often attribute to each other moral scores and normative judgments (McElroy 1992, 30, 46, and 51).

The above six paths of influence overlap and complement each other, reflecting a range of possible impact from a mere functionalist/rationalist logic to a much more comprehensive Grotian or constructivist perspective. They are summarized in Table 2.1.

To sum up, the impact of international norms on international relations, both at the individual state and regional levels, is a function of two clusters of variables, as composed of domestic and international factors. The domestic variables include a focus on the salience of domestic actors who mobilize international norms (individual and collective moral entrepreneurs, social groups, interest groups, epistemic communities, advocacy networks, NGOs, domestic institutions, national leaders), as well as the domestic circumstances that those

Table 2.1. "Paths of Influence" of International Norms

Path of Influence	Impact
General International norms (regional and international) affect international and domestic politics.	Shaping of foreign and domestic politics Structural (normative) constraining Setting the domestic and international agendas Teaching actors how to behave Promotion of norms because of moral scruples, legal considerations, reputation, and emulation
Domestic International norms (regional and international) affect the domestic political discourse and behavior of states.	Influence on beliefs and values of decision makers Norms become part of domestic law SOPs of bureaucratic agencies Mobilization of and by nonstate actors ("bottom-up") Social learning by political leaders ("top-down")
Functional/Rationalist International norms are exogenously coordinating mechanisms that enable actors to overcome problems of collective action.	Predictability in world politics Norms promote and keep the international order Norms act as signposts and heuristic devices Routinization of international and transnational relations (SOPs) Tripwire against possible transgressions
Constructivism International norms help to shape state interests and state identities.	Norms provide direction and goals for action Norms define interests Norms constitute/shape basic identities Norms prescribe and proscribe behaviors Social learning (cognitive evolution)
Grotian approach International norms constitute and institutionalize the international society.	Multilateral instruments of regional law Institutions of the international society Processes of legitimation of behavior
International law International society constitute the non-material structure of the international system.	Norms enshrine sovereignty Norms establish criteria for membership in society Norms provide rules for binding (of other rules) Norms establish diplomacy Norms give normative value and justification for action Considerations of reputation and prestige Internalization (through domestic institutionalization)

actors confront (for instance, type of political regime, peaceful or crisis times). In turn, the international variables refer to the distribution of power at the regional and international levels, the presence or absence of an hegemonic power, the degree of institutionalization of the international society, the degree of fitness between the preexisting normative framework and the relevant normative case, and the degree of "contagion effect" (of adherence) to certain international norms. These variables are summarized in Table 2.2.

From the reading of Table 2.2 we can then hypothesize that international norms will be more influential (1) the more salient the domestic actors who mobilize them are; (2) the more open and liberal-democratic the political regimes are; (3) the more peaceful (in other words, absence of war) conditions reign within the country involved; (4) the more stable and recognized the distribution of power is; (5) the more visible the presence of an hegemonic power is vis-à-vis the local power and the regional system; (6) the more institutionalized the international society is; and (7) the higher the degree of fitness between the preexisting international normative framework and the relevant normative case.

Table 2.2.   Conditions for the Impact of International Norms

---

Domestic Variables

Salience of domestic actors who mobilize international norms
(individual/collective "moral entrepeneurs," social groups,
interest groups, epistemic communities, advocacy networks,
domestic NGOs, domestic institutions, and national leaders)

Domestic circumstances
type of political regime, "normal" (peace) or crisis times

International Variables

---

distribution of power (regional and global); presence
(or absence) of an hegemonic power; degree of
institutionalization of the international society
(regional and global); degree of adherence by
neighbors to regional norms; fitness between the
existing normative framework and the normative case

Conclusion: An Argument for Pluralism and Modesty

In this chapter I have presented a framework for the study of regional inter-national norms. This framework is composed of several elements: the defini-tion and classification of international norms; their importance as attributed by different approaches in the field; the genealogy and evolution of norms; and the assessment of their impact. I have traced six alternative paths of influence for the impact of international norms on international relations—general, domestic, functionalist/rationalist, constructivist, Grotian, and international law and morality. Moreover, I have identified two clusters of variables that might explain the variance in the impact of norms across different cases in terms of time and space, domestic and international. The domestic variables focus on the salience of domestic actors who mobilize international norms and the domestic circumstances they face. The international variables refer to the distribution of power, the presence of an hegemonic power, the degree of institutionalization of the international society, the fitness between the pre-existing normative framework and new international norms, and the degree of adherence to international norms by the neighboring states in the regional milieu ("contagion effect").

To examine the conditions under which norms might have an impact on international society, we should turn to their empirical evidence, through the analysis of international law and practices. At the same time, this is a challeng-ing theoretical and methodological exercise, since we should be wary of coun-terfactual validity or refutation. No single counterfactual occurrence refutes the existence of a norm. In other words, even when a norm is violated, that does not mean that it is insignificant or that it does not have any political effect at all. In that case, we need the insights of the sociological/interpretative approaches, whether they are found in the late Hedley Bull's writings from the English School or in more recent constructivist explorations. In any case, we cannot empirically study international norms without knowing the instru-ments of international law, and without at least being aware of their ethical dimension and connotations.

Malign tendencies in the field of international relations to draw lines, form camps, celebrate new and old fads, and constantly reinvent old and for-gotten wheels have led in the last two decades to a "third debate" confronting positivists (or rationalists) with constructivists and postmodernists. This debate has been exacerbated and taken to absurd extremes. Constructivist and other post-positivist approaches have been insightful enough in denouncing realism (and especially the neorealist version of Kenneth Waltz's theory) as the hegemonic and distorted paradigm of international relations until the late 1980s. Thus, the major contribution of constructivism for international relations has been to readdress the distorted balance between interests and norms in the direction of reasserting the importance of ideas, culture, norms, and identities.

Yet, in an interesting reversal of fortune typical of the study of political science and particularly of international relations, constructivism has become the new "fad" and almost the new hegemonic "ism" and ideological (if not dogmatic) magnet for the new and recent legions of Ph.D. students in search of new challenges and areas of exploration (as related to "the social construction" of . . .). The focus on norms and identities, essential for constructivism, has become in itself distorted when it is isolated from international law and from international ethics, especially when it is wrapped in obscure if not incomprehensible language. The absurdity resides in the fact that sometimes, in the process of applying the constructivist approach, the study of international norms seems to be a mere pretext to justify sterile metatheoretical and espistemological debates such as the agent/structure or the material/ideational divides. Hence, it seems that our discipline is suffering from an overdose of "epistemologism." What about the *problematique* related to the content and impact of international norms? Can we turn these norms into more effective instruments of foreign policy for the international community as a whole in order to improve the world we all share?

Nobody will dispute that international relations are socially constructed, as nobody will argue with Monsieur Jourdain in Molière's comedy when he lately realized that all his life he was "talking prose." But just being aware of having "talked prose" all our lives (by socially constructing our reality) will not improve our normative condition, in ethical and nonethical terms. By adopting an eclectic neo–Grotian approach, as a kind of proto–constructivism I suggest taking the best of these different schools and reconciling them through the empirical analysis of the instruments of international law. After all, the distances among the different schools are not irreconcilable; they overlap and complement each other much more than they are ready to mutually acknowledge. If we then combine in our empirical examination the six alternative paths of influence for international norms, this will help us examine and understand their impact in the international society in general, and in a regional context in particular. I turn now to an overview of the Latin American case as a regional international society.

CHAPTER THREE

Latin America as an International Society

IN THIS CHAPTER I ADOPT HEDLEY BULL'S (1977) CONCEPT OF INTER-national society in terms of common interests, values, norms, and institutions to assess the claim that Latin America can be analyzed as a regional international society. Since their independence in the early nineteenth century the Latin American countries have gradually built up a sophisticated and highly developed system of regional international law and institutions. This system has included a series of regional norms that have regulated their international and domestic behavior.

The reality of a regional international society is puzzling in the Latin American context because of the evident contrast between the rhetorical and practical levels, and between the international and domestic arenas. No other region of the world has as many bilateral and multilateral documents, treaties, charters, conventions, and resolutions imposing obligations for the peaceful settlement of international disputes. Among the more prominent documents, one can mention the Treaty on the Maintenance of Peace (Lima 1865), the General Treaty of Arbitration between Argentina and Chile (Pactos de Mayo) of 1902, the Bogotá Pact on Peaceful Settlement of 1948, and the Charter of the Organization of American States (OAS). While few of these legal instruments contain compulsory procedures, many of them have been frequently invoked to suggest a rich regime of peaceful conflict resolution norms (Holsti 1996, 156). Conversely, in practical terms, the Latin American nations have been more inclined to adopt prejurisdictional or political forms of settlement, usually through diplomatic negotiations and - procedures. Moreover, when some of the juridical procedures (such as compulsory arbitration) were agreed upon, usually they were only enforced for a few states or they were displaced by diplomatic negotiations (Puig 1983, 11). This disjunction between the formal and legalistic organizational principles and the informal and pragmatic workings of their institutions is related to the shaping of the collective identity of the region, which can be traced back to colonial times. At that time, Spanish people in the Americas coined the famous expression "I obey but I do not carry out," in reaction to royal ordinances (quoted in Roniger and Sznajder 1998, 5).

As for the domestic realm, with its recurrent cycles of democratization and authoritarianism until the 1980s, the practical assessment of the impact of international norms has been a most difficult task. By contrast, the international scene, with the maintenance of regional peace in South America since 1883, seems to indicate a greater receptivity to the norms and institutions of that international society (see Holsti 1996, 150–82; Kacowicz 1998, 67–124).

The domain of the Latin American regional society overlaps with the greater vision of the Americas, or the "Western Hemisphere," as a whole. This great design of a New World as a continent culturally and politically distinct from Europe has permeated the diplomatic rhetoric, if not the foreign policy, of the Latin American states. There have always been discussions about a special "American international law," as distinct from the general international law binding upon all of the members of the international community. From the Monroe Doctrine of 1823, through the Treaty of Perpetual Union sponsored by Bolívar and signed at the Panama Congress of 1826, to the contemporary Inter-American institutions, there has been a recurrent theme of exceptionalism, regarding the Americas as a special place ruled by international law in contradiction to the power politics of Europe.[1]

In Latin America in particular there has been a strong tradition of support for international law, partly as a vehicle for preventing war and opposing the potential intervention by stronger extraregional powers, first and foremost the United States. In this regard, the major principles that Latin Americans have contributed to the more general American international law are the nontransfer of territories; *uti possidetis;* nonintervention; nonrecognition of territorial conquests; the use of morality in international relations; solidarity; and equality of states and respect for their sovereignty.

Defining International Society and Its Main Elements

The idea of an "international society" or "society of states" is directly related to the Grotian tradition of international politics, carving a middle ground between the realist conception of a mere system of states and the universalistic/idealistic (Kantian) view of a potential community of humankind. For Bull, the Grotian prescription for international behavior is that "all states, in their dealings with one another, are bound by the rules and institutions of the society they form" (Bull 1977, 27). According to Bull's definition (1977, 13),

> A *society of states* (or international society) exists when a group of states, conscious of certain common interests and common values, form a society in the sense that they conceive themselves to be bound by a common set of rules in their relations with one another, and share in the working of common institutions. If states today form an international society, this is because recognizing certain common interests and perhaps some common values, they regard themselves as bound by certain rules in their dealings with one another, such as they should respect one another's claims to independence, that they should honor agreements into which they enter, and that they should be subject to certain limitations in exercising force against one another. At the same time they cooperate in the working of institutions such as the forms of procedures of international law, the machinery of diplomacy and general international organization, and the customs and conventions of war.

International societies can be traced at different levels of aggregation, from the global to the local. Historically, international societies have been located at the level of regions, sharing a common culture or civilization. The European international society, evolving from medieval Europe through the nineteenth-century Concert of Europe, became a global international society after World War II in the contemporary age of decolonization, nuclear weapons, and economic globalization. At the same time, in our contemporary global society we can recognize distinctive regional settings, such as Latin America.

There are basically three major elements of any international society: common interests and values, common norms and rules, and common institutions. Like any other society, an *international* society includes a set of actors who share a sense of *common interests* in the elementary goals of social interaction, including the preservation of life, freedom, and the limitation of violence. At the level of the international society we can identify four such goals: (1) the preservation of the system and the society of states themselves; (2) maintaining the independence and sovereignty of the individual member-states; (3) the maintenance of peace, defined as the normal absence of war among the members of the society; and (4) the limitation of violence resulting in death or bodily harm, the keeping of promises, and the stabilization of possession by rules of property (Bull 1977, 16–19). In addition to these common interests, the members of an international society share common beliefs, values, and attitudes, usually within the framework of a single culture.

Among many other possibilities, norms have been defined in chapter 2 as standards of behavior spelled out in terms of rights and obligations (Krasner 1982, 186). Similarly, rules are general imperative principles that require or authorize prescribed classes of persons or groups to behave in prescribed ways (Bull 1977, 54–55). The essential norm of the international society is the principle of state sovereignty. This norm includes the principles of territorial integrity, political independence of existing states, legal equality, and nonintervention as its corollary.

Common interests, values, norms, and rules have a certain impact on the member-states of the international society through their articulation, formulation, and formalization into common *institutions*. Thus, institutions can be considered as a set of habits and practices shaped toward the realization of common goals (Bull 1977, 74).

According to Bull, the major institutions of the international society are the nation-states themselves, in the absence of a recognized supranational authority. States cooperate and collaborate with each other, shaping institutions such as the balance of power, international law, diplomatic mechanisms, great power management, and even the regulation of war. Institutions might sustain several and changing degrees of formalization and institutionalization, ranging from informal diplomatic contacts through elaborated schemes of economic and political integration.

Historical Background of the Contemporary Latin American Society

The Evolution of Latin American Society since Independence

Since their independence the Latin American countries have gradually built up a sophisticated and highly developed system of regional international law, which includes a series of regional norms that have regulated their international and domestic political behavior. The legal evolution of Latin American society has been expressed at the levels of public international law, private international law, and the establishment of a regional institutional system, which has advanced international law in general. Since the Panama Congress of 1826, summoned by Simón Bolívar, legal issues had always been a priority of the nineteenth-century Latin American Congresses that preceded the Inter-

American Conferences launched in the 1890s, and since then in the innumerable conferences and meetings of the Inter-American system.

The Latin American countries, especially those in South America, through a gradual historical and learning process, have managed to establish a unique Latin "diplomatic culture" that has helped their governments to resolve their international conflicts short of war. There has been a long tradition in the region of gaining honor by meeting legal obligations, not divorced from considerations of national interest such as prestige and reputation (see Holsti 1993, 19; Holsti 1996, 169–70). The Latin American nations have succeeded in developing a theory and practice of exceptionalism regarding their recourse to international law—arbitration of disputes, mediation, bilateral negotiations, and other techniques for the peaceful settlement of international disputes—rather than the use of force.[2] Based on a common historical and cultural framework, the Latin American nations have built a strong normative consensus that has been institutionalized in legal instruments since the beginning of the nineteenth century.

In few other parts of the world is the culture of a given region perceived to be so distinctive, identifiable, and at the same time so influential in the political process, both domestic and international, as is Latin America (Ebel, Taras, and Cochrane 1991, 5). To understand this peculiar legal (or legalist) culture, one has to refer to its origins in Spain and Portugal (Wiarda 1995, 186–87). As a "fragmented" culture or offshoot of its Iberian mother culture, Latin America reflected the different and competing cultural strains that arose in the Spanish empire: political centralization and authoritarianism, in juxtaposition with decentralization and resistance to authority (Ebel and Taras 1990, 193; Dealy 1984/1985, 111). The strain of political centralization and authoritarianism stemmed from the Habsburg model of absolutism, which emphasized top-down hierarchical rule, a rigid social system based on principles of patrimonialism and seignorial authority, and an authoritarian body of beliefs and institutions from a religious and intellectual point of view. A second, venerable (Machiavellian or even Lockeian) tradition emphasized political rebelliousness and resistance to authority. This was reflected in the tendency of "taking to the streets, or taking to the hills" in order to reach political and social goals. The people could collectively overthrow an unjust prince, but for them to exercise effective checks and balances on his (rather than her) behavior or stay in power was practically unheard of (Dealy 1984/1985, 115–16; see also Ebel, Taras, and Cochrane 1991, 50).

The Spanish Empire was a medieval colonial Christiandom, essentially a feudal and patrimonial system already dying in a modernizing Europe at the beginning of the colonial period. Its transplantation to the New World, combined with the absolute necessity on the part of colonial and postcolonial elites to control the local population, resulted in inherently unstable political regimes, confronting domestic as well as external threats. The inevitable result of this clash of cultural strains was a chronic condition of domestic political instability, stemming from a basic opposition to accept and play by the rules of the (democratic) game, resulting in recurrent cycles of transitions from and to democracy and authoritarianism until the 1980s. In turn, this instability created and perpetuated a relatively weak position for Latin American nations in the hierarchy of the international system. Paradoxically, these two factors— domestic political instability and external weakness vis-à-vis the international system—explain the Latin American anomaly with respect to its regular normative behavior. On the one hand, there has been a deliberate willingness to accept certain norms in international relations (such as the rule of law, or the recourse to nonviolent means of conflict resolution). On the other hand, those same norms, or similar ones, were constantly violated in the domestic scene until the return to (or installation of) democratic regimes in the last two decades. Hence, the Latin American regional society has been characterized since the late nineteenth century by a paradoxical contrast between domestic violence and instability and relatively peaceful international relations.

The early years of the Latin American states were punctuated by civil wars, domestic anarchy, disintegration, and a lack of regional unity. The continental unity of the Spanish Empire broke down into small entities, following the failure of confederative schemes. The wars of independence and the process of state formation in the region were long and bloody—fifteen years of independence wars against Spain (1810–1824), followed by another fifty years or so of intraregional and civil wars. Furthermore, given the political instability and domestic anarchy that characterized most of the new states, with the exceptions of Brazil and Chile, some of these wars overlapped with civil wars and other domestic conflicts.

During these formative years, boundary disputes were a high priority in the foreign relations of the Latin American states, leading to wars and consequent problems of irredentism, revanchism, and nationalism that extended well into the twentieth century. At the same time, the Latin American states accepted by the mid-1830s the principle of *uti possidetis,* whereby the boundaries of the new states should coincide with those of the former administrative colonial divisions (Clissold and Hennesy 1968, 403). Moreover, throughout this period many of the new states entertained a lingering spirit of solidarity, keeping the idea of Latin American cooperation alive in a series of congresses designed to implement some form of political integration. Hence, even in their initial chaotic period one can identify a recurrent paradoxical pattern that is basic to the conception and reality of the Latin American international society. A practical failure in the aspirations for larger forms of political union in Central America and in Bolívar's Gran Colombia did motivate a lingering sense of frustration. This frustration, in turn, explains the ambivalence and ambiguity of several Latin American states in proclaiming at the same time strident declarations of nationalism, along with a vigorous concern and formal adoption of international institutions and international (regional) law with even a supranational tinge (Davis 1959, 10).

Despite the practical failure to achieve power through political unions and integration, the theme of unity has remained an important one in the formal discourse of the Latin American nations and their common regional identity. Unity has been bolstered by arguments stressing their common origin, history, and institutions, as well as references to "one family" of Spanish (if not Latin) American nations. This unfulfilled aspiration for unity partly explains the recurrent patterns of regional cooperation, consensus seeking, and harmonization (*concertación*) in limiting the recourse to interstate war, and the relatively peaceful settlement of disputes that has characterized the international relations of the region, especially in South America, since 1883 (Meyer 1997, 160–61).

Bolivarianism and Panamericanism

As a basic theme in the formation and evolution of the Latin American international society, the supranational aspirations for regional unity have been developed by two overlapping and sometimes opposing ideological movements: Bolivarianism and Panamericanism. Bolivarianism has been expressed in the Latin American Congresses of the nineteenth century, the regional efforts to resolve the Central American civil wars in the 1980s (by the Contadora and Rio Groups), and the invigorated schemes for economic integration throughout Latin America. Conversely, Panamericanism has been reflected in a series of Inter-American Conferences held since 1889, the work of the Organization of American States (OAS) since 1948, and numerous Inter-American institutions, including the recent Presidential Summits of the Americas in 1994, 1998, and 2001. In sum, while Bolivarianism focuses on the internal (intraregional) dynamics of the emergence of norms among the Latin American states themselves, Panamericanism includes the external (i.e., U.S.-centered) dynamics of that process. In other words, Panamericanism (or Inter-Americanism) can be considered a form of hemispheric regionalism. In contrast, Bolivarianism (or Latin Americanism) refers to a sort of nationalism, or pan-nationalism (Ardao 1986, 170).

The Latin American nations in general, and the Hispanoamerican states of South America in particular, have always sought to build upon a structure of political cooperation on the basis of their common historical, cultural, and institutional heritage. Schemes of political integration, such as Bolívar's dream of a South American political union, or even more modest confederation schemes such as the Gran Colombia (Colombia-Venezuela-Ecuador), Mexico with Central America, the small states of Central America, and Peru-Bolivia, broke down a couple of decades after independence. However, the idea of a Latin American consciousness and identity, of a regional society based on a common history, culture, and language, never disappeared.

Bolivarianism—that is, Bolívar's basic concept of a loose confederation of Hispanoamerican states—derived from the external threat posed by Europe's powers to the nascent South American states. According to this view, the political solidarity, cooperation, and integration among the Latin American states were inherently defensive and externally driven. In the 1820s Bolívar called for the establishment of an international or supranational entity that would "serve as a council in great conflict, as a point of contact in common dangers, and as a faithful interpreter of public treaties where difficulties occur, as a conciliator, in short, of our differences" (quoted in Perera 1985, 133; my translation). In his view, "Iberoamerica can only operate in the world as an economic and political union" (quoted in Amescua 1986, 51; my translation). However, the 1826 Congress of Panama convened by Bolívar ultimately failed, so that the political union among the new Latin American nations never materialized. While the formal institutions sponsored by Bolívar and his successors remained ephemeral, the principles and norms underlying them became a permanent part of the Latin American and American landscapes of regional international law, well after the initial failure of the political schemes of integration. Those were national-populist ideas that rejected imperialism and the Panamerican system, defended sovereignty, self-determination, and nonintervention, and encouraged Latin American coordination and cooperation.

The major norms of the contemporary Latin American society were already spelled out by Bolívar in the early 1820s, including: (1) the regional society should be governed by a democratic supranational assembly; (2) the goals of the Latin American union should include keeping the peace and prosperity of its member-states; (3) peaceful settlement of international disputes, including the recourse to compulsory mechanisms of arbitration; (4) a system of collective security, including common and mutual defense and neutrality; (5) adoption of the norms of equality of states and sovereignty, including the principle of nonintervention; (6) recognition of the principle of *uti possidetis juris;* (7) nonrecognition of territorial conquests following wars; (8) protection of human rights, including the abolition of slavery; and (9) regulation of territorial and diplomatic relations, with specific references to the issues of extradition and the granting of political asylum.[3]

Bolivarianism as an expression of regional (i.e., Latin American) nationalism declined with the ascendance of the Panamerican movement after 1889.[4] It was resuscitated only with the Central American peace process after 1982, when the Contadora Group and, later, the Rio Group adopted a "concerted diplomacy" of peacemaking in Central America distinctive from the Inter-American framework. The wish to develop policies toward the Central American conflict that were different from those of the United States led to the creation of the Contadora Group in 1983, formed by Colombia, Mexico, Panama, and Venezuela. The peace plans sponsored by the Contadora Group were adhered to by the Support Group formed in 1985 by Argentina, Brazil, Peru, and Uruguay. Finally, in 1986 a Permanent Mechanism for Consultation and Concert was formed in Rio de Janeiro (the Rio Group). Nowadays it includes most of the countries of the region and it has become an effective forum for policy coordination and political cooperation among the Latin American countries (Meyer 1997, 166–67; Espíndola 1998, 16).

While the Rio Group represents the political expression of Bolivarianism, the Inter-American system and the Organization of American States are the political expression of Panamericanism, which predates the formal, post-1945 institutions. Starting with the Monroe Doctrine of 1823, the concept of a "special relationship" among the Americas has provided the ideological underpinning for Inter-American cooperation and the building of institutions, based on common principles and norms. Among the essential American norms and rules, one can mention the following: (1) the principle of *uti possidetis;* (2) recognition of relatively free and unimpeded fluvial navigation; (3) recognition of the legal status of rebels; (4) recognition of political asylum; (5) acceptance of the principle of *ius soli* against the generally applied continental (European) principle of *ius sanguinis;* (6) the rule that there is no *res nullius* in America; (7) the equality of states; (8) respect for sovereignty and nonintervention; (9) the acceptance of codification of international law; (10) peaceful settlement of disputes; (11) the establishment of arrangements for the defense of the hemisphere; and (12) the promotion of republicanism, liberty, and democracy (see Jacobini 1954, 129; Atkins 1995, 197).

Interestingly, at the normative level there has been a high degree of overlap between these two ideological movements. The Spanish American congresses of the nineteenth century and the principles and institutions of international law that emanated from the treaties signed in those congresses gravitated considerably on the origin and evolution of the Inter-American system. For instance, the current Charter of the OAS contains specific references to the same topics that were on the agenda of the Panama Congress of 1826, such as the collective security of the fledgling Latin American states against Spain (see García-Amador 1983, 59; De Vries 1972, 105). Among these common norms, the Latin American states have traditionally emphasized the overarching principle of nonintervention.

If Bolivarianism and Panamericanism share the same norms, though within different formal institutions, what are their major differences at the conceptual level? Panamericanism has been based on the notion of a special relationship among the Americas, particularly their geographical proximity, similar historical experiences, and common republican ideas. It can be best understood in terms of a theory and ideology of regionalism that has provided the rationale for the practices and institutions of the Inter-American system. Conversely, Bolivarianism can be considered as a case of cultural identity and nationalism at the regional level, beyond their common historical and ideological experiences. The difference between the two movements stems from the divergent roles assigned to the United States in the definition and shaping of the Latin American regional identity. Panamericanism implies the recognition of the preponderance, if not the hegemony, of the United States in shaping the political agenda and establishing the common norms on the continent. Conversely, Bolivarianism suggests a series of regional norms as a nonmaterial (ideational, normative) balance against the use (and abuse) of U.S. power in its relations with its Southern neighbors.

The Role of the United States in Shaping the Latin American Regional Identity and Society

The Latin American conception of an Inter-American legal order has shown an obsession with the norms of sovereignty and independence of its member-states, with a concomitant emphasis on the principle of nonintervention. This conception has been more than justified against the historical background of recurrent U.S. interventions in Mexico, the Caribbean, and Central America, especially between 1904 and 1938. By the turn of the twentieth century, the external European threat to Latin America was replaced by the aggressive foreign policy of the United States in the region. The behavior of the United States did cause mixed feelings of fear and hatred toward a coercive hegemon and predator. At the same time, the United States also garnered admiration because of the need for its protection and leadership as a regional *caudillo* or even benevolent *patrón* (see Ronning 1963, 160; Ebel and Taras 1990, 200–1).

As a perceived external threat, the United States has fulfilled an important role in shaping the Latin American identity and its conception of an international society. The constant U.S. threat of intervention in the early twentieth century had the effect of inhibiting some Latin American states from using force to settle their international differences. Many precepts of international law developed by prominent South American jurists, such as the Calvo and Drago doctrines, defended the principle of nonintervention and peaceful settlement of disputes. These principles constituted the legal weapon and response of the weak Latin American states to the possibility of forcible interventions by extraregional powers, first and foremost the United States. Hence, the development of a regional international law can be understood as a sensible and practical response of weaker actors in the international arena vis-à-vis predatory stronger powers.

In addition to these legal aspects, the concept of a Latin American international society evolved partially from a complex identity relationship with the United States that included both "negative" and "positive" elements. The negative identity developed as the result of the political and cultural shocks caused by the Spanish defeat in the 1898 Spanish-American War. In its aftermath, some Latin American intellectuals soul-searched and redefined themselves partly in contrast to their North American counterparts, especially at the cultural and ideological levels. For instance, the work of José Enrique Rodó at the beginning of the twentieth century epitomized the antinomies between Latin American and North American cultures and ideologies.[5] This ideological schism existed until the 1980s, when the Latin American countries as a whole (with the notorious exception of Cuba) finally adopted the global tenets of political democracy and economic neoliberalism, in convergence with the United States' own ideology and political culture.

The positive identity relations with the United States derived from the identification of many ruling political elites in Latin America with the U.S. political and strategic interests in the region. Many analysts tend to identify the normative consensus of the Latin American international society, including its peaceful international relations, with the U.S. hegemony. After all, the pacifying role of the United States seems to offer a plausible explanation for why Latin America (and especially South America) was more peaceful in the twentieth century than in the nineteenth century. The United States has both the motive and the capacity to deter wars among the Latin American countries.

Yet this argument is flawed for three reasons. First, it cannot explain why no wars occurred in South America between 1883 and 1930, when the United States competed with the still-large economic influence of the United Kingdom in the region, as well as with Germany and France. Second, the two exceptional South American wars of the twentieth century—Chaco from 1932 to 1935 and Peru-Ecuador in 1941 occurred at the time of U.S. preponderance. Third, a clear distinction should be drawn between Central America and South America. Central America has been more conflict-ridden, in both domestic and international terms, than South America. Moreover, unlike the U.S. role in Central America and the Caribbean basin, the U.S. hegemony has been steadily declining in South America, at least until the end of the Cold War, when it became paramount again but at the same time strategically irrelevant. This process has been linked to the consolidation of local powers such as Brazil, Argentina, Chile, and Venezuela, and the diversification of foreign links between the South American countries and Western Europe, Japan, China, and the former Soviet Union.[6]

Genealogy and Evolution of Norms in Latin America

From a reading of the historical background of the Latin American society we learn that it has gradually evolved since independence; Bolivarianism and Panamericanism have been two strong ideological currents that shaped it; and the United States has fulfilled a certain role in setting its identity. Thus, we can suggest that the international norms of Latin America have emerged and developed as a result of social practices, ecological processes, and social and internal processes.

Genealogy of Norms

Social Practices

International norms are based on preexisting cultural knowledge and institutions, including other, previous norms. The emergence of norms in Latin America is associated, first and foremost, with the political culture of the "mother country," especially Spain. In more specific terms, the Spanish legalistic culture, including its features of idealism, paternalism, legalism, and formalism can explain the emergence of norms such as sovereignty and equality of states, *uti possidetis,* and political legalism.

Moreover, if social practices are associated with ordinary practice, imitation, and learning, then many of the norms stem from the evolution and institutionalization of Bolivarianism and Panamericanism in the course of the nineteenth and twentieth centuries, including the norms of peaceful settlement of international disputes, arms control, and collective security. Many norms have been "built" upon the foundations of multilateral institutions, such as the nineteenth-century Latin American congresses.

Ecological Processes

An ecological process implies an explicit interaction between actors and their environment. In the Latin American case, norms have emerged as the result of conscious promotion of actors, they have been negotiated among the different actors, and they have been imposed from a hegemonic position, as in the case of the Inter-American system promoted by the United States.

A positivist argument will explain the emergence of norms in the Latin American society as a functional necessity or response of a weak region confronting a hostile environment of great powers in general, and of the United States in particular. The emergence of Latin American norms and institutions was supposed to serve the interests of the countries of the region. Thus, the attempt to focus the intraregional international relations of Latin America in legalistic terms can be derived from the structural and domestic weaknesses, as well as the international disadvantages, of the Latin American states. For instance, prominent Argentine jurists like Carlos Calvo and Luis María Drago suggested doctrines that enhanced sovereignty and nonintervention to confront, by juridical means, the paramountcy of extraregional powers. Conversely, from a realist perspective, some of the norms of peace and security in the Western Hemisphere, especially by the turn of the twentieth century, have been associated with the "entrepreneurial" role adopted by the United States, from its unique hegemonic position, in promoting Panamericanism and the Inter-American institutions.

Social and Internal Processes

Similarly, the etiology and evolution of international norms are linked to social processes such as social diffusion, transgovernmental networks, epistemic communities, and transnational movements. Some of these processes are international and transnational, while others are domestic.

In the Latin American case a substantial body of supranational Latin American law has emerged and evolved via a regional network of treaties and conventions (Karst and Rosenn 1975). This has resulted from the weakness of much of Latin American national law enforcement machinery; the universalistic, natural law perspective of the region's jurists; and the common legal, cultural, and linguistic backgrounds of most of Latin America.

As for the internal or domestic processes in Latin America, the internalization of regional norms has led to their adoption within the domestic political sphere. This has been evident in the case of the norms of democratization and promotion of human rights, in the "third wave" of democratization in the late 1970s and early 1980s.

Evolution of Norms

Norms have evolved in Latin America as a function of the historical trajectory of the Latin American states since their early stages of independence. The frustrating record of Latin American (especially Spanish American) leaders in the nineteenth century to establish larger forms of union explains their ambivalence toward strident nationalism, as well as their vigorous concern and formal support for international law (Davis 1959, 10). To explain the evolution of norms in the region, we can turn to the theoretical models regarding processes of inheritance, dominance and reputation, and cognitive evolution.

Processes of Inheritance (Norms as Genes)

Several prominent norms in the region, such as sovereignty and nonintervention, *uti possidetis,* and peaceful settlement of international disputes, can be explained according to this mechanistic or deterministic model. For instance, *uti possidetis* and peaceful settlement have been coherent with the preexisting concern with sovereignty and nonintervention, and have grown and evolved in a favorable regional environment, especially with the consolidation of the new Latin American states in the second half of the nineteenth century.

Behavioralist Processes: The Importance of Dominance and Reputation

In terms of dominance, norms might evolve as the result of a hegemonic power that imposes norms as a means of systemic diffusion. With the decline of Bolivarianism by the end of the nineteenth century, many of its essential norms were transplanted into the emerging Panamericanism, leading to their institutionalization within the Inter-American system before, and especially after, World War II. Moreover, within Latin America itself, the adoption and evolution of agreed-upon norms of peace and security can be explained through a regional demonstration of "contagion," according to which states care about their self-image, so they adapt to the "peer pressure" of their normative environment. This was evident in the case of the domino effect (*la moda*), which sought to democratize the region in the late 1970s and 1980s. It has also affected the evolution and prominence of the norm of peaceful settlement of international disputes throughout the twentieth century.

Cognitive Processes: Cognitive Evolution as Learning

Finally, the evolution of norms in Latin America has been linked to a historical process of learning and adaptation over time. Through a long and painstaking process, many of the regional norms have become institutionalized, within both the Latin American and the Inter-American systems. This has been evident in the adoption of the principle of nonintervention as a corollary of the paramount norms of sovereignty and equality among states. As for the norm of *uti possidetis,* it was selected and diffused as an effective legal and normative mechanism to cope with territorial disputes in the nineteenth and twentieth centuries. Regarding the norms of peaceful settlement of international disputes, *convivencia,* and *concertación,* these have been diffused on both international and transnational bases, leading to their more recent adoption and implementation involving domestic conflicts, such as civil wars—as in the case of Central America in the 1980s and early 1990s. Finally, the norms of democracy and protection of human rights evolved on a cognitive basis through a regional "contagion effect," disseminated through international and transnational agents, leading to the sweeping wave of democratization and redemocratization in the region in the late 1970s and 1980s.

The Elements of Latin American Society

Having discussed the historical and ideological bases of Latin American international society, what are its major elements? As stated above, these are common interests and values; common norms and rules; and common institutions.

Common Interests and Values

In the Latin American region we can identify the general goals of any international society as follows:

1. The Latin American states have been obviously interested since their independence in preserving their regional system of independent states.
2. They have remained adamant regarding the respect for their sovereignty and independence, as evident in their promotion of the principle of nonintervention.
3. They have maintained regional peace, the absence of war being considered the normal condition in their international relations.
4. They have limited violence in their relations by turning to mechanisms of peaceful settlement and by keeping their diplomatic relations within a general framework of international law.

Paradoxically, these common goals have enabled the Latin American countries to reach a high degree of civility in their international relations, juxtaposed with uncivilized (if not brutal) political relations within their own borders. Thus, an international society could coexist for many decades with the lack of basic societal relationships between authoritarian regimes and their own societies. This paradox stems from the common values and the particular political culture of the region.

In contrast to other regions of the developing world, the basic social, political, and economic values of Latin America directly derive from its European tradition; hence, its values are part of the Western Christian culture (or "civilization"). An entrenched culture of legalism characterizes the political and diplomatic systems of the region. Among the most important factors that have conditioned this legal culture are idealism, paternalism, legalism, formalism, and lack of penetration into their own societies. Moreover, the Hispanic tradition of political monism, organicism, legal idealism, and patrimonialism has forged the dominant political value system of Latin America, discouraging the development of pluralistic tendencies in favor of a difficult, if not impossible, collective harmony at the domestic level embodied by a long tradition of "civil law." In terms of international relations, this legalist culture helps us to understand the unique (and sometimes exaggerated) importance of legal considerations and formal(istic) procedures in Latin American policy making and approaches to international conflicts.[7]

Common Norms and Rules

This common cultural framework, together with the development of a distinctive regional identity, has helped to consolidate the basis for a normative consensus related to the way international relations should be conducted among the Latin American nations. A discussion of the five essential norms follows, though the list is by no means exhaustive.[8]

Sovereignty and Equality of States

In Latin America and the Caribbean the norm of sovereignty initially reflected the early-sixteenth-century notion of an independent, self-sufficient, and geographically defined state. It also reflected the authoritarian political position of the Spanish Empire in the New World at that time. Following the emergence of the new republics in the early nineteenth century, the concept of constitutional sovereignty was grafted onto the tradition of the monarchical absolutism associated with Castilla and the Spanish Empire (Knight 1992, 11 and 15).

The norms of sovereignty and equality of states are deeply rooted in the tradition of Latin American and Inter-American international law, despite their inconsistency with the actual practice of powerful states—first and foremost the United States. As a corollary, the principle of nonintervention has received special attention, reflecting the Latin American resistance to unilateral acts of intervention by the European powers and the United States. This principle was clearly exposed in the Calvo Doctrine of 1896 and the Drago Doctrine of 1903. Both doctrines stressed the absolute juridical equality of states and the inviolability of sovereignty, pointing out that intervention to enforce pecuniary claims under any circumstances was legally invalid.[9] Eventually, the principle of nonintervention was formally recognized and incorporated into the Inter-American system in 1933, at the Seventh Inter-American Conference in Montevideo. Its brief formulation included the clause that "No state has the right to intervene in the internal or external affairs of another" (quoted in García-Amador 1983, 90).

Uti Possidetis *and Territorial Integrity*

In Latin America, and especially in the South American subregion, the majority of border disputes throughout the nineteenth and twentieth centuries have been resolved peacefully, leading to some cession or exchange of territories.

The basis for a peaceful settlement of those disputes was established through the principle of *uti possidetis, ita possideatis* ("as you possess, you may possess"). The main goal of the doctrine has been to proclaim the right of the Latin American states to replace their mother country in exercising their territorial rights. It is based on the premise that there was no *terra nullius* on the American continent by the end of the colonial age. The doctrine was explicitly mentioned in the Panama Congress of 1826, the Lima Congress of 1847–1848, and the Caracas Treaty of 1883 (Bachler 1975, 288; Bachler 1976, 259).

According to Cukwurah, "The new states of Latin America, for convenience and expediency, adopted as the basis for their boundaries the administrative divisions of the mother country which existed at the date when the movement for independence broke out. That 'critical date,' in the case of South America, was generally taken to be 1810" (Cukwurah 1967, 112–13).

The principle of *uti possidetis* did not preclude the emergence of boundary disputes among the Latin American states, since uncertainty characterized the demarcation of borders and frontiers of the new states. However, by recognizing the same norm of international law, the parties at least managed to resolve their border disputes, in most cases, peacefully. For instance, thirty attempts at arbitration in the nineteenth and twentieth centuries applied the principle of *uti possidetis,* especially among the Spanish American republics, but also between Argentina and Brazil (Bachler 1976, 233). The principle was invoked in several territorial disputes that resulted in cases of peaceful change (see Kacowicz 1994). The norm of *uti possidetis* has fulfilled a crucial role in the peaceful settlement and management of territorial disputes and conflicts. It directly relates to the norm of territorial integrity, according to which force should not be used to alter interstate boundaries (Zacher 2001, 215).

Peaceful Settlement of International Disputes, "Convivencia," *and* "Concertación"

These three interrelated norms encompass a pattern of regional cooperation that has resulted in mediation, arbitration, and diplomatic solutions rather than war. Sometimes peaceful settlement was arranged through international congresses and multilateral diplomacy; more frequently, it took place through bilateral solutions with noncompulsory, ad hoc resources for the management and resolution of international conflicts (see Meyer 1997, 160; Puig 1983).

The principle that Latin American disputes should be settled by peaceful procedures goes back to Bolívar's original plan of confederation at Panama in 1826. Later, after more than half a century, it took shape in the 1890 Plan of Arbitration at the Inter-American level and in a long succession of declarations, treaties, resolutions, and conventions on the subject. That disputes should be settled peacefully is one of the firmest principles of both the Latin American international society and the larger Inter-American system; the problem has always been how to implement it.

In the last part of the nineteenth century and throughout the twentieth century, Latin America in general, and South America in particular, saw exceptionally high rates of peaceful conflict resolution and/or toleration of conflicts that remain unresolved but are not likely to be settled by recourse to war. Arbitration procedures have been used in the area at extraordinarily high rates compared to other regions of the world. From the 1820s until the 1970s, eight states alone—Argentina, Bolivia, Brazil, Colombia, Chile, Ecuador, Peru, and Venezuela—used arbitration procedures 151 times (see Puig 1985; Mares 1997, 204). Many of the bilateral border disputes involving the Latin American states have been submitted to arbitration (a total of twenty-two). Out of these twenty-two cases, almost half of them were accepted.

Arms Control, Collective Security, and Confidence-Building Measures

Compared to other areas of the developing world, such as the Middle East, Southeast Asia, or parts of Africa, militarism in Latin America never represented a danger to the peace of the world, or even to the peace of the region and the territorial integrity of its nations. Except for the virulent Chaco War of 1932–1935, there were no major violent international conflicts involving Latin American countries in the twentieth century. Hence, Latin American states have enjoyed a respectable (though qualified) tradition of moderation in military affairs, at least at the international level. Enduring rivalries such as those between Argentina and Chile, or between Argentina and Brazil, did not escalate into armed conflicts, though militarization and arms races have characterized these two dyads until the wave of democratization that swept Latin America in the 1980s.

Throughout the history of Latin America there have been many calls for disarmament, and even some limited success in achieving demilitarized frontiers or zones. Latin American governments set forth a variety of arms limitations, proposals, and agreements, such as the demilitarization of the Magellan Strait between Argentina and Chile (1881); the Mayo Pacts of 1902 calling for comprehensive naval arms control between Argentina and Chile; the Treaty of Tlatelolco in 1967, which established a nuclear-free zone in Latin America; and the Ayacucho Declaration of 1974. Moreover, the Argentine-Brazilian nuclear cooperation in the 1980s and 1990s, including bilateral and multilateral agreements on nuclear arms control and disarmament, led to the joint ratification (together with Chile) of the Tlatelolco regime in 1994.

The norm of arms control is directly linked to the principles of collective, mutual, and comprehensive security among the Latin American states, as well as at the Inter-American level. Like the principle of peaceful settlement of international disputes, the principle of Inter-American mutual defense (i.e., collective security) was originally embodied in Bolívar's plan of confederation, though it did not take shape until more than a century later. Formally, the OAS Charter and the Rio Treaty can be interpreted as farsighted collective security instruments, sponsoring peaceful settlement of disputes, military cooperation against aggression, and even the promotion of democracy and human rights throughout the region. In practice, however, these instruments were not very effective in reaching these normative goals.

Political Legalism, Democracy, and Human Rights

In addition to the norms of peaceful settlement and arms control, the strong legalist tradition in Latin America has also been expressed—in theory, if not always in practice—in a clear commitment to the rule of law, political liberalism, republicanism, and political democracy. At the same time, there have been other features of political culture, such as patrimonialism, a heritage of elitism and authoritarianism, organic statism, and corporatism, which had always eroded any viable pluralistic tradition or translation of those principles into a coherent and viable practice (Dealy 1984/1985, 115; Wiarda 1995, 9). Thus, in many cases throughout its political history, much of Latin American democracy has consisted chiefly of formalism and verbalisms, which we might call legalism or constitutionalism, principles and ideals of political democracy that seem to have been more breached than honored. And yet the consistency with which political leaders, elites, and public opinion in general have adhered to these principles, such as republicanism and the rule of law, represents in itself an important political and social fact (Davis 1959, 8). In this sense, as Kathryn Sikkink (1996, 1–10) forcefully states, the assumed contradiction between support for sovereignty and nonintervention and the promotion of human rights and democracy is not as severe as often portrayed. Legalism has been primarily identified with support for sovereignty and nonintervention in international relations, although there has also been a strong, long-lasting, and under-studied tradition of formal support for democracy and human rights in the region.

Nowadays the commitment to democratic norms has become broad and widespread. The end of the Cold War has furthered the promotion and defense of democracy and human rights by removing the ideological and strategic connotations attached to democracy for many years. The contemporary perception is that representative democracy can be defended in the Western Hemisphere without running the risk of being trapped in the logic of the former East-West confrontation (Muñoz 1994, 194; Whitehead 1991, 217). Since the mid-1980s, the Latin American normative consensus has therefore been enhanced by an additional norm associated with peace in a broader sense: the commitment and promotion of political democracy. For instance, on June 8, 1991, the General Assembly of the OAS proclaimed the Declaration of Santiago de Chile, by which all member-states committed themselves to the defense and enhancement of representative democracy in the Western Hemisphere.

Common Institutions

The five major norms described above have been formalized in an intricate network of formal institutions that have regulated the relations of Latin American nations within their regional society. These institutions include the Latin American states themselves; their regional international law and regulation of diplomatic relations; multilateral forums of cooperation, such as nineteenth-century Latin American Congresses; and recent schemes of economic integration and interdependence.

Compared with other developing world regions, Latin America has avoided major sources of identity conflicts, such as ethnicity, irredentist claims, tribalism, and religion. Thus, in a continuum between the strong and democratic states of Western Europe and the weak and undemocratic states of Africa, the typical Latin American state occupies an intermediate position. In Latin America, weak though consolidated nation-states have confronted their civil societies and their international environment through different types of political regimes, both authoritarian and democratic. While political regimes were in dispute until two decades ago, the state as an institution has enjoyed widespread political legitimacy, as the result of a long period of independence and the consolidation of international boundaries.

A second, major institution in Latin America has been the law and the rule of law itself, at both the domestic and the international levels. At the domestic level, law does matter in the politics of the region, though it has not always been effective or respected (Becker 1997, 1). At the international level, the recourse to a regional international law as a common institution of the Latin American international society has facilitated the foreign and international relations of the Latin American states, both among themselves and vis-à-vis extraregional powers. The international congresses of the nineteenth century, which sought to deter, limit, and resolve military conflicts both within the region and through extraregional powers, are examples of multilateral frameworks of international law. In most of these congresses, a series of treaties and resolutions were discussed and adopted, spelling out many of the current norms mentioned above. Beginning with the Congress of Panama in 1826, the issue of the maintenance of peace was addressed and formalized in a series of treaties—such as Lima (1848), Santiago de Chile (1856), and Lima again (1865). Later on, before World War II, a series of multilateral treaties were signed regarding the peaceful settlement of disputes, such as the Anti-War Treaty of Non-Aggression and Conciliation (Saavedra Lamas Treaty) of 1933.

In turn, the Pan-American movement since the end of the nineteenth century also incorporated this normative consensus in the form of twelve treaties signed between 1890 and 1945, dealing with good offices, mediation, investigation, conciliation, arbitration, and judicial settlement (Bailey 1967, 75). Especially after World War II, the norms associated with peace and security were institutionalized in three major legal instruments of the Inter-American system: the Inter-American Treaty of Reciprocal Assistance (Rio Pact) in 1947, the Charter of the Organization of American States in 1948, and the American Treaty on Pacific Settlement (the Pact of Bogotá) in 1948.

In addition to these formal institutions within the broader framework of the Inter-American system, more recent schemes of economic and political integration in Latin America can also be considered important. Integration has both political and economic components. Political integration, implying several forms of union, federation, and confederation, was the ephemeral political attempt of some of Latin America's early great liberators and statesmen. For example, Simón Bolívar himself created Gran Colombia, which did not outlast him. Similarly, Central American leaders fought until 1907 to recreate the United Provinces of Central America, which had been dismantled in the civil wars of 1838–1842.

Economic integration has been another important expression of the Latin American international society, through the institutionalization of cooperation and the promotion of economic, if not political, interdependence. Moreover, frameworks of economic integration have fulfilled important political roles in the assertion of the Latin American society, as in the case of CEPAL (Comisión Económica para América Latina y el Caribe) after World War II, with a concomitant economic ideology of "developmentalism" and the adoption of economic policies of Import-Substitution-Industrialization (ISI) (Lagos 1987, 111). In recent years subregional schemes of economic integration, such as the Andean Group, the Central American Common Market, and especially Mercosur, have become important vehicles in the region's political assertion and its consolidation as a regional international society.

The Impact of the International Society on Its Members

It is evident from this cursory description that Latin America contains the three major elements that compose and define any international society:

1. The Latin American nations sustain common goals and interests, related to common values derived from the same cultural heritage.
2. There is an elaborated set of norms and rules that prescribes the behavior of the Latin American states in their international relations.
3. These norms have been formalized and translated into a complex network of formal institutions, both at the Latin American and the Inter-American levels.

Yet the interesting policy issue that has remained unexplored so far is an assessment of the impact of the Latin American international society on its constituent members, in terms of both domestic and international politics. Does the existence of a Latin American international society make any difference in the domestic and foreign political behaviors of the Latin American states? If the answer is yes, as we presume in this book, then we should find evidence regarding the impact on the foreign policies of the member-states, as well as in their domestic politics. Thus, we should look for examples of the six paths of influence through which international norms and institutions affect international and domestic political processes in the Latin American region.

Impact on the Foreign Policies of the Member-States
(International Processes)

The evolution and development of the Latin American international society has had a benign and peaceful effect on the foreign policies of its member-states. More specifically, three influences can be traced from the common values, interests, norms, and institutions that compose the international society in shaping the international relations of Latin America:

1. Regional norms and institutions have contributed to the maintenance of the "long peace" in South America since 1883 (Kacowicz 1998, 102–5).
2. The elements of the regional international society (common interests, values, norms, and institutions) have reshaped the definition of state interests in terms of their foreign relations. This has been evident with regard to norms of peace (such as *uti possidetis* and peaceful settlement of international disputes), as well as norms of security (arms control, collective security, and confidence-building measures).
3. In some cases, norms such as democracy have moved and "upgraded" the peaceful relations in Latin America in the direction of a pluralistic security community.

Without ruling out competing explanations of *Realpolitik* and self-interest, it is clear that the norms of peaceful settlement, *convivencia, concertación,* and *uti possidetis* help to explain the maintenance of regional peace since 1883. Moreover, norms and institutions in the Latin American international society have promoted recurrent attempts at regional integration, have kept the rigidity of the international borders, and have maintained international disputes without escalating them to war.

Furthermore, these regional values, norms, and institutions have, to a certain extent, contributed to the redefinition of the national interests of its member-states to "fit" the normative consensus of the Latin American society. For instance, the diffusion of democratization has reshaped the way states define their security policies, even in matters such as nuclear policy, as in the cases of Argentina and Brazil in the 1990s. Finally, these norms and institutions have expanded and "deepened" the preexisting peaceful relations among the member-states in the direction of a pluralistic security community. There are several examples to illustrate the impact of norms and institutions on the members of the Latin American international society.

First, between 1851 and 1922 at least fourteen peaceful cessions and exchanges of territory took place in South America. Eight of these disputes were resolved following arbitration and the rest through direct negotiations, good offices, and mediation. In many cases, the arbitration award was followed by further negotiations about its implementation, such as in the cases of Misiones (1895) and Tacna and Arica (1929).

Second, it can be argued that norms of peaceful settlement and *convivencia,* as well as the institutions of the Latin American society as a whole, have had a restraining effect in the direction of de-escalation and resolution of international conflicts and civil wars. This has been evident in the cases of the

Leticia dispute between Peru and Colombia (1932–1934); the resolution of the Beagle crisis of 1978 and the subsequent negotiations between Argentina and Chile (1979–1984); the regional initiatives of Contadora (1984) and Esquipulas (1987) to resolve the civil wars in El Salvador and Nicaragua; and, more recently, the final and peaceful resolution of the long conflict between Peru and Ecuador in October of 1998.

Third, in the Southern Cone of South America the return to democracy in Argentina (1983), Brazil (1985), and Chile (1989) has clearly affected and "upgraded" the quality of the peace among these three countries and the level of *rapprochement* and security cooperation between Argentina and Brazil since 1985, and between Argentina and Chile since 1990. These three countries have collaborated not only on nuclear nonproliferation, but also on the prohibition of chemical and biological weapons and the development of regional CBMs in 1995 and 1996. Moreover, the formation of Mercosur among Argentina, Brazil, Paraguay, and Uruguay in 1991 has changed and reshaped the perception of the (formerly narrow) national interests of its member-states in the direction of enhanced cooperation. Mercosur epitomizes a serious effort to increase interdependence and to move in the direction of economic, if not political, integration.

Impact On Domestic Politics (Domestic Processes)

The impact of the Latin American international society on the domestic politics of its constituent members—unlike the impact of its international relations—is more difficult to ascertain. Yet we can still recognize three direct and indirect effects of the common values, norms, rules, and institutions in Latin America on the domestic processes within their member-states:

1. The benign effects of the international society on the international relations of the region have indirectly shaped the political agenda of the Latin American states by focusing it on domestic politics.
2. The commitment to political democracy and legalism, at least at the formal level, has shaped the "transitional" character of the authoritarian regimes in the region, as manifested by the recurrent waves from and to democracy until the 1980s.
3. Membership in the Latin American international society has produced "domino effects" of recurrent cycles of authoritarianism and democratization in the region, following considerations of prestige and reputation.

Since international relations in Latin America have been overall peaceful since 1883, this benign international society has also shaped the domestic political agenda and the behavior of its member-states. Hence, the paramount political problems of Latin America have been associated with state consolidation and political legitimacy, as well as political and economic development. In general, domestic politics in Latin America have been considered much more important than international politics. This has to do with the character of the state in Latin America: it has been strong enough not to fall apart as in other postcolonial situations (like those in Africa). At the same time, it has been weak enough to find it hard to mobilize its society for war and conquest (see Centeno 2002). With the possible exceptions of Chile, Uruguay, and Costa Rica, most of the states in the region were captured by exclusive and restricted groups. Thus, the military and the oligarchic upper classes tended to rule by force rather than by legitimacy, at the expense of the rest of their societies. Moreover, the transitory character of the authoritarian regimes in the region, by definition, has been directly affected by the strong tradition of political legalism, which has contributed to the spread of democratization and the gradual consolidation of precarious democracies in the region since the 1980s.

Finally, membership in the Latin American society has led to a focus on domestic linkages and reverberations of political stability and instability across borders. It is precisely because of their common values, norms, and institutions that the Latin American states have been concerned with both the domestic politics of their neighbors and how their political regimes are regarded by other states, as "members of the same family" (*el qué dirán,* "what would they say . . ."). This partly explains *la moda* (the fashion) of domino effects through cycles of authoritarianism and democratization in the region. There are several illustrations to these possible impacts.

First, according to the legalist tradition, new military regimes, upon their accession to power, tried to regularize (i.e., legitimize) their de facto regimes in a somewhat formalistic fashion. They established constituent assemblies that drafted new constitutions that legalized, ex post facto, the existence and authority of the usurping leadership that had convened the assembly in the first place. This was the typical case of bureaucratic-authoritarian (BA) regimes in Argentina, Brazil, and Uruguay in the 1960s and 1970s (Golbert and Nun 1982, 35–36).

Second, the cycles of transitions back and forth between authoritarianism and democracy can be characterized as Latin American "waves." For instance, the "second reverse wave" (in the direction of authoritarianism) affected

Latin America in sequential terms: Peru (1962), Brazil and Bolivia (1964), Argentina (1966), Ecuador (1972), and Uruguay and Chile (1973). The military governments in Brazil, Argentina, Chile, and Uruguay became examples of bureaucratic-authoritarian regimes. Conversely, the "third wave of democracy" affected Latin America again as a domino or ripple effect. The sequence of democratization included Ecuador (1979), Peru (1980), Bolivia (1979–1982), Honduras (1982), Argentina (1983), Uruguay and El Salvador (1984), Brazil and Guatemala (1985), and, finally, Chile and Paraguay (1989) (see Huntington 1991, 19–23; Linz and Stepan 1978; O'Donnell and Schmitter, 1986).

Third, following the Santiago Commitment of 1991 on the promotion of democracy, coups and attempted coups in Latin America in the 1990s led to verbal and even active responses by the OAS and other subregional institutions such as Mercosur to restore democracy in the region. The results were uneven. In Guatemala (1993) and Paraguay (1996) some success was achieved, Peru (1992) was a failure, and Haiti (1991–1994) saw mixed results. That representative democracy has become a serious trigger for diplomatic and even military intervention in the region is a remarkable development (Acevedo and Grossman 1996, 132–41).

Latin America as a Unique Case?

Is the Latin American regional international society a unique case? In a way, the answer to this question is both "yes" and "no." In affirmative terms, Latin America is fairly unique in its plethora of stated norms and declarative intentions of prescriptive behavior, dating back to the beginning of the nineteenth century. Moreover, the contrast between its "civilized" and relatively peaceful international relations and the anarchy, lack of governance, civil wars, and recurrent cycles of authoritarianism until the 1980s within the borders of its member-states is quite peculiar.

At the same time, it is clear that the case of the Latin American international society is not completely exceptional. As we will further examine in chapter 6, there are other regional examples of contemporary international societies that have reached higher levels of institutionalization and societal relations, moving in the direction of pluralistic security communities, such as North America, Western Europe, or Southeast Asia. Only the Southern Cone of Latin America might qualify nowadays as an incipient pluralistic security community, with higher degrees of social links and institutionalization, as compared to other areas of Latin America.

The core of the Latin American international society has been its common values, norms, and institutions characterized by its legalistic tradition, with a very formalistic and sophisticated corpus of legal norms enhancing the principles of sovereignty and nonintervention. From that core derive a series of norms regarding peace and security, such as the peaceful settlement of disputes, *uti possidetis,* and the prohibition of deployment of nuclear weapons in the region. Finally, the norm of commitment to political democracy and protection of human rights, with its direct association with the maintenance of domestic and international peace, has been an integral part of this long tradition of political legalism and preference for the rule of law.

The effects of these regional norms and institutions on Latin American politics can be considered both constitutive and regulative, both shaping interests and identities as well as reflecting them. Moreover, the effects have had a "double" or combined impact, both domestic and international, or what I call *intermestic.* After all, it is only through their domestic internalization within the different Latin American states, and their institutionalization at bilateral and multilateral levels, that these norms and institutions have become effective, if at all.

The impact of the Latin American international society on the domestic and international politics of the region should be gauged against alternative explanations for the phenomena of the long South American peace and successful economic integration. Alternative explanations such as balance of power, U.S. or Brazilian hegemony, geographic isolation, irrelevance, and impotence to fight wars, threats by third parties, economic development and prosperity, dependency and interdependence are also feasible, without necessarily contradicting the normative argument advanced in this chapter.

Since most of the Latin American political regimes were authoritarian until the late 1970s and 1980s, it is quite striking to notice that norms of peaceful settlement, arms control, and even political legalism have had any effect at all on them, within the framework of a regional society. In other words, the Latin American case has proved that nondemocratic regimes can share some of the normative perspectives and institutional restraints that seem to characterize democracies. In this sense, the Latin American international society has been a successful Grotian laboratory to test the presence, effect, impact, and resilience of regional values, norms, and institutions associated with peace. While this has not been particularly unique—as witnessed by the example of ASEAN (Association of South East Asian Nations) and its authoritarian member-states—it is quite remarkable, given the former lack of civility of many of the Latin American states toward their own citizens.

CHAPTER FOUR

Norms of Peace
Peaceful Settlement and *Uti Possidetis*

IN THIS CHAPTER I EXAMINE THE RELEVANT NORMS OF PEACE IN LATIN America in the context of six territorial disputes that took place in the second half of the nineteenth century and throughout the twentieth. These six cases encompass a broad continuum of serious international conflicts, some of them long and enduring rivalries, ranging from peaceful settlement through war.

Since colonial days, there has been a notorious number of disputed borders in the region. A striking fact about post-independence Latin America has been the frequency and intensity of territorial conflicts and wars in its first sixty years (up to 1883) and its relative peacefulness thereafter. Although there were a few exceptions in the twentieth century—notably the Chaco War of 1932–1935—armed conflict between states declined as their economies developed and their governmental structures became stronger and better organized. The disputes and wars of the nineteenth century were largely about implementing the agreed-upon principle of *uti possidetis;* that is, resolving the legal ambiguities of boundaries inherited from the Spanish Empire. Many of these border disputes were diplomatically resolved, while a few ended after military action. Once these disputes were settled, diplomacy rather than force became the common practice in the region, as illustrated by the extraordinarily peaceful expansion of Brazil westward in the late nineteenth and early twentieth centuries, with almost no recourse to violence. Moreover, as a natural result of their preoccupation with boundary questions, by the end of the nineteenth century Latin Americans had developed a keen interest in the development of regional international law and legal mechanisms for the peaceful settlement of their international disputes, such as the recourse to arbitration. Even today many of the Latin American states still have territorial disputes with at least one neighbor (see Little 1986/1987, 594; Mares 1997, 198–99; Calvert 1983, 5; Treverton 1984, 5). Yet most of these remaining conflicts have been contained short of war, without escalating into serious international crises. The assumption of this chapter is that the fact that "dogs have not barked" (states have not fought) is directly related to the existence and persistence of a peculiar Latin American normative framework.[1]

At the rhetorical and formal levels, we can find a myriad of evidence regarding the existence of a normative system of peace in Latin America that regulates the peaceful settlement of conflicts within the Inter-American system in general and in Latin America in particular. In methodological terms, one can identify the pertinent norms through written recognition (documents of international law), as part of formal institutions (institutionalized through multilateral mechanisms of cooperation), and as part of customs and practices of international law. And yet the paradox remains that this battery of norms has not always been applied and implemented as such. In other words, there seems to be a normative inaccuracy (what I might refer to here as a kind of *normative dissonance*) between the legalistic and formal aspects of the norms and their translation into a more "plastic," open, and political reality. As we will learn from several of the case studies, at times leaders have preferred political and pragmatic solutions to legalistic ones.

In the following pages I present in further detail the two major relevant norms of peace for Latin America: peaceful settlement of disputes and *uti possidetis*. I focus on the empirical examination of six cases of territorial disputes. In each instance I introduce the historical and legal background of the case, assess the impact of norms of peace as opposed to other alternative explanations, and examine the conditions under which norms might have an impact.

Peaceful Settlement of International Disputes

In formal terms, multilateral mechanisms for peaceful settlement were established in the early nineteenth century, when several Spanish American states signed treaties regarding the peaceful management and resolution of their disputes, as well as the maintenance of regional peace. For instance, the Treaty of Perpetual Union, League, and Confederation, signed in 1826 at the Congress of Panama, obliged the signatories to bring their disputes before a general assembly for conciliation or mediation and to accept the decisions as final. Later on, in 1856 at Santiago de Chile and in 1865 at Lima, three more instruments were signed, urging the signatories to resolve peacefully their disputes through arbitration if direct diplomacy had failed to reach a settlement (Atkins 1997, 93–94).

The Pan-American movement, propelled by the United States at the end of the nineteenth century, had also incorporated and institutionalized this normative framework of peaceful settlement in the form of twelve treaties signed between 1890 and 1945, dealing with good offices, mediation, investigation, conciliation, arbitration, and judicial settlement (Bailey 1967, 75). Before World War II, a series of important multilateral treaties were signed on the subject, including the Treaty to Avoid or Prevent Conflicts between the American States (Gondra Treaty) of 1923, and the Anti-War Treaty of Non-Aggression and Conciliation (Saavedra Lamas Treaty) of 1933.[2] Especially after World War II, these mechanisms were institutionalized in three major legal instruments: the Inter-American Treaty of Reciprocal Assistance (Rio Pact) of 1947; the Charter of the OAS in 1948; and the American Treaty on Pacific Settlement (the Pact of Bogotá) of 1948, which superseded the never-implemented Gondra Treaty. Despite this impressive panoply of documents and treaties, the Inter-American record of conflict resolution, both prior to and after World War II, has not been impressive, and the mechanisms provided for it rarely have been used. Instead, certain OAS bodies such as the Inter-American Peace Committee carried out conflict resolution functions on an ad hoc basis. Similarly, in the 1980s the Latin American countries recreated a political mechanism of consultation and agreement (*concertación*) to foster similar principles within the Rio Group.

In practical terms, between 1851 and 1922 at least fourteen peaceful cessions and exchanges of territory related to territorial disputes took place in South America. Eight of these disputes were resolved following arbitration and the rest through direct negotiations, good offices, and mediation. In several cases, the arbitration award was followed by further negotiations about its implementation. In practice, many Latin American nations have shown a consistent preference for noncompulsory, ad hoc resources for the management and resolution of their international conflicts. Moreover, these nations seem to have preferred the continuation of the status quo, even if it led to continuing tensions, rather than escalate their disputes into full-scale wars (Puig 1983, 21–22).

Similarly, it can be argued that norms of peaceful settlement have had a restraining effect in the direction of de-escalation and resolution of international conflicts, and even of civil wars. This has been evident in the cases of the Leticia dispute of 1932–1934 between Peru and Colombia, the resolution of the Beagle Channel crisis of 1978 and the subsequent papal mediation and negotiations between Argentina and Chile in 1979–1984, the regional initiatives of Contadora (1984) and Esquipulas (1987) to peacefully resolve the civil wars in El Salvador and Nicaragua, and, more recently, the final and peaceful resolution of the long conflict between Peru and Ecuador in October 1998.

As for arbitration, up to the 1930s there were approximately 250 treaties for arbitration and for the advancement of peace involving American (both Latin and North American) states, including treaties of a general character and those dealing with particular disputes (Hughes 1929, 17–19). More than any other area of the world, border disputes in the region have been subject to formal legal and quasi-legal processes, such as adjudication and arbitration, in which the disputing states request a neutral third party to make an authoritative ruling resolving their territorial questions (Simmons 1999, v). From the 1820s until the 1970s, eight states—Argentina, Bolivia, Brazil, Colombia, Chile, Ecuador, Peru, and Venezuela—turned to arbitration 151 times in a myriad of issue-areas (Puig 1985). Many of the bilateral border disputes involving Latin American states have been submitted to arbitration (about twenty-two), in itself a puzzling phenomenon given the political sensitivity of territorial issues and their centrality to notions of state sovereignty and national identity. Out of these twenty-two cases, there were ten or eleven in which the parties complied completely with the ruling and eleven or twelve in which at least one of the parties partially or utterly rejected the ruling (see Table 4.1).

What is the explanation for this widespread tendency among Latin American countries to use arbitration? First, as mentioned in the previous chapter, there has been a relatively strong tradition in the region of using formal legal procedures to resolve territorial disputes. Second, states that have been more or less symmetrical in their military capabilities have been more likely to submit a territorial dispute to arbitration than highly asymmetric dyads. Third, countries that have had a history of difficulty getting territorial agreements ratified by their national congresses prefer to use arbitration, as a way of bypassing continued domestic obstruction to the resolution of border disputes. Fourth, prior experience with quasi-legal procedures tends to repeat itself over time. For instance, Argentina and Chile turned to arbitration five times, and Argentina itself has been involved in seven out of the twenty-two cases (Simmons 1999, 6–7).

Table 4.1.   Cases Involving Authoritative Third-Party Rulings

Parties complying with the rulings

Parties	Dates of dispute	Ruling date	By	"Loser"	Comments
Argentina/Brazil	1858–1898	1895	U.S.	Argentina	
Argentina/Chile	1872–1903	1899	U.S.	not clear	Los Andes
Argentina/Chile	1847–1966	1966	U.K.	Chile	Palena sector
Argentina/Chile	1847–1994	1994	regional	Chile	Laguna del Desierto
Argentina/Paraguay	1840–1939	1878	U.S.	Argentina	
Colombia/Venezuela	1838–1932	1891	Spain	Venezuela	compliance delayed
El Salvador/Honduras	1861–1992	1992	ICJ	El Salvador	80 percent to Honduras
Guatemala/Honduras	1842–1933	1933	U.S./ Costa Rica	not clear	
Guyana (U.K.)/Venezuela	1880–1899	1899	U.S.	Venezuela	34,000 sq km to U.K.; 20,000 sq km to Venezuela

Parties not complying with the ruling

Parties	Dates of dispute	Ruling date	By	Rejecter	Comments
Argentina/Chile	1847–1984	1977	U.K.	Argentina	Beagle Channel Islands
Argentina/Chile	1847–1994	1902	U.K.	Chile	partially rejected
Bolivia/Peru	1825–1911	1909	Argentina	Bolivia	
Chile/Peru	1881–1929	1925	U.S.	Peru	Tacna and Arica
Costa Rica/Nicaragua	1842–1900s	1888	U.S.	Nicaragua	
Costa Rica/Nicaragua	1842–1900s	1916	CACJ	Nicaragua	
Costa Rica/Panama	1903–1944	1900	France	Costa Rica	
Costa Rica/Panama	1903–1944	1914	U.S.	Panama	
Ecuador/Peru	1842–1998	1910	Spain	Ecuador	no ruling
Ecuador/Peru	1842–1998	1945	Brazil	Ecuador	rejects in 1960
Guyana/Venezuela	1951–present	1899	U.S.	Venezuela	
Honduras/Nicaragua	1858–1960	1906	Spain	Nicaragua	

Source: Based on Simmons 1999, 5.

In more general terms, there are alternative explanations for the disposition of the countries in the region to comply with arbitration awards. In the first place, the acceptance of awards enhances the reputations and thus the self-interests of the parties involved, assuming the principle of reciprocity. The strengthening of legal institutions and mechanisms has generally served the interests of the countries in the region, which have submitted their disputes to arbitration of their own volition. Second, as emphasized throughout this book, there is a strong normative framework that socializes and induces states to comply with arbitration awards. Argentina, with the notorious exception of its rejection of the 1977 British award on the Beagle Channel dispute, is a case in point. Traditionally, Argentina had accepted the principles of peaceful settlement of international disputes and pacifism, as well as recourse to international law and moralism (see Piñero 1924, 129; Ruiz Moreno 1961, 19; Paradiso 1996, 15). This normative framework is directly related to the legalist culture that characterizes the whole Latin American region. Third, the structure of the international system, characterized by the subordinated position of the Latin American states to Europe and the United States, has also enhanced their disposition to accept the arbitral ruling of the more powerful countries or former colonial powers such as Spain.

Uti Possidetis and Territorial Integrity

Many border disputes in Latin America throughout the nineteenth century and the first two decades of the twentieth century were resolved peacefully through the cession or exchange of territories, where the basis for peaceful settlement was the principle of *uti possidetis, ita possideatis* ("as you possess, so you may possess") discussed earlier. The principle became the basis by which the new Spanish American republics wished to settle permanently their claims to possession of territory, by replacing their mother country in the exercise of their territorial rights. The norm of *uti possidetis* has been incorporated into hundreds of cases dealing with border disputes in Latin America, Africa, and Asia. It has been widely accepted as a regional norm and has been established as a general principle in international law.[3]

The principle of *uti possidetis* did not preclude the emergence of boundary disputes in Latin America, since uncertainty characterized the demarcation of borders of the new states. The boundaries with which the doctrine dealt were not apparent, since they were not delineated carefully by the previous

Spanish and Portuguese authorities. What it did accomplish, however, was to establish the framework by which the newly formed countries of Latin America decide on the final dispositions of their territories peacefully. In their choice of *uti possidetis,* the new republics insisted on figuring out their borders diplomatically rather than turning to war. In this sense, *uti possidetis* was a precursor, as a strong normative basis, for the large number of cases of peaceful territorial change in the region (Roy 1997, 3).

As with other legal norms, the doctrine of *uti possidetis* faced practical difficulties in its implementation. Due to the trouble that the new states had in fixing their boundaries, two arguments arose that developed into two different versions of the doctrine, *uti possidetis juris* and *uti possidetis facto.* According to the former, states favored a juridical boundary line; that is to say, the rule applied to territorial limits legally in force when the act of decolonization took place. Conversely, according to *uti possidetis facto,* an opposing borderline is preferred, namely, that of the actual possession at the time of independence. The two lines—the juridical and the practical—did not always coincide, as was evident in the multitude of border disputes that have plagued Latin American countries. The Spanish-speaking Latin American states tended to prefer the *juris* version, in which only Spanish legal documents were pertinent for locating borders. In contrast, Brazil preferred in its negotiations a *de facto* interpretation of the doctrine, as stemming from the actual possession of some of the territories in question.

The application of the doctrine was extremely difficult. Owning land in every direction for huge distances, the Spanish Empire was not very precise about its administrative boundaries in colonial times. The formidable geography of South America made accurate map making almost impossible. It seems that each new state had a set of maps showing different boundaries from those of its neighbors (Calvert 1983, 4–5). Thus, even when two Spanish-speaking states both recognized the principle of *uti possidetis juris,* that in itself was not always a panacea to avoid armed conflict between them, as in the cases of Chaco (Bolivia and Paraguay) and the Oriente (Peru and Ecuador).

Similarly, the norm of territorial integrity is linked to the respect for sovereignty, the application of *uti possidetis,* and the principle of avoiding the use of force in the resolution of territorial disputes. In Latin America the norm was formalized in the Saavedra Lamas Anti-War Pact of 1933 and the Inter-American Conference for the Consolidation of Peace in 1936. Overall, the Latin American countries have been consistent opponents of coercive territorial agrandizement.

Territorial Disputes and Norms of Peace in South America

The central section of this chapter addresses the impact of norms of peace on six serious territorial disputes in South America. I analyze here not only the overall impact of norms, but also the specific conditions under which norms could have made an impact. In other words, if there was an eventual failure (a crisis and a war), does that mean that norms of peace were not important? And conversely, if there was a clear success (peaceful management, settlement, or resolution) does that necessarily mean that norms of peace were present and vital?

Misiones, 1858–1898

On February 6, 1895, the U.S. Secretary of State delivered to the representatives of Brazil and Argentina in Washington the arbitral award of U.S. President Grover Cleveland, dated February 5, 1895. According to the sentence, the boundary line between the two countries was the rivers Pepiri and San Antonio, as designated by Brazil as the "westerly system." Thus, the award favored Brazil and was loyally accepted by Argentina, which gave up its claims over the 31,000-square-kilometer territory of "Misiones" (Ireland 1938, 16).

Historical and Legal Background

According to the Treaty of San Ildefonso of October 7, 1777, Spain and Portugal agreed that the boundary line between their colonial possessions should be from the Uruguay River up the river Piquiry, or Pepiri-Guazú, across by the highest land, and down the San Antonio to the Curityba rivers. Yet the provisions of this treaty for survey and demarcation of the border on the ground never took place. After independence, the Empire of Brazil and the Argentine Republic fought a war that ended in 1828 with their mutual recognition of the independence of Uruguay. Later on, in 1856 and 1857, the two countries established a regime of free navigation and commerce in its common rivers. At this time they sustained a territorial controversy over their limits in the Misiones region. In 1885 they set up a mixed commission to explore and map the rivers Pepiri-Guazú and San Antonio, and the two rivers to the east of these known in Brazil as the Chapeco and the Chopim, as well as the disputed territory between the four rivers. The commission ended its work in 1891.[4]

On September 7, 1889, Brazil and Argentina agreed to submit their territorial dispute to the arbitration of the president of the United States.[5] Following the proclamation of the Republic of Brazil in November 1889, the two parties renewed direct negotiations and reached an agreement on January 25, 1890, by which they divided the disputed territory across the *divortia aquarum* of the Iguazú and the Uruguay rivers.[6] Yet the Brazilian House of Deputies rejected the treaty in August 1891 by a vote of 142 to 5. Hence, Argentina insisted on proceeding with the previously accorded arbitration. In the arbitration treaty of 1889 it was stipulated that the frontier must be constituted of the rivers that Argentina and Brazil had designated. The arbitrator was then invited to decide which of two rival systems constituted the boundary of Brazil and Argentina, in view of the arguments and documents that the parties might produce (Ireland 1938, 14–15; Scenna 1975, 274–75). On February 5, 1895, President Cleveland decided that the boundary line should be the rivers that Brazil had designated in its argument and documents, to be called the Westerly System (Argentina 1901, 411).

Argentina accepted the sentence and fulfilled the award in good faith, ceding to Brazil territories that today are within the Brazilian State of Santa Catarina. After the arbitral award, friendly messages were exchanged between the two countries. For instance, the Argentine consul in Petrópolis, García Merou, referred to the "great example in America to the entire humanity of two young nations . . . for the international law and justice, and for the improvement of moral and spiritual conditions of all people" (quoted in Lobo 1952, 168; my translation). There were three logical ways of settling the question of Misiones: by war, by direct negotiations, and by arbitration. In less than a century all of these methods were tried.

Evidence and Impact of the Normative Framework

To understand the Argentine position, we should locate its specific attitude in the early 1890s vis-à-vis Brazil within the general doctrine of pacifism and recourse to peaceful settlement of international disputes that traditionally characterized its foreign policy. The parameters of Argentina's foreign policy included pacifism, isolationism, recourse to international law, moralism, confrontation with the United States, affiliation with the British (and generally European) sphere of influence, and a general weakness in the articulation of its territorial policy (see Silva 1946, 159; Paradiso 1996, 15–18). "Argentina carried on the [normative] principle and practice of arbitration. Its acceptance of the award was an example of its behavior in international relations, inspired by an ideal of harmony and justice" (Piñero 1924, 129; my translation). Beyond the obvious eulogy of Argentine conduct, it seems that the country's behavior could be considered at that time and context as the *normal* one, as part of the acceptance of the principle of peaceful settlement of international disputes, if not sheer pacifism (Ruiz Moreno 1961, 19). As part of the "arguments" submitted to the arbitration process in 1893–1894, Argentina contended that "the question to be determined was one of law" (Zeballos 1894, 187). Moreover, by mentioning the truncated treaty of 1890, the Argentine chief negotiator, Estanislao Zeballos, also emphasized that by agreeing to the partition of the disputed territory, he always preferred "a noble and stable peace to the small territorial advantages of the past" (Zeballos 1894, 10).

As for the specific normative arguments invoked during the arbitration, the Argentine position was much more ambiguous than the Brazilian one. At one time Argentina contended that the principle of *uti possidetis,* applicable to the relations between nations whose territory was formerly under a common sovereignty (such as Spanish America), had no place in a controversy between states whose territory had always belonged to two different nations (such as Portugal and Spain).[7] Yet, later on in the arbitration process, Zeballos argued that the principle of *uti possidetis* favored the Argentine claims over the disputed territory (Ireland 1938, 15; Zeballos 1894, 319). In addition, Zeballos claimed that: (a) Spain discovered and settled the territory submitted to the arbitrator; (b) Argentina was successor to Spain in its possession and its territorial rights; (c) these rights were contained in the Treaty of 1777; (d) the colonies founded by Brazil in the disputed territory were established by mistake, because neither Argentina nor Brazil knew the true position of its boundaries; and (e) the international exploration carried out by virtue of the Treaty of 1885 showed the error of the two governments regarding the eastern boundary of the territory in dispute (Zeballos 1894, 315–18).

The Brazilian position, as clearly articulated by the Baron of Rio Branco, was rather simple and effective: the Brazilian and Argentine governments agreed on the borders of the Iguazú and the Uruguay rivers, but they disagreed regarding the determination of which two rivers formed their international border (Rio Branco 1894, 2). For the Brazilians, the relevant norm was that of *uti possidetis facto.* Brazil established its right based on the fact that since the seventeenth century the territory to the east of the Pepiri-Guazú, discovered by Paulistas, was Brazilian. The right was that of *uti possidetis* from the time of independence (1822); moreover, Argentina did not demand the territory in question between 1810 and 1881 (Lobo 1952, 69–70; Petrocelli 1995, 38–39).

Conditions for the Impact of Norms

Type of political regimes and peaceful conditions within the countries. The Argentines regarded the question that came before the arbitrator as an "eminently political one, between the irreconcilable tendencies of traditional imperialists and modern republicans," the latter represented by a peaceful and powerful Argentina (Zeballos 1894, 13; Lobo 1952, 59). Despite the fact that Argentina had also experienced a serious political crisis in 1893 (Palacio 1965, 296–97), its economic boom and the subsequent political stability in the 1880s contributed to the adoption of its doctrine of pacifism, including the recourse to arbitration (see Mosquera 1994, 128–29, 133, and 146).

Fitness between the regional normative framework and the given case; degree of institutionalization of the international society. According to the Argentine newspaper *La Nación*, the Argentines attributed more importance to arbitration than to territory as a peaceful means and a mechanism to reach harmony between two American peoples (quoted in Lobo 1952, 171; my translation). It is clear, then, that in 1895 the Argentines managed to find a high degree of coherence among the norms of peaceful settlement, their economic boom and political stability, and their peaceful behavior in international relations.

Alternative Explanations

The Argentine nationalist critique of the arbitration award of 1895 argued, among other things, that President Cleveland reached his decision because of economics and the U.S. alliance with Brazil. Moreover, the Argentine representative, Zeballos, later declared that Argentina, in contrast to Brazil, "does not know how to negotiate, and that Misiones was a lost cause" (quoted in Etchepareborda 1982, 50 and 55; my translation).

Common interests between the two countries contributed to the peaceful resolution of the dispute, including realist and geopolitical considerations. For Brazil, the territory had geopolitical implications in terms of land communication (Soares 1973, 274). For Argentina, confronted at that time with much more serious territorial disputes with Chile, there was an inherent benefit in improving its relations with its large neighbor, Brazil (Scenna 1975, 266). Moreover, the resolution of the dispute paved the way to improve the common political and economic interests of the two parties.[8] In this case, as in many others, there was a convergence of the normative framework with more pragmatic interests.

Tacna and Arica, 1883–1929

The story of the Tacna-Arica territorial dispute involving Chile and Peru started with the expansion of Chile northward along the Pacific coast in quest of nitrates and guano. Following Chile's victory in the Pacific War (1879–1883) and the Peruvian loss of Tacna and Arica, settling the problem of Tacna-Arica meant to Peru morally what the reincorporation of Alsace-Lorraine meant to France (Dennis 1967, xv–xvi). The disputed territories included about 24,000 square kilometers, 7,500 in Tacna and 16,400 in Arica. The importance of Tacna-Arica has been strategic, and in the broader sense, historical. Deprived of its Pacific littoral as a consequence of the Pacific War, Arica has been the natural outlet to the sea for a third party, Bolivia. Moreover, the "question of the Pacific" has been a sentimental powder keg for the two (and even three) countries. What explains, then, the political compromise of dividing the disputed territories, almost fifty years after the end of the war, between Peru and Chile?

Historical and Legal Background

The long-standing dispute about the sovereignty of Tacna and Arica developed as a result of the failure of Chile and Peru to settle the issue in the Treaty of Ancón after the Pacific War (1879–1883). The war had begun as a quarrel between Chile and Bolivia over nitrates and guano. On February 14, 1879, Chilean troops occupied the Bolivian province of Antofagasta, and Bolivia, counting on Peru's support under a "secret" treaty of 1873, declared war. The Chileans demanded that the Peruvians remain neutral, and when they refused, Chile declared war on them as well. The result was a disaster for the allies. The Peruvian navy was destroyed by the Chileans, who occupied Tarapacá, Arica, and Tacna,—which had previously belonged to Peru—and in 1881, in a surprise attack up the coast, Lima itself (Calvert 1983, 12).

Chile's stunning victory forced Bolivia to sign a Pact of Truce in 1884, and Peru to sign the Treaty of Ancón in 1883. By the provisions of these treaties, Chile annexed the Bolivian littoral of Atacama, received the province of Tarapacá from Peru, and obtained the right to occupy the Peruvian provinces of Tacna and Arica for ten years. Article III of the Treaty of Ancón mandated a plebiscite after ten years to decide whether the area would remain a part of Chile or revert to Peru. The winner of the plebiscite was to pay the loser 10 million Chilean pesos or the equivalent in Peruvian soles.[9]

Although the Treaty of Ancón technically ended the war between Chile and Peru, it did not assure a stable peace between the two countries. There was no plebiscite at the end of the ten-year period (in 1894), and Chile continued to benefit from the vast nitrate revenues. Peru protested the failure to implement the Treaty of 1883 and focused its diplomatic efforts on the complete recovery of the two provinces. In 1888 and 1890 Chile offered to buy them from Peru. In 1898 Peru agreed to a compromise—the Billinghurst-La Torre Protocol—that was later truncated by the Chilean Congress. Peru severed diplomatic relations with Chile in 1910, and negotiations did not proceed until the end of World War I.

It was not until the early 1920s that the quest for a peaceful solution was pursued, under strong pressure from the U.S. government. On January 17, 1922, U.S. President Warren G. Harding invited the governments of Chile and Peru to send delegates to Washington to devise a means of reaching an agreement, either by direct negotiations or through recourse to arbitration. On July 20, 1922, the two parties signed a protocol of arbitration and a complementary act defining its scope, regarding the execution of Article III of the Treaty of Ancón.[10] On March 4, 1925, U.S. President Calvin Coolidge handed down his opinion and award, deciding that a plebiscite should be held after all.[11] Since by that time the disputed territories had already become Chileanized, Chile immediately accepted the award, while Peru asked for its modification based on the legal argument of *rebus sic stantibus* ("change of conditions") (Ireland 1938, 167–69).[12] The preparations for the plebiscite did not materialize in 1925 and 1926, so the whole idea of holding it was definitively abandoned. Ultimately, the failure of the plebiscite was due to the fact that neither Chile nor Peru could have afforded to allow the other party to win an absolute title to Tacna and Arica (Dennis 1967, 264).

Having exhausted the legal option, the U.S. government pressed for the renewal of diplomatic relations and direct negotiations between the parties in 1928. With its mediation and "good offices," the talks led to the second Treaty of Ancón, signed at Lima on June 3, 1929, which resolved the dispute through a political compromise. The disputed territories were partitioned between the parties; Arica remained in the hands of Chile, and Tacna reverted to Peru. Chile was to grant Peru port facilities at its harbor in Arica, a process that was completed only recently, in the 1990s. Interestingly, neither of the parties (Peru and Chile) could alienate any of the territories (Tacna and/or Arica) to a third party (Bolivia), so the Bolivians obtained nothing from this agreement, except a continuation of their guaranteed access to (Chilean) Arica.

The Treaty of 1929 was well received by the majority of the people in both nations. For Chile, the settlement of the long dispute with Peru freed it from a long economic and military burden. Compared with its prize, Arica, Tacna had little economic significance or strategic value. For Peru, a negotiated solution was the only way to recover at least part of the territories lost in the Pacific War.

Evidence and Impact of the Normative Framework

The Tacna–Arica question represented for both countries a paramount normative and political issue rather than a legal one. The award to either country of a permanent title to *both* Tacna and Arica should have constituted a verdict of "guilt" or "innocence" in the significant moral question of defining who the aggressor was in the Pacific War (Dennis 1967, xv).

Moreover, the two countries agreed on the need to reach a peaceful settlement of their long territorial dispute, as part of the "exemplary system of peaceful coexistence and common responsibilities" that had always characterized the Latin American nations (Ríos Gallardo 1959, 435; my translation). Moreover, they mutually recognized their territorial sovereignty. Yet at the same time they could not agree on the political and legal significance of the plebiscite clause in the Treaty of Ancón regarding Tacna and Arica. From the Chilean perspective, the plebiscite clause served as either a military expedient or a disguised cession that guaranteed its sovereignty over the disputed territories (Chile 1923, 1–7). In Peru, however, it was interpreted as a bona fide way to determine their ultimate disposition. Although Chile retained Tacna and Arica, the failure to hold the plebiscite in 1894 terminated its temporary occupation and possession. Therefore, Peru recovered after that its "right to the unencumbered possession and sovereignty of her provinces" (Peru 1923, 249–51; Willis 1918, 71–72).

Furthermore, the two countries held different normative and legal arguments in justifying their conflicting positions. For Peru, its cause was one of "justice and American solidarity," of "international morality against the 'might is right' attitude of Chile" (J. Prado y Ugarteche, quoted in Maurtua 1919, xxxiii–xxxiv; my translation). The Peruvians appealed to arguments of justice in stark terms.[13] From their perspective, in 1894 about 80 percent of the population of Tacna and Arica was Peruvian, so that a plebiscite then held would have resulted in an "overwhelming decision by the popular will that the provinces should continue under the sovereignty of Peru" (Peru 1923, 251). Peru linked the principle of self-determination to its sovereign claims. Moreover, Peru argued in 1923 that the principle of *rebus sic stantibus* made the holding of a plebiscite in Tacna and Arica a "manifestly impossible condition" in the "present circumstances" (Peru 1923, 25). Its case was based on more than 340 certified and witnessed reports from Peruvian citizens who had allegedly experienced various forms of Chilean persecution and had been forced to flee from Tacna and Arica (see Peru 1924, 8; Wilson 1979, 38).

In normative terms, the Chilean position remained consistent over the fifty-years period of the dispute. According to the Treaty of Ancón of 1883, the sovereignty over Tacna and Arica was granted to Chile, and the plebiscite clause should be interpreted as a "practical and honorable form for facilitating the annexation of those territories" (Alvarez, quoted in Willis 1918, 34). Chile's conciliatory attitude toward Peru also translated into a series of functional and economic agreements celebrated between the parties and the Chilean disposition to submit the dispute to arbitration in 1922 (Chile 1923, 180). Moreover, Chilean Ambassador (later foreign minister) Conrado Ríos Gallardo argued that "the inspirations of concord and harmony that motivated always the foreign policy of Chile" led his country to open direct negotiations with Peru in 1928, leading to the peaceful resolution of 1929 (Ríos Gallardo 1959, 457–58; my translation).

Conditions for the Impact of Norms

Salience of domestic actors and types of political regimes.   During the forty-six years of the dispute, both Peru and Chile were governed by civilian and military regimes. Domestic politics in both Chile and Peru combined to frustrate the advance toward a workable solution. After 1919, only the charismatic leadership of President Augusto Salcedo Leguía in Peru was able to accomplish reconciliation with Chile. Leguía had managed to resolve the conflicts with Bolivia and Brazil, and to achieve progress in the disputes with Colombia and Ecuador. In Leguía's view Chile preferred to support Colombia and Ecuador, and to promote Bolivian aspirations on Arica, rather than fighting a new war with Peru. Conversely, the election of Arturo Alessandri in Chile indicated a stronger executive leadership, prone to end two decades of weak "parliamentary" government. Hence, the road to find a peaceful compromise between the leaders of the two countries was opened. It should be mentioned that each country's congress ratified the treaty of 1929 with large majorities. Moreover, the public opinion in both countries supported the treaties (see *El Mercurio's* editorial of May 18, 1929, quoted in Ríos Gallardo 1959, 381).

Presence of an hegemonic power.   While Chile was more advanced and developed than Peru at that time, both countries were economically dependent upon the United States and, to a lesser extent, the European markets (Benavídes Correa 1988, 100–1). In this regard, the United States exercised a strong normative leadership in moving the two parties toward a peaceful solution.

Distribution of power between the parties.   In the immediate aftermath of the Pacific War the power distribution was obviously unbalanced to the benefit of Chile. Yet in the decades that followed the war the power distribution was perceived as becoming more even between Chile and Peru. Thus, the prolongation of the dispute over time—with the concomitant change in the power distribution—led Chile to consider more seriously the normative position of its neighbor-rival, Peru, in order to find a suitable solution.

Fitness between the regional normative framework and the given case; degree of institutionalization of the international society.   Both Chile and Peru were well aware of the regional consensus regarding the peaceful settlement of international disputes and the predilection for political solutions. For instance, President Leguía of Peru referred to the treaties of 1929 as choosing "life to mourning, and reality to utopia . . . for the purpose of bringing peace to the continent" (quoted in Ríos Gallardo 1959, 358; my translation).

Alternative Explanations

As in the case of Misiones, the impact of the normative framework explains part of the very delayed happy ending of Tacna and Arica, but not all of it. In addition, substantial interests led the two countries to opt, eventually, for a political compromise.

In the first place, the regional balance of power was weighted against either Chile or Peru seeking to escalate their territorial dispute into another war. Both countries were (pre)occupied by other territorial disputes with third parties: Argentina in the case of Chile, Colombia and Ecuador in the case of Peru. Furthermore, Bolivia's persistent clamor to regain an outlet to the Pacific Ocean was a concern—if not a potential threat—to both countries.

Furthermore, Chile and Peru sustained asymmetrical interests regarding the territory of Tacna and Arica. From an economic point of view, Tacna-Arica became a white elephant, producing little revenue and possessing meager material resources. The profits from nitrates declined so drastically after

World War I that the provinces had lost almost any economic value, drawing Chile in the direction of finding a compromise with Peru.

Chile's main interest in the area was strategic; Tacna and Arica afforded a protective northern boundary against any Peruvian attempt to regain Tarapacá, a rich nitrate province. Conversely, Peru's attraction to Tacna and Arica was mainly symbolic, if not sentimental. The attempt to regain at least Tacna was a matter of national pride. A moral victory would have been more desirable to Peru than another war, successful or not. Furthermore, both Chile and Peru had common interests that transcended their dispute over those territories. The continuation of their arms race was detrimental to both. Peru and Chile needed each other in economic terms, in order to further "the progress and well-being of both peoples" through bilateral trade and better communications (Ambassador Conrados Ríos Gallardo in 1930, quoted in Lagos Carmona 1966, 79; my translation. See also Dennis 1967, 280; Pérez Canto 1918, 43).

In sum, it seems that neither Chile nor Peru wanted to maintain the status quo in Tacna and Arica indefinitively. Converging interests and geopolitical realities moved them toward a compromise, which was embedded within a regional normative consensus that promoted the peaceful settlement of territorial disputes. Once the juridical procedure of arbitration was terminated, and with substantial help from the United States, the two countries turned to a political solution that proved satisfactory to both of them, by partitioning the disputed territory between the two.

The Chaco Dispute, 1906–1938

The only major war that took place in South America in the twentieth century began in 1932 between Bolivia and Paraguay. Known as the Chaco War (1932–1935), it concerned a territorial dispute over sovereignty in the region of the Chaco Boreal (Northern Chaco), the upland area of the Chaco bounded by the Pilcomayo, Paraguay, and Parapeti rivers, an area of about 384,000 square kilometers (see Calvert 1983, 14–15; Atkins 1997, 68). It is probably one of the least hospitable places on earth. Not exactly either a desert or a jungle, it manages to combine the worst characteristics of both regions (Farcau 1996, 5). This territorial dispute led to a long and bloody war with about one hundred thousand soldiers killed. Both Bolivia and Paraguay had recognized and agreed on the principle of *uti possidetis,* but not on its implementation. How can one explain the catastrophic failure of the normative framework in avoiding war?

The eventual peace agreement of 1938 was reached through the intervention of third parties. What was the role of norms in bringing about peace after war?

Historical and Legal Background

The origins of the Chaco dispute stem from conflicting jurisdictions during the Spanish American colonial period and the subsequent undetermined national frontiers. In the colonial period the disputed area had been administered at various times as part of either Paraguay or Bolivia. Paraguay claimed that the Chaco had always been included in the jurisdiction of the governor in the Paraguayan capital of Asunción, while Bolivia claimed that the Chaco had been part of the Audiencia of Charcas in Upper Peru, which later became Bolivia (Windass 1970, 69).

Only in the latter part of the nineteenth century did both Paraguay and Bolivia take increasing interest in the disputed area. Both countries were the major losers of the two significant wars of the nineteenth century—Paraguay lost territory to Brazil and Argentina in the War of the Triple Alliance (1865–1870); Bolivia lost its seacoast to Chile in the Pacific War in 1879–1883. Rumors that the area contained large oil reserves added an important element to the conflict. Since 1906 Bolivia had looked for a port on the Pilcomayo River in the Chaco to get access to the River Plate system and the Atlantic Ocean. It began bolstering its territorial claims by constructing a series of military posts (*fortines*) in the Chaco (Rout 1970, 11). Conversely, Paraguay was searching for a way to recover and defend its lost national honor, so it considered the Chaco Boreal dispute as a matter of national survival. Both Paraguay and Bolivia were revisionist and frustrated states, landlocked countries dependent on others for their trade route with the outside world.

As far as Paraguay was concerned, the edge of the Chaco lay just across the Paraguay River, facing its capital city, Asunción, and had from the earliest days of the *conquistadores* been regarded as a legitimate area for adventure, conquest, expansion, and exploitation. Since the mid-nineteenth century large agricultural settlements were established on the Chaco side of the river. The Bolivians, for their part, had done little to position themselves in the Chaco until 1906. Yet the region became strategically important to them since its possession could provide Bolivia with access to the Atlantic Ocean down the Paraguay River (Windass 1970, 69).

Since November 12, 1878, when Paraguay was awarded the disputed territory with Argentina between the Pilcomayo and the Verde rivers, until the late 1920s, Paraguay and Bolivia conducted intermittent negotiations to establish a clear boundary line between them. On April 5, 1913, the parties signed the Ayala-Mujía Protocol, in which they promised to negotiate a final boundary treaty within two years by direct arrangement if possible, and, if not possible, to submit the boundary question to arbitration. Meanwhile, they committed themselves to maintaining the status quo as stipulated in previous agreements (Ireland 1938, 69–70). In 1927 Paraguay proposed a nonaggression pact between the two countries, a permanent commission to study the border dispute, and a return to the status quo line of 1907. Bolivia rejected these suggestions (Farcau 1996, 12).

Following these futile negotiations, the two countries moved rapidly toward military confrontation. The continued construction of advanced military posts (*fortines*) along the unclear border, coupled with recurring incursions by armed patrols, culminated in a series of bloody encounters in 1927 and 1928. The military crisis was aggravated by the ineffectiveness of the existing Inter-American peace machinery (see Rout 1970, 14–15). Fortunately for the parties, the International Conference of American States on Conciliation and Arbitration offered its good offices to deescalate the conflict. On January 3, 1929, both countries signed in Washington, D. C., a protocol agreeing to create a commission of investigation and conciliation regarding the violent events of the preceeding few years and to foster a diplomatic solution. In September 1929 the commission adopted a resolution on conciliation, asking for the renewal of diplomatic relations and calling for arbitration. Yet further negotiations between 1929 and 1932 remained inconclusive.

When war broke out in July 1932, the Bolivians were confident of achieving a quick victory. Their country was richer and more populous than Paraguay, and their armed forces were larger, better trained, and better equipped. These advantages quickly proved irrelevant in the face of the Paraguayans' zeal to protect their homeland. The highly motivated Paraguayans knew the geography of the Chaco, which was closer to their homeland, better than the more distant Bolivians. In contrast, Indians from the Bolivian high plateau (the *Altiplano*) who were forced into the Bolivian army had no real interest in fighting the war, and failed to adapt to the hot and humid Chaco climate. In addition, long supply lines, poor roads, and poor logistics hindered the Bolivian campaign. Finally, the Paraguayan leaders proved more united and capable than their Bolivian counterparts—as President Eusebio Ayala and Chief of Staff General Estigarribia worked well together throughout the war.

On the diplomatic front, the eruption of armed conflict in 1932 led to several attempts at mediation to reach a cease-fire and a further truce. Those included a "neutral commission" of representatives of various Latin American states under a U.S. chairmanship; a committee of neighboring states (Argentina, Brazil, Chile, and Peru, or ABCP); and a special commission of the League of Nations, which produced a special report dealing with techniques of reconciliation that proved ineffective.

In the summer of 1934, when it was losing the war, Bolivia brought the dispute before the League of Nations, under Article 15. Paraguay would thus become an aggressor in terms of the League Covenant if it continued to make war on Bolivia, liable to all the sanctions of Article 16. As a result, Paraguay announced its withdrawal from the League (see Windass 1970, 74).

Meanwhile, the resolution of the conflict was gradually worked out in military terms. By 1935 Paraguayan armed forces had established full control of most of the Chaco region, yet Bolivia refused to surrender. With the military campaign at an impasse, no hope of total victory for either side, and both countries exhausted by bloody conflict, financial ruin, and internal strife, they finally turned to third parties to help end the war (Atkins 1997, 70–71). Peace became practical since both sides were reaching the limits of their capabilities. Thus, a truce was negotiated through the good offices of the United States and Argentina. This was followed by a difficult peace process, which included an international peace conference (1935–1939) and the signature of a Treaty of Peace, Friendship, and Boundaries on July 21, 1938.

The treaty established a procedure similar to arbitration, providing that the six presidents of the mediatory ("neutral") states (Argentina, Brazil, Chile, Peru, Uruguay, and the United States) should determine the territorial outcome of the dispute. On October 10, 1938, they eventually gave Paraguay control over most of the contested area, while Bolivia gained port facilities and rights of passage through Paraguay, though those rights still have not been completely implemented (see Torres Armas 2001). On the one hand, Bolivians could take heart because Paraguay had been driven back from the Oriente (Eastern) oil fields, drawing the boundary line at a distance of 60 to 100 miles from the area of oil production. On the other hand, Paraguayans could point out with satisfaction their exclusive retention of the Paraguay River littoral and extensive territorial acquisitions over most of the Chaco Boreal (see Calvert 1983, 15; Rout 1970, 207; Garner 1966, 106).

After three years of painful negotiations to reach peace, the treaty of 1938 confirmed military victory for Paraguay, at the cost of about three Bolivians and two Paraguayans for each square mile. It was estimated that during the war there had been total casualties of 250,000, of which Bolivia, with a population of 2,911,000, had lost 55,000, with 83,000 ill or wounded; and Paraguay, with a population of 836,000, lost 45,000, 67,000 ill or wounded (Ireland 1938, 94).

Evidence and Impact of the Normative Framework

Despite the failure to avoid the virulent war of 1932–1935, the norms of *uti possidetis* and peaceful settlement of disputes played an important role in explaining several dimensions of the territorial conflict between Bolivia and Paraguay, which was, after all, a dispute over sovereignty. Bolivia maintained that the dispute involved a territorial question, and insisted that a definition of the area of any (limited) arbitration should precede the suspension of military hostilities. Conversely, Paraguay argued that the dispute involved only a boundary question, not including any of the territory awarded to it in 1878, and demanded a suspension of military hostilities with third-party guarantees before an (unlimited) arbitration agreement could take place (Ireland 1938, 95).

Regarding peaceful settlement, the Chaco War can be considered a major failure for the Inter-American system in general and the Latin American normative consensus in particular. Even a last-minute attempt to reach a diplomatic solution was made at the beginning of the conflagration, in August 1932.[14] At least rhetorically, Bolivia and Paraguay each constantly argued that it had always accepted the principle of peaceful settlement, the other party being the recurrent violator of that norm (see *Proceedings* 1929, 1–3, 188, 195, and 963).

The respective territorial claims of Bolivia and Paraguay were always cloaked in the purest of judicial and legal formulations. For instance, both countries claimed the territory based on the norm of *uti possidetis*. The Bolivian case rested firmly on the original *uti possidetis juris* of 1810, which gave Bolivia jurisdiction over the territory originally encompassed by the Audiencia of Charcas. From the Bolivian legal standpoint, "Paraguay could not conquer the Chaco, because at the time when she came into legal existence the region had already ceased to be *res nullius* and was a Spanish possession which was transmitted integrally to the successor State, the Republic of Bolivia" (*Proceedings* 1929, 944).

Conversely, Paraguay sustained its sovereignty claims by right of *uti possidetis de facto,* due to its physical occupation of the area. Paraguay's basic argument was that its citizens had conducted virtually all the explorations of the region and established the only viable settlements in the Chaco, while the nearest Bolivian outposts were hundreds of kilometers away. Thus, in its Report to the Commission of Inquiry in 1929 Paraguay argued that "it holds possession of the Chaco since the year 1536 in which she discovered, explored, and occupied it" (*Proceedings* 1929, 1145). Relatively speaking, the Paraguayan case appeared to be the stronger in terms of international law, on the basis of colonization and possession (see Garner 1966, 49; Farcau 1996, 8).

Conditions for the Impact of Norms

Fitness between the regional normative framework and the given case; degree of institutionalization of norms in the international society.   In the Chaco dispute there was a serious "normative dissonance" between the regional norms sponsored by the alarmed Latin American neighbors, on the one hand, and their adoption by Bolivia, Paraguay, and even the mediators themselves, on the other. In the declaration of August 3, 1932, the American nations argued that "the Chaco dispute is susceptible to a peaceful solution" and that "they will not recognize any territorial arrangement . . . which has not been obtained by peaceful means" (quoted in Rout 1970, 68). In practice, the dispute was resolved by military means, and the mediation/arbitration of 1938 that followed the formal Peace Treaty actually recognized and legalized most of the military gains that Paraguay obtained on the battlefield. Moreover, the diplomatic and legal arena of the dispute after the war (1935–1938) was expanded to encompass not only the norms, but also the interests of the third-party peace makers. Thus, important diplomatic participants such as Argentina promoted their national interests, which could appear somewhat incongruous with the lofty normative aspirations they themselves proclaimed (see Garner 1966, 51; Saavedra Lamas 1937, 41–45).

Alternative Explanations

The Declaration of the American nations (the so-called Neutrals) of August 2, 1932, regarding a peaceful settlement of the Chaco dispute was a diplomatic fiasco. The Latin American nations in particular and the international community in general failed to avoid war, and they even failed to impose a serious arms embargo on the belligerents. Paradoxically, this normative failure surrounding the Chaco dispute was exacerbated by the (relative) success of the resolution of the Tacna and Arica dispute between Chile and Peru in 1929, which explicitly excluded Bolivia. Hence, Bolivia intensified its diplomatic and military pressures to find a prompt settlement in the other direction—the Chaco, the River Plate basin, and ultimately an outlet to the Atlantic Ocean. As for Paraguay, it also intensified its military preparations, as in the Vanguardia incident of December 8, 1928, which was provoked by Paraguayan forces (Garner 1966, 38). Yet naming Paraguay the legal aggressor in that incident was a futile and irrelevant exercise, since it seemed that Bolivia had more to gain from any military conflagration.

Farcau brilliantly summarized the Bolivian rationale for opting for war:

> Bolivia had lost huge slices of its original territory to her other neighbors, and given their strength, there was slim chance Bolivia would ever recover any of it. However, here was minuscule Paraguay playing the same dangerous game. Not only was there no reason why Bolivia should let itself be 'pushed around' by a dwarf, but here was a heaven-sent opportunity safely and easily to turn the tide of Bolivia's fortunes with a short, glorious little war and leave Paraguay as the military laughing stock of the continent. (Farcau 1996, 13)[15]

All in all, the failure of legal recourses, such as arbitration and conciliation, and of diplomatic solutions, such as finding a sensible political compromise, led to the escalation of the conflict and ultimately to an unnecessary war. This war was the logical culmination of a century of diplomatic frustrations and erratic contacts, previous loss of territory by both countries, and what might be termed "the territorial instinct in nationalism," leading to geopolitical excesses (see Garner 1966, 35; Porcelli 1991, 29 and 103). The Bolivians at first saw the Chaco War as an adventure and an opportunity, but later on as a curse and a tragedy. The Paraguayans were far more consistent; from the beginning they referred to the military conflict as a struggle for national survival. It is thus not surprising that the Paraguayans performed so much better on the battlefield, assisted at least logistically by the "neutral" Argentines (Farcau 1996, 24; Rout 1970, 40–41).

When peace was finally established in 1938, the altruistic declarations and moral pretenses of the "neutral" third parties were abandoned in favor of the realities created by the military outcome of the war. Throughout the escalation of the conflict between 1928 and 1938, we can trace a transition from legal and juridical (normative) argumentation to political formulations and a tendency to establish facts on the ground (*fait accompli*).

What remained after 1935 was to translate the relative Paraguayan military victory into some palatable political formula that the two former belligerents could live with. The Treaty of Peace, Friendship, and Borders of July 21, 1938, reestablished peace and stipulated the arbitration of the area, which eventually reflected the military results of the war. Yet the wisdom of the six mediators ensured that in their final settlement Paraguay got less than it had originally demanded, and Bolivia got "something." Paraguay could be pleased with the final award, which gave it most of the Chaco region. But Bolivia could be contented as well, at least in the retention of its Chaco oil fields and its guaranteed free access to the Paraguay River. Indeed, peace has been maintained since, and both countries have greatly improved their bilateral relations.

The Leticia Dispute, 1932–1934

Unlike the Chaco dispute, the conflict between Peru and Colombia over the Leticia Trapezium developed into a serious militarized crisis without escalating into a full-fledged war. The dispute, which was the result of rubber exploitation and the lack of a clear definition of the borders since 1826, was initially resolved by negotiations in 1922 (Donadio 1995). It erupted again when Peru illegally occupied the disputed territory next to the Amazon River. Threats of war and skirmishes between the two countries took place in 1933. Yet the crisis was peacefully managed through the Council of the League of Nations and the good offices and mediation of the United States and Brazil. An agreement was reached in May 1934, leading to the Colombian reoccupation of the disputed area.

Historical and Legal Background

The Leticia dispute arose over a Peruvian attempt to repudiate a valid international treaty and to regain by violence territory ceded to Colombia in 1922 (see Ireland 1938, 166–206). From 1911 to 1922 Peru and Colombia feuded over possession of the strategic Amazon port city of Leticia. Peru's economic interests, particularly its search for raw materials after its defeat in the Pacific War against Chile, led it to claim this area in the Upper Amazon basin. The Leticia Trapezium had a psychological importance for both Peru and Colombia that was not commensurable to its economic or demographic development, because of its proximity to the Amazonas.

In 1922 Peru and Colombia had concluded the Salomon-Lozano Treaty, by which an area of about 10,240 square kilometers was ceded to Colombia, including the left bank of the Putumayo River and a corridor to Leticia, in exchange for other border areas with Ecuador that were in Colombian possession. The Leticia area included fewer than 500 white inhabitants—300 of them in Leticia—and about 1,500 Indians. At its northeast corner on the Putumayo stood the town of Tarapacá, and at its southeast corner on the Amazon River, 4,000 kilometers from the Atlantic Ocean, the town of Leticia. The agreement, which was very unpopular in Peru, was reached by the authoritarian government of Augusto Leguía without consulting the Peruvian inhabitants of the adjacent Loreto area.

A military revolt led by Colonel Luis M. Sánchez Cerro deposed President Leguía on August 25, 1930. Following a chaotic year in Peruvian politics, elections were held on October 11, 1931, and Sánchez Cerro was elected president. The new Peruvian regime was supported by the army and several groups of conservatives that wished to cancel the Salomon-Lozano Treaty (see Wood 1966, 174–75; St. John 1976, 328–36).

On the night of August 31, 1932, an armed band of some three hundred Peruvian civilians entered Leticia, seized the public buildings and town offices, expelled the Colombian officials, and raised the Peruvian flag. Later, they extended their occupation to the entire area. Although the Peruvian government disavowed the action at the beginning of the crisis, local Peruvian authorities in Loreto furnished military support, and on November 26, 1932, Peruvian regular troops were said to have occupied Leticia.

Colombia decided to take measures to restore "normal conditions" in the Leticia area, "under the aegis of Colombian laws and Colombian authorities." Colombia prepared a naval expedition of six vessels and 1,500 men under the leadership of General Alfredo Vázquez Cobo; it was to sail around the Atlantic coast and all the way up the Amazon River as a police expedition to restore the law in the usurped territory. Yet what was regarded by Colombia as a "police expedition," sent to operate in Colombian territory, was perceived by Peruvians as a "punitive expedition" designed as a show of aggression against Peruvian troops and civilians (see Hudson 1933, 5–6; Ireland 1938, 198–200).

During January and February 1933 the Colombian naval expedition slowly approached the Leticia area, while diplomatic efforts to avoid war were undertaken by Brazil, the Pan-American Union, the United States, Argentina, Chile, and the League of Nations. As early as September 1932 the Peruvian government sought to submit the dispute to the Washington Conciliation Commission, as provided by the Gondra Treaty of 1923. Colombia rejected the arbitration plea, arguing that the events at Leticia were "strictly and exclusively of an internal nature." The Colombian expedition reached Manaos, Brazil, on January 9 and remained there until January 23, when it sailed for the upper Amazon. On January 24 Colombia sought the intervention of the parties to the Kellogg-Briand Anti-War Pact, and of the League of Nations, to remind Peru of its international obligations. The following day U.S. Secretary of State Henry L. Stimson condemned the Peruvian occupation of Leticia and decided to intervene through the League of Nations to avert war (see Hudson 1933, 8; St. John 1976, 338).

On February 14, 1933, Peru and Colombia clashed on Brazilian territory, near the Leticia area, as Peruvian planes unsuccessfully attacked the Colombian flotilla. The following days the countries broke off diplomatic relations. Colombia recaptured Tarapacá and moved in the direction of Leticia. Moreover, on February 17 it appealed to the Council of the League under Article 15 in order to effect a peaceful settlement of the dispute. On February 25 a League mediation committee proposed that a League commission administrate the disputed territory for a transitional period.

Following the battle of Tarapacá, the crisis further escalated as the two countries finalized their preparations for a general war, including levying war taxes and mobilizing personnel. On February 28 the League of Nations ordered a halt to the conflict. On March 1 the League adopted a peace plan to administer the territory, and on March 18 the League Council demanded that Peru surrender "Colombian territory." On March 26 the Colombian expedition reported it had captured the Peruvian Fort Guepi on the south bank of the Putumayo. In April Peru sent its own naval expedition, including warships and submarines, through the Panama Canal. A general war seemed imminent.

On April 30, 1933, Peruvian president General Sánchez Cerro was assassinated. His death unexpectedly opened the way to resolve the Leticia crisis by peaceful means; he was known to be the moving spirit both of the illegal occupation of Leticia and of Peru's refusal to accept the decision of the League of Nations to restore Leticia to Colombia. The new Peruvian president, General Oscar Benavides, happened to be a personal friend of a prominent Colombian diplomat and Liberal presidential candidate, Alfonso López. In a matter of days, the crisis deescalated as López flew to Bogotá and conferred with Colombian President Enrique Olaya Herrera, and then flew to Lima to directly negotiate with President Benavides from May 15 to 20.

On May 10 the League advisory committee proposed a temporary occupation of the territory in the name of Colombia for one year, followed by direct negotiations for a permanent settlement of the territorial question. Colombia accepted these proposals on May 12, and Peru on May 24, after the López-Benavides meetings (see López 1936, 19–25; St. John 1976, 340). A preliminary agreement to end the military crisis was reached on May 25, 1933. One year later, on May 24, 1934, the two countries signed the Protocol of Friendship and Cooperation in Rio de Janeiro, Brazil, ending their conflict. Their agreement included a mutual guarantee of free access to the Amazon and the Putumayo Rivers in order to develop their respective trading interests (Windass 1970, 82). Leticia was transferred back to Colombia from the temporary League administration on June 19, 1934. The war over Leticia never took place.

Evidence and Impact of the Normative Framework

In the Leticia dispute the regional normative consensus facilitated the peaceful management and resolution of the crisis. One can argue that the issue over Leticia stemmed from the practical difficulties of implementing the accepted norms of peaceful settlement and *uti possidetis,* and was aggravated by domestic problems and a limited use of force. While Colombia insisted that the problem was a domestic one, Peru attempted to internationalize the crisis under the pretext that it threatened the South American peace.

Peru's normative arguments were convoluted and ambiguous. On the one hand, it recognized the treaty of 1922 as a legal fact; on the other, it called the treaty into question. Similarly, it both dissociated itself from the original occupation of Leticia and justified and supported those who had carried it out.[16] Moreover, Peru's legal position against the norm of the observance of treaties (*pacta sunt servanda*) was based upon three arguments. First, since the occupation of Leticia, the relevance of the principle of *rebus sic stantibus* led to a change in the current legal conditions. Second, the 1922 treaty was finalized by the dictator Leguía without democratic approval. And third, the self-determination of the inhabitants of the Leticia area should be respected. In addition, Peru directly appealed to the Latin American normative consensus against war with the expectation that this would prevent Colombia from escalating the crisis into a full-fledged war. A Peruvian editorial summarized the country's normative position as follows:

> The attitude of Colombia would have been quite different if, instead of making its declaration on the intangible sanctity of treaties, and instead of peremptorily recommending to Peru the acceptance of Brazilian mediation without changes, . . . it should understand that the peace of America stands above all other considerations, and that the keeping of the peace should never be sacrificed to the text of a diplomatic agreement which, while negotiated to promote harmony among peoples, was converted into an instrument of hatred and a cause of war.[17]

Similarly, the Colombian government, following its traditional recourse to legalism and diplomatic procedures, emphasized the need to avoid the war to maintain Latin America's normative consensus on peace. In an exchange of telegrams with Peruvian President Benavides, the Colombian negotiator Alfonso López underlined this point:

The peaceful resolution [of the crisis] will set a precedent for the Latin American peoples, underlining the norm that among them there should not be territorial conflicts that would lead to armed interventions.... We have to respect the diplomatic tradition and the international conventions."[18]

At the same time, Colombia's normative position was based on the defense of the legal situation as it existed before the Peruvian invasion of Leticia, its treaty rights, the norm of sovereignty, and its corollary of nonintervention. The Colombian case was crystal clear and unambiguous. According to international law, Colombia could demand from Peru the respect of their bilateral treaties, especially those of 1911 and 1922. In this sense, there was no valid juridical or political argument in Peru's claims that the national Peruvian sentiment should be taken into consideration, or that Peru could submit the dispute to the conciliation committee in Washington or to arbitration. From the Colombian standpoint, Leticia was part of its domestic jurisdiction, so the government had an obligation to restore the legal domestic order there, according to its sovereignty rights over the territory in question (see Latorre 1932, 23–26; Santos, in Colombia 1933, 15–16; Hudson 1933, 9; Windass 1970, 78–79). Moreover, this situation could not create a right or a pretext for another state (such as Peru) to discuss the effectiveness or legality of the juridical preestablished order (see Santos in Colombia 1933, 17–19; Latorre 1932, 12).[19]

Although the normative consensus that existed between Peru and Columbia could not keep their dispute from becoming a serious military conflict, it helped to prevent the Leticia crisis from exceeding the bounds of a fragile peace. In contrast to Peru, Colombia was in better shape from a normative point of view, though it stood on weak grounds in terms of defending its own territory. As for the Peruvians, they called for arbitration and conciliation, trying to make a domestic (in other words Colombian) "situation" into an international crisis that threatened the continental peace (see Vázquez Cobo 1985, 25, 86–87, and 106).

Conditions for the Impact of Norms

Type of political regimes and peaceful conditions within the countries.   Unlike Peru and most of the South American republics at the time, Colombia in 1932–1933 was a democracy. The picture that emerges from Colombia's management of the Leticia crisis in those years is of a cautious, even reluctant, escalation in the direction of an armed confrontation. The Colombian leadership did not want a general war, but it decided to regain the occupied territory by diplomacy if

possible and by force if necessary. Paradoxically, precisely because the population could vote freely, public opinion and the existence of a free press pushed
in the direction of war. As for Peru, Sánchez Cerro transformed his regime
into a repressive autocracy, crushing a revolutionary movement in the town of
Trujillo in 1932 with more than a thousand casualties. In response, the Aprista
Party (APRA) escalated the cycle of violence, which eventually led to the
assassination of Sánchez Cerro.

*Presence of hegemonic power and institutionalized international society; fitness between
the regional normative framework and the given case.*   The normative consensus in
favor of keeping the peace has been facilitated by the action of several third
parties, which played the roles of mediators, peace makers, and peace keepers.
Several international and regional actors played a significant role in defusing
the Leticia dispute in the early months of 1933. Brazil, the prospective South
American hegemon, was particularly prominent in the peaceful resolution of
the crisis. Both Colombia and Peru had agreed to the Brazilian mediation
since the beginning of the crisis, with the support of the United States. On
December 30, 1932, Brazilian Foreign Minister Afranio de Mello Franco had
proposed to Colombia a plan for Peru to deliver Leticia to Brazil, and for Brazil
to restore it to Colombia, with the understanding that Colombia and Peru
would settle their territorial dispute through talks in Rio de Janeiro and Brazil
would act as mediator. Although the parties rejected this plan, the League of
Nations adopted it in March 1933 as a basis for its own interim administration
of Leticia. Peru and Colombia accepted the League plan by the end of May
1933, initiated negotiations under Brazilian auspices, and signed a final peace
agreement in Rio de Janeiro the following year (Barros 1938, 29–34).

   The United States, Argentina, Chile, the Pan-American Union, and the
League of Nations also played important roles in deterring the parties from
escalating their crisis into a full-fledged war. For instance, on January 25, 1933,
U.S. Secretary of State Henry L. Stimson consulted the Kellogg-Briand Anti-
War Pact signatories about Colombia's insistence that Peru was an aggressor,
and decided to condemn Peru's occupation of Leticia in strong terms.[20] Similarly, on March 18, 1933, the League Council demanded the complete evacu-
ation by the Peruvian forces of the whole territory of Leticia (see Windass
1970, 77–81; Ireland 1938, 200; Hudson 1933, 34 and 43).

Alternative Explanations

It would be naive to argue that norms of peace alone avoided the escalation
of the Leticia dispute into a full-fledged war. The abrupt leadership change

that took place as a result of the assassination of Sánchez Cerro on April 30, 1933, presents an alternative and plausible explanation for the eventual peaceful outcome. Only two days after his death, direct negotiations over Leticia commenced between the two countries. Thus, serendipity seems to play a crucial role in this case.[21]

Furthermore, a series of material factors, including the geographical location of the territory and the economic situation in both countries, contributed to the eventual resolution of the crisis. The lack of economic resources by both Peru and Colombia affected their disposition to engage in a full-fledged war.

For both countries, Leticia was a remote place. Trans-Andean communications were extremely difficult, and the only way either Peru or Colombia could bring heavy military equipment to the Leticia area was to bring it up over the top of South America, to the Amazon River, through Brazil. Leticia was 2,700 kilometers from Pará, Brazil, at the mouth of the Amazon. From Pará to Barranquilla, the nearest port in Colombia, the distance was about 3,500 kilometers. From Callao, the closest port in Peru on the Pacific Ocean, the voyage through the Panama Canal to Pará and then to Leticia was about 8,800 kilometers (see Wood 1966, 180).

Both countries encountered serious financial problems in preparing for war, but neither could expect any financial return from the control over Leticia that could compensate for the exorbitant costs of a prolonged conflict. For Peru, one reason to accept the peace plan in May 1933 was the lamentable condition of its navy as compared with that of Colombia. Colombia also was well aware of the ruinous consequences of an armed conflict, especially given the economic situation of both nations. For example, in May 1933 Alfonso López wrote to his former diplomatic colleague, Peruvian President Benavides, asking him to cooperate and to improve Colombia's political and economic links with Peru, rather than fight a futile war. In response, President Benavides wrote:

> Under the present economic conditions, the armed conflict cannot be sustained over long time without bringing misery and mourning to two fraternal peoples. There is a need to end the war preparations in both sides of the border. . . . As you say, the Bolivarian nations need to cooperate to defend their common economic interests.[22]

In sum, economic and financial conditions, as well as serious difficulties in mobilizing the national economies for a long war, acted to defuse the crisis and enact a peaceful resolution of the dispute over Leticia. These conditions converged with the normative framework in favoring an ultimate peaceful settlement. Hence, although the dispute was resolved in accordance with the existing power structures, it did not necessarily contradict the normative premises of justice and fairness (Windass 1970, 83).

The Oriente/Mainas (Marañón) Dispute, 1828–1998

The conflicting claims of Ecuador and Peru over the territory of Mainas (the "Oriente") dated back to the early nineteenth century and have continued unresolved until October 1998. The Peruvian-Ecuadorian conflict has been by far the longest territorial dispute in Latin America. Moreover, in area and importance to the countries concerned and to their neighbors, the controversy was second only to that over the Chaco Boreal (Ireland 1938, 229–30; Zook 1964, 11). The dispute escalated several times into war in July 1941, January 1981, and, most recently, January 1995. Only after the brief war of 1995 did negotiations succeed, leading to the Peace Treaty of October 1998.

Historical and Legal Background

Peru and Ecuador have had an old territorial dispute from their time of independence in the early nineteenth century, claiming an area of about 256,000 square kilometers lying to the north of the Marañón River, not far from the Amazon River. Their boundary conflict over the Mainas region resulted from the ambiguous border definition of the former colonial units. As in many other cases, the Spanish colonial government made little effort to carefully delimit the boundaries of its vast possessions. Thus, even if Peru and Ecuador could agree on the doctrine of *uti possidetis,* they still found it difficult, if not impossible, to delineate their common frontiers (St. John 1994, 1–2).

Peru became independent from Spain in 1821, and in the following year Ecuador achieved independence as part of the new state of Gran Colombia, which included Colombia, Venezuela, and Ecuador. A dispute arose between Peru and Gran Colombia over the sovereignty of the border provinces of Jaén and Mainas. During the Spanish period they had at various times been ruled by the vice-royalty of Nueva Granada (which formed the basis for Gran Colombia), and by the vice-royalty of Peru. Both provinces had joined with Peru in 1821, but in 1822 Gran Colombia claimed that they should belong to it. The dispute escalated into the war of 1828–1829. By the Treaty of Guayaquil of September 22, 1829, both parties recognized their boundaries as being those of the old vice-royalties. A boundary commission was to be appointed to fix the frontier. Subsequent efforts to define the border failed, leading to the continuation of the conflict (see Goldstein 1992, 187–88; Zook 1964, 20).

With the secession of Ecuador from Gran Colombia in 1830, Peru's boundary dispute with Colombia shifted to Ecuador as the western part of the line, from the Pacific Ocean over the mountains to the Marañón River, in the upper Amazon River Basin (Ireland 1938, 228–29). During the negotiations of 1841–1842, the Ecuadorians proposed recognizing the vice-royal borders prior to independence; consequently, Peru should return Jaén and Mainas to Ecuador, since they had belonged to the *Audiencia* of Quito. Yet the Peruvians asserted that the doctrine of *uti possidetis* should be applied to a time *after* independence. Since the representatives of the disputed provinces had chosen freely to become part of Peru in 1821, and they had previously been a part of the vice-royalty of Peru, they indeed belonged to Peru (Zook 1964, 25). In 1887 the parties agreed to submit their territorial dispute to the arbitration of the King of Spain. This led to a projected award in 1910 that largely recognized Peru's juridical theses, which was rejected a priori by Ecuador.

Despite occasional efforts at mediation, such as in 1936–1938, no diplomatic solution could be found. As in the Chaco dispute, the parties disagreed about the substance of their dispute. For Ecuador, this was a territorial dispute that involved the ownership of large areas of the Oriente. Conversely, for Peru this was only a border dispute. Border skirmishes became frequent in 1940. One escalated in June–August 1941 into a short but intensive undeclared war, culminating with a Peruvian blitzkrieg into Ecuadorian territory and a resonant Peruvian military victory.

On January 29, 1942, Ecuador was compelled to accept the Protocol of Rio de Janeiro, negotiated between the parties through the mediation of the United States and the "ABC powers," Argentina, Brazil, and Chile, as "guarantor powers." Its terms were stern. Ecuador recognized the Peruvian sovereignty over most of the disputed territory and surrendered another 12,800 square kilometers. The new boundary line not only caused Ecuador to lose two-thirds of the Oriente Province, which it had considered its own, but also deprived it of an outlet to the Amazon River. Yet the agreement generally followed what was known as the "status quo line of 1936," which both Peru and Ecuador had agreed to, since it corresponded roughly to areas occupied by citizens of the two countries. The settlement gave to Peru a net territorial increase of some 18,500 square kilometers. Yet, since Ecuador received some 5,000 square kilometers in the far north, Ecuadorian Foreign Minister Tobar honestly estimated that Peru gained "only" 13,481 square kilometers over the 1936 status quo line. Thus, Ecuadorian claims that the Rio Protocol of 1942 deprived Ecuador of half of its national territory were inaccurate (Tobar, quoted in Wood 1978, 171; see also Simmons 1999, 10; Marcella and Downes 1999, 6).

For Peru the Rio Protocol was a major diplomatic triumph, since it gained for the first time territories to which it had possessed titles but had never held before. For Ecuador the result was a bad outcome that was nonetheless preferable to the worse alternative of imperiling the nation's very existence. By accepting the protocol, Ecuador formally renounced to its claims in the Oriente region. Moreover, while the treaty stipulated that Ecuador should have navigation rights on the Amazon and its upper tributaries, Ecuador forfeited its claim of any sovereign access to the Amazon River (see Calvert 1983, 17; Zook 1964, 202).

In implementing the Rio Protocol, more than 95 percent of the border was demarcated, except for a small section of seventy-eight kilometers along the Cordillera del Cóndor. This area was the subject of an arbitral award contemplated in the Rio Protocol and rendered by a Brazilian naval officer, Captain Braz Dias de Aguilar, in July 1945. The two countries initially accepted the award unconditionally, and began to demarcate their common border (see Simmons 1999, 10–11; Atkins 1997, 164–65).

Yet Ecuador asserted that a new piece of geographical information came to light in 1946–1947 as a result of aerial photography, regarding the location of a new watershed (the *divortium aquarum*) between the Zamora and Santiago rivers—the Cenepa River. This discovery invalidated the location of the border in the Cordillera del Cóndor area. As a result, Ecuador became increasingly revisionist, formally declaring the Rio Protocol (and the subsequent arbitration of 1945) as null and void in August 1960. At that time, Ecuadorian President José María Velasco Ibarra initiated a critical and destructive campaign for reelection, in which he asserted that the protocol could not be executed due to its geographical flaws and inherent unfairness. In his view the protocol was an unjust settlement imposed by the force of Peruvian arms in defiance of international law. Ecuador sustained a valid and just claim to its territorial rights regarding the headwaters of the Amazon River. Peru, for its part, has regarded the border problem as being definitively resolved by the Rio Protocol. The guarantor states also upheld the validity of the 1942 treaty and urged the two parties to finish charting the area in question (see Mares 1999, 173; St. John 1994, 15; Marcella and Downes 1999, 7; Delgado Jara 1985, 17–23; Atkins 1997, 165; Simmons 1999, 11).

For about the next thirty years, Ecuadorian foreign policy actively pursued in numerous international forums the nullification of the entire Rio Protocol and the rejection of the 1945 arbitration. The territorial conflict persisted, and it further escalated into armed confrontations in January 1981 and, more recently, in January 1995, always around the anniversary of the Rio Protocol. In 1981 Ecuadorian troops occupied outposts in Peru; Peru responded with jungle fighting and bombing raids conducted by helicopters, driving the Ecuadorians out by the time a cease-fire was arranged. In 1995 there was another round of fighting for thirty-four days. This time there were relatively high casualty figures (about 500) and a limited Ecuadorian victory in the upper Cenepa Valley and around the Tiwintza military base, which both sides claimed to be within their own territory. This was the first time Ecuador inflicted any kind of military defeat on Peru since the 1829 battle of Tarqui.

Following the brief war of 1995, Ecuador surprisingly changed its previous revisionist attitude, accepting the Rio Protocol of 1942 as mostly valid but with "shortcomings" (Marcella and Downes 1999, 7). The end of the war of 1995 opened the way to negotiations and mediation and to the active participation, good offices, and even arbitration of the guarantor powers. On October 29, 1996, Peru and Ecuador signed an agreement that committed them to addressing the remaining "impasses" surrounding their dispute: the final demarcation of the common border and the free access to the Marañón and Amazon rivers.

By the beginning of October 1998 the direct negotiations between the parties remained in a stalemate. At this point, both Presidents Mahuad (from Ecuador) and Fujimori (from Peru) sent letters to Brazilian President Cardoso, indicating their inability to agree on the final demarcation of their common border and asking for a binding arbitration by the presidents of the four guarantor states. Ecuador and Peru asked the guarantors to suggest a viable compromise and committed themselves to ratifying it in their legislatures (see Marcella 1999, 232–34; Simmons 1999, 20). This unusual procedure, reminiscent of the award of the "neutral" parties to the Chaco dispute in 1938, facilitated the signature of the Peace Treaty in October 26, 1998, ending the longest territorial dispute in Latin America.

According to the guarantors' award, the disputed stretch of border was to be demarcated according to the Rio Protocol's line of division, along the high peaks of the Cordillera del Cóndor range. In exchange, Ecuador received a square kilometer of private property across the Peruvian side of the border at Tiwintza, where scores of Ecuadorean soldiers lied buried. In addition, both countries established an ecological park and a demilitarized zone in their common border. The treaty also gave Ecuador navigation rights—though no sovereign access—to the Amazon River and its tributaries in Peru, and the possibility of establishing two trading centers there (Simmons 1999, 20).

Evidence and Impact of the Normative Framework

Throughout their 160 years of disputing the Oriente, Ecuador and Peru articulated their conflicting claims in distinctive normative and legal terms. The alleged rights in the dispute included discovery (claimed by both parties), legal titles (disputed as well), and possession (with a clear advantage to the Peruvians). Moreover, both countries recognized the doctrine of *uti possidetis juris* and the need to settle their dispute by peaceful means, according to the regional framework that favored peace.

In spite of their consensual and formal adoption of *uti possidetis,* the two countries diverged sharply in the definition of their conflict and the relevant principles for its resolution. Ecuador sustained sovereign rights to an area that Peru considered part of its own national territory. For Peru any such sovereign rights ended with the Rio Protocol of 1942 and the Braz Dias de Aguilar award of 1945. Peru insisted upon the principle of self-determination, according to which the establishment of American nationalities stemmed from their own free determination following their break with the mother country. Ecuador rejected this principle, given the historical trajectory chosen by the people of Mainas to opt for Peru. Furthermore, Ecuador pointed out the dangerous consequences of the application of the principle of self-determination, as it could be appreciated in the Leticia crisis (Ecuador 1938, 13). In addition, Ecuador felt that Peru attempted to shrink the conflict in time and space—by making a territorial question into a border one, and by focusing on the latest de facto advances that obviously favored Peru. From the Ecuadorian perspective, there could not be a common normative ground, since the controversy consisted of the contraposition of Quito's titles against Lima's allegations and Peru's illegal retention of Ecuadorian territory. Furthermore, since the imposition of the Rio Protocol of 1942, the question was interpreted in Ecuadorian terms as one of justice and equity, thus demanding modification (Zook 1964, 131).

The Ecuadorian legal case was based on several arguments. First, Ecuador claimed the discovery of the Amazon River in 1542. Second, the application of *uti possidetis* followed a series of Spanish decrees issued after 1563 when a *cédula* awarded Mainas, Quijos, Jaén, and any adjoining land to the *Audiencia* of Quito. Third, the Treaty of Guayaquil of 1829 reaffirmed the boundary between the previous vice-royalties. Fourth, Ecuador dismissed the right of possession argued by Peru, since possession could not generate any juridical right against the legitimate sovereign (see Wood 1978, 2 and 19; St. John 1994, 4; and Ecuador 1938, 9–15, 217).

In addition, following the war of 1941 and the Rio Protocol of 1942, Ecuador argued that the force of a Peruvian occupying army acting in defiance of international law had imposed an unjust settlement. The Protocol in itself represented a contradiction to the norms of peaceful settlement of international disputes and no recourse to force (see Carrión Mena 1989, 318). President Ibarra summarized in 1961 the major arguments for noncompliance, including legal and equity claims, as follows:

- "Ecuador cannot be far away, maintained apart from the Amazonas." (Ibarra 1961, 16; my translation)
- "Can Ecuador, which discovered and colonized the Amazon basin, be confined between the sea and the mountain ranges in the East? Is that justice? Is that Americanism? Is that an expression of South American cooperation?" (Ibarra 1961, 17; my translation)
- "Can a treaty be signed when a[n Ecuadorian] province is being invaded? Is it possible to formulate a contract when a pistol is pointed at one of the parties? [Hence] the Treaty of Rio is a null treaty." (Ibarra 1961, 17; my translation)
- "In the so-called Declaration of Costa Rica, it is stated that the controversies among the American nations should be resolved by peaceful and juridical means. . . . Hence, we have the right to say that, according to the Inter-American norms, the treaties imposed by force are null and void." (Ibarra 1961, 23; my translation)
- "The Protocol of Rio de Janeiro is null because it was imposed by force, when the country was invaded and its cities put to fire. Thus, from a legal point of view, it is null and void. This [Ecuadorian] position is entirely legal." (Ibarra 1961, 26; my translation)
- "The 1942 Protocol contradicts the substance of American [international] law, according to which one cannot earn advantages from military conquests, as it was proclaimed in all the Pan-American Conferences since 1890 up to the consultation among American Foreign Ministers in 1940." (Ibarra 1961, 46; my translation)

In sum, Ecuador dismissed the Rio Protocol as legally null because (a) it was imposed by force; (b) it could not be executed on the watershed between the Zamora and Santiago rivers; (c) it had not been signed by competent and legitimate representatives; (d) it opposed positive norms of international law in Latin America regarding the nullity of territorial cessions if effected under pressure or by force; and (e) it opposed legal and historical facts, essentially the principle of *uti possidetis* and the Guayaquil Treaty of September 22, 1829 (Delgado Jara 1985, 16–23). Only after the 1995 war did Ecuador change its normative stance regarding the validity of the 1942 agreement.

Peru's legal claims of *uti possidetis juris* stemmed from a Spanish royal decree of July 15, 1802, adjudicating to the vice-royalty of Peru the vaguely defined former captaincy general of Mainas. Peruvian territorial claims consolidated in 1851, when Peru and Brazil agreed on their present boundary line north of the Amazonas (Wood 1978, 2). However, more important and even superseding the principle of *uti possidetis* was the norm of self-determination, which encompassed the essence of independence in the Americas. Peru argued that all of the disputed territories were Peruvian because their populations had voluntarily adhered to Peru at the time of its independence (1821), several years before the independence of Ecuador (1830), and expressed their free will to do so through their *cabildos* (popular assemblies) (see St. John 1994, 4; Zook 1964, 134; Luis Alvarado in Peru 1961, 45).

In addition to the norms of *uti possidetis* and self-determination, which somehow contradicted each other, Peru sustained strong juridical and legal principles as the status quo party. First, in a position similar to that of Paraguay in the Chaco dispute, Peru argued for a right of possession in the disputed territories since 1821. Second, and especially vis-à-vis the Rio Protocol of 1942, Peru upheld the principle of *pacta sunt servanda*.[23] Third, Peru presented itself vis-à-vis the Latin American international society as the peaceful side, while Ecuador "attempted to break the regime of *convivencia* built by the American republics, creating chaos and becoming a threat to the continental peace" (Peru 1961, 59).

To counter the Ecuadorian accusations about the alleged injustice of the Rio Protocol, the Peruvian Foreign Ministry quoted profusely from a report compiled by George M. McBride, the U.S. assistant to the Brazilian arbitrator Braz Dias de Aguilar, who suggested from 1942 to 1949 the following conclusions:

- The Rio Protocol was based on the status quo line of 1936, a de facto border that was accepted on a voluntary basis by both countries.
- In the division of the disputed territory Peru received most of it, but Ecuador got the best part.

- Ecuador lost few of the territories that it ever controlled.
- In compensation for that, Ecuador received lands that it had given up, in the region of Sucumbios-Gueppi.
- Ecuador had never established itself on the Amazon River or near it, either by colonies or by military posts.
- The aggression, in the sense of penetrating the disputed territory, was committed apparently by both countries, despite the 1936 agreement. The confrontation of 1941 was a result of that.
- The mediation [by the ABC powers and the United States] was in favor of, rather than against, Ecuador. Mediation had saved Ecuador from being completely occupied by the Peruvian forces, and provided Ecuador with a guarantee for a just solution to the long conflict with its more powerful neighbor.
- The decisions of the mediators regarding the disagreements in the demarcation [in the Cordillera del Cóndor] were fair and just for both parties. (McBride, quoted in Peru 1996, 19–20, my translation)

From this standpoint, the Rio Protocol of 1942 could be considered more of a compromise than a dictate imposed on Ecuador, since each party had to rennounce a part of the territory it claimed. Though Ecuador had to give up its sovereign claims for direct access to the Amazon River, Peru ceded as well territory that was not disputed. This territory had been previously transferred from Ecuador to Colombia, and from Colombia to Peru (McBride in Peru 1996, 146–47). Moreover, the Protocol offered Ecuador the possibility of "free navigation" in the Amazon River.

Conditions for the Impact of Norms

The Oriente case is a complex one that encompasses a serious failure of peaceful change that led to successive rounds of war in 1941, 1981, and 1995. At the same time, the last four years of the conflict (1995–1998) did witness a diplomatic transition from conflict management to peaceful resolution, with a final, though delayed, "happy ending" Hence, while assessing the conditions for the impact of norms in a time period that spans 160 years of conflict, we focus particularly on its last decade.

Salience of domestic actors who mobilize norms; role of leaders.   It is evident that in the last two years of the dispute, Presidents Mahuad (from Ecuador) and Fujimori (from Peru) played a crucial role in concluding the process. Their commitment to peaceful resolution was evidenced by unprecedented levels of political contact and communication and by their agreement to submit the last unresolved territorial issues to the arbitration of the four Guarantor states, upon acceptance of the congresses of Ecuador and Peru (Simmons 1999, 16).

Type of political regime and peaceful conditions within the countries. It is not clear whether there is a direct link between the democratization processes that have affected Peru and Ecuador since the early 1980s and their disposition for peaceful resolution from 1995 to 1998. After all, the wars of 1981 and 1995 took place when one or even both countries were ruled by civilian regimes, though in the case of Peru under Fujimori it is difficult to characterize the regime as democratic at all. Moreover, Peru was affected by a virulent civil war against *Sendero Luminoso* ("Shining Path") that ended only in the early 1990s. Notwithstanding their changing political regimes, both countries tended to assess the history of their conflict through nationalistic filters heavily influenced by domestic politics and militarized politics (Marcella and Downes 1999, 6). At the same time, difficult political and economic conditions within both countries might have moved them in the direction of a political compromise, especially after realizing the futility of the recourse to violence in 1995. Thus, after the last war, there was a detectable change in popular attitudes toward the dispute, especially in Ecuador, where the conflict was felt much more deeply than in Peru (Simmons 1999, 17–18).

Fitness between the regional normative framework and the given case. In the Presidential Act of Brasilia of October 26, 1998, both presidents finally recognized the need for the peaceful settlement of their dispute, in accordance with the norms established in the Americas.[24] In this sense, the resolution of this dispute ended what it might be called a Latin American anomaly, in contradiction to the accepted norms of peace in the region. As Ecuadorian President Jamil Mahuad declared, "After so many decades of trying to defeat each other and win these wars, together, both countries are winning the peace" (Mahuad 1998, 1–2).

Presence of hegemonic power and degree of institutionalization of the international society. The resolution of the dispute in 1998 offers an illuminating example of how a multilateral mechanism devised within a formal treaty can facilitate the final peaceful settlement of a conflict involving two parties (Scott Palmer 1999, 21). The role of the four guarantors, especially that of the United States and Brazil since 1995, has been crucial in devising and articulating a successful process of peaceful negotiations. According to the 1942 Protocol, the four guarantors were legally obligated to mediate, and even to arbitrate, all the aspects of the Ecuador-Peru border dispute. The Protocol of 1942 was in fact multilateral, since the mediators were also guarantors adopting a more active role than just offering a simple "moral guarantee" for the implementation of the treaty (see McBride, in Peru 1996, 148; Simmons 1999, v). Indeed, in their letter dated October 23, 1998, the four guarantors emitted their "binding point of view" that ultimately resolved the remaining "impasses" and the boundary differences between the two countries (Marcella 1999, 244).

Alternative Explanations

Norms have played an important role in the last phase of the territorial dispute between Peru and Ecuador, especially through the intervention of the four guarantor states. Moreover, both countries liked to present their almost perennial conflicting claims in legal, judicial, and moral (in other words, justice and equity) terms. Yet the Oriente dispute can be interpreted as well in terms of power politics and national interests, like the Chaco and Leticia disputes.

Moreover, Ecuador sustained a misperceived sense regarding its territorial losses. It always carried a sense of having been wronged and deceived by the international society. As former Ecuadorian Foreign Minister Julio Tobar candidly recognized, "Our boundary litigation has been a problem of illusion. Confident in the justice of our cause, we have disdained realistic solutions, in pursuit of dreams and of unattainable hopes" (Tobar, quoted in Zook 1964, 202). The difference between Ecuador's alleged rights and its actual possession in the Oriente in 1936 reflected a century of errors. The net loss in 1942 was only about 13,500 square kilometers, since Peru had retired from some of its 1941 military conquests. Ecuador thus managed to preserve a small but valuable section of the Oriente, the higher land lying at the foot of the Andes (Tobar, quoted in Zook 1964, 203).

In addition to the psychological misrepresentation of the territorial dispute, national pride exacerbated the dispute in both countries, contributing to the lack of empathy and understanding between the parties (see Simmons 1999, 3). With many other points of access to the Amazon River, Peru had no particular economic need for the disputed territory. Moreover, given the relative weakness of Ecuador, it seems that there was no great strategic urgency for it either (Calvert 1983, 17–18). And yet Peru opposed consistently any Ecuadorian sovereign claim that would give it a certain access to the Amazon basin.

With the conclusion of the Rio Protocol of 1942 the Ecuadorian case was closed from a legal standpoint. Hence, its subsequent rejection of the protocol between 1960 and 1995 could be regarded as a subversive challenge of the accepted rules of international law, in the name of justice and morality. Unfortunately for Ecuador, it has been the weaker side both in terms of its legal arguments and in terms of its power relation with Peru, though the results of the war of 1995 slightly changed the power equation between the two countries. The change was more psychological than real. It opened the way for some form of political compromise between the two parties. Yet the final agreement remained within the preestablished legal and territorial parameters of the Rio Protocol of 1942.

Only in the years following the 1995 war did the parties change their nationalistic rhetoric, agreeing that trade and development were more important than nationalist symbols. Alongside their conflict, there were a series of common interests and institutions involving the two countries that pushed them in the direction of resolving their dispute. Both had a common stance on the Latin American thesis of the 200 miles in the debates on the Law of the Sea; and both were partners in the Andean Group and the Amazon Treaty (Denegri Luna 1996, 322–23). Moreover, both governments faced a poor economy and few resources to devote to another military round. Ecuador's stronger performance in the 1995 war meant that any concessions it would make in the near future would not be interpreted as an act of coercion. As economic and trade integration in the Andean Group proceeded, Ecuador and Peru became increasingly aware of the opportunity costs that their dispute enacted by denying them the advantages of normal economic and political relations (Simmons 1999, 21).

The Beagle Channel Dispute, 1847–1984[25]

In contrast to the violent Peruvian-Ecuadorian dispute, Argentina and Chile confronted the problems of one of the longest land frontiers in the world and a history of territorial disputes and militarized crises with action that led to occasional armed clashes but always stopped just short of war. The dispute turned into a serious militarized crisis in 1978, following Argentina's rejection of a British arbitration award giving three Beagle Channel Islands to Chile in 1977. In December 1978 war was narrowly avoided, perhaps providentially, by a severe South Atlantic storm that prevented a naval confrontation between the two countries, and by a last-minute papal diplomatic intervention. After intense negotiations that lasted for more than five years, Argentina and Chile signed the Treaty of Peace and Friendship on November 29, 1984, which had previously been endorsed by a vast majority of Argentine citizens in a referendum. In the treaty Chile's sovereignty over the Beagle Channel Islands was recognized, though there was an explicit limitation about projecting its sovereignty beyond a surrounding three-mile-wide zone. Why did Argentina reject the 1977 award? How did it manage to improve its position, turning the conflict outcome from a juridical to a political solution?

Historical and Legal Background

The definition of the boundary between Argentina and Chile has historically been a source of conflict between the two states. Longstanding, intractable territorial disputes marked the relations between Chile and Argentina since their early postcolonial days. Throughout the nineteenth century both Chile and Argentina claimed the southern Patagonia region. After concluding a boundary agreement in 1881 that included the neutralization of the Strait of Magellan (see chapter 5), they resolved most of their territorial differences, although the conflict over the Beagle Channel lingered until 1984. Throughout the twentieth century their territorial conflicts focused on three areas in particular. One was the precise location of the Beagle Channel, a strait separating Argentina's part of Tierra del Fuego from Chile's Navarino Island. The dispute involved the possession of a group of three islands in the Channel (Picton, Lennox, and Nueva, or PLN group) and the maritime rights regarding their surrounding sea. A second was the Palena area, involving a 38-kilometer stretch of sparsely inhabited territory along the Andes frontier, eventually resolved in 1966 by an arbitration award that granted Argentina 70 percent of the disputed territory. The Laguna del Desierto region was a third area of conflict, also located on the Andean frontier to the south. It was resolved in 1994 by a regional arbitration award in favor of Argentina.

The 200-kilometer-long Beagle Channel both links the Atlantic and Pacific Oceans and separates Tierra del Fuego from the small islands that dot the way south in the direction of Cape Horn. Under the terms of the Treaty of 1881, all territory south of the Beagle Channel was considered Chilean.[26] Although the treaty's terms were explicit and clear, the two countries did not agree on the exact position of the channel, so they diverged on their interpretation of which territory was deemed "south" of the Beagle Channel (Garrett 1985, 82).

From the Argentine standpoint, the Beagle Channel turned south along the coast of the large Chilean island of Navarino before reaching the PLN group situated at the channel's eastern mouth. This position maintained Argentina's "bioceanic principle," according to which Atlantic territory was Argentine and Pacific areas were Chilean. Conversely, according to Chile, the channel flowed north of the PLN group after passing Navarino and then emptied into the Atlantic. This position gave Chile control over a significant portion of the waters of the South Atlantic, including an additional 30,000 square maritime miles, in terms of the 200-mile limit (see Garrett 1985, 82–83; Golbert and Nun 1982, 191; Calvert 1983, 9). Thus, the Beagle Channel "question" revolved around the issue of how and where to define the dividing line between the South Atlantic (Argentina's sphere of influence) and the South Pacific (Chile's sphere).

In July 1971 the two countries agreed to submit the Beagle Channel dispute to the arbitration of the United Kingdom. Under the terms of the accord (*compromis*), the British government was restricted to accepting or rejecting whatever award was given by an international court of five jurists of the International Court of Justice. The major task of the court was to find the correct interpretation of Article 3 of the Treaty of 1881, which specifically referred to the Beagle Channel. The award was to be legally binding on both parties unless based on factual error (see Golbert and Nun 1982, 192; Millán and Morris 1990, 9–10; Scenna 1981, 211–12; Garrett 1985, 90–91).

In May 1977 Argentina and Chile received the arbitration decision, which awarded the disputed islands to Chile, which already was in possession of them. On January 25, 1978, Argentina officially rejected the arbitration award, arguing that the decision contained errors about the geography of the area and was null in juridical and legal terms. According to Argentina's legal opinion, the award violated the agreement of 1881 on spheres of influence in the Southern region and the principle of *uti possidetis*. This rejection precipitated a serious military and political crisis between the two countries. As Chile became Argentina's major security concern—replacing Brazil and the United Kingdom—the two countries prepared for war, including the massing of troops and equipment along their Southern border and the general mobilization of their armed forces.

In the first half of 1978 a series of meetings and bilateral negotiations took place in order to manage and defuse the militarized crisis. Presidents Videla (from Argentina) and Pinochet (from Chile) met in Mendoza on January 19, 1978, and again in Puerto Montt on February 20, 1978, in order to negotiate "a peaceful solution of our controversies and, subsequently, to determine our two nations' respective rights under the legal system" (quoted in Day 1982, 336). Under the Act of Puerto Montt, a joint negotiating commission was established with a limited mandate of 180 days to resolve the dispute by peaceful means. Six rounds of negotiations followed, without any results. By November of 1978 the two countries acknowledged the failure of their negotiations. Chile threatened to appeal to the International Court of Justice. On December 12, 1978, there was a final encounter between the two foreign ministers, to no avail. War then became imminent in the third week of December, when a last-minute intervention by Pope John Paul II managed to defuse the crisis on December 21, 1978 (Pastor 1996, 265).

The Montevideo Act of January 8, 1979, which recognized the diplomatic role of the pope, paved the way for an eventual peaceful resolution of the dispute. Negotiations were conducted for almost six years with the mediation of the pope, ultimately leading to the conclusion of the Treaty of Peace and Friendship on November 29, 1984. In December 1980 the pope suggested the recognition of Chile's ownership of the PLN group, but with a maritime limit extended only to ten, instead of 200, miles east of Nueva. The area between mile twelve and mile 200 was to be a zone of "shared resources," or a "sea of peace," over which Chile and Argentina would exercise joint sovereignty (Garrett 1985, 98). In January 1984 the parties accepted the papal proposal as a basis for their final negotiations.

The 1984 Treaty of Peace and Friendship represented a watershed in the relations of Chile and Argentina, which at least three times in their long history came to the verge of war, though they never fought against each other. The agreement allowed common developmental and economic concerns to come to the fore, replacing divisive national security and geopolitical matters previously raised.

Evidence and Impact of the Normative Framework

The Beagle Channel conflict, like several other territorial disputes analyzed in this chapter, was considered in both Chile and Argentina in terms of legal obligations arising from nineteenth-century treaties and standard legal and juridical practices that located sea and other territorial boundaries, including the interpretation of the norm of *uti possidetis* (Holsti 1996, 170). Some of these practices have become anachronistic, when confronted with recent developments in international law like the claim for a 200-mile "economic exclusive zone," according to the Law of the Sea. Thus, the unfortunate legal and political conflict between Argentina and Chile shows very clearly that an arbitral award delivered following a preestablished hermetical procedure is neither a guarantee of a final agreement nor an obstacle for further crisis and escalation.

Throughout their long history of boundary disputes, Argentina and Chile did recognize the 1810 doctrine of *uti possidetis juris* as the basis for boundary determination. Three other patterns associated with the normative framework emerge from the record of their bilateral relations. First, when they could not settle their boundaries, they postponed the issue many times, pushing it aside and agreeing to tackle it at some point in the distant future. Second, they formally agreed not to resort to violence and pledged to accept the norm of peaceful settlement. Third, they agreed to submit their boundary disputes to the arbitration of third parties. At the same time they disagreed on their interpretation of *uti possidetis* regarding their maritime boundaries and on the rights of possession over the disputed territory. For instance, Chile claimed the PLN group based on its right of discovery and possession since the end of the nineteenth century, while Argentina disputed the existence of a single possession act in any of the three islands neither before nor after 1881 (Lanús 1984, 514).

Between 1971 and 1977 the juridical process of arbitration took place. In its Report of July 1973 submitted to the arbitration court, Argentina included documents to prove its claims that "the Beagle began to the north of Lennox." Moreover, Argentina argued that Chile had recognized the bioceanic principle in a series of negotiations and treaties, including the Treaty of 1881, the Protocol of 1893, and the May Pacts of 1902 (Lanús 1984, 51 and 513–14; see also chapter 5). On April 18, 1977, Queen Elizabeth II accepted the decision of the Arbitral Court and published it on May 2, 1977. The award recognized Chile's claims.

Although the parties had agreed to submit their dispute to arbitration in 1971, the 1977 award created a serious normative schism between them. As a matter of fact, the award was more declarative than attributive. Thus, it did not grant the islands to Chile, as Argentina argued, but rather recognized the legitimate sovereign rights that Chile already had over them (see Holguín Pelaez 1980, 11).

By unilaterally rejecting the arbitral award of 1977, Argentina violated the principle of *pacta sunt servanda*. It became the renegade party in terms of international law, like Ecuador after 1960. Its normative justification for the unilateral rejection included the following points:

- Argentina acknowledged that, while it had traditionally upheld international agreements and had a long tradition of peaceful settlement of disputes, it had no obligation to comply with any decision that damaged its vital national interests.

- The award was null and void, and it was "dictated in violation of international norms." The arguments were based on (1) excess of power, including opinions to questions not submitted to the court, such as the eastern mouth of the Magellan Strait; (2) defects of argumentation; (3) mistakes related to the application of international law ("defective"); (4) the Court's reasoning was deemed "contradictory"; and (5) distortion of Argentine arguments (see Montes 1978, 87–91; my translation; Lanús 1984, 520).
- There were "geographical and historical errors" in the award. Moreover, the Court exhibited a clear "imbalance in the evaluation of the respective arguments and evidence submitted by the two parties" (Montes, quoted in Golbert and Nun 1982, 201–2).

The arguments presented by Argentina in its Declaration of Nullity attempted to justify the noncompliance with the execution of an arbitral award. Officially, Argentina claimed that its rejection stood "according to the *jus cogens* and a series of international precedents, regarding the rejection of an award if it violates in content and procedures basic rules of international law" (Argentina in Holguín Pelaez 1980, 178; my translation). In practice, many of these assertions were far more subjective than the Argentine Declaration of Nullity suggests.

From the Chilean point of view, the award of the United Kingdom in 1977 resolved definitively the jurisdiction in the Southern region, according to the norms of the Treaty of 1902 and the terms of the arbitral *compromis* of 1971. In response to the Argentine Declaration of Nullity, Chile stated that the unilateral rejection was a clear violation of international law and norms of behavior within the international community. Moreover, the court's ruling remained mandatory and fully valid, so that Chile reaffirmed its legitimate rights over the disputed territory. Thus, even if Chile was ready to contemplate negotiations with Argentina in 1978 and after, they were not supposed to affect its sovereign rights (Carrasco 1978, 243–44).

From a legal and juridical point of view, the Argentine rights could not be sustained. The legal controversy reached (literally) a dead end. As Argentine President General Jorge Videla argued, "for Argentina the arbitral award does not exist, the juridical road is finished" (Videla, quoted in Carrasco 1978, 338–39). At this point, Argentina preferred a political solution that could be reached by peaceful settlement if possible, but by military means if necessary.

Paradoxically, the rejection of the award in 1977 and the escalation toward a serious militarized crisis, as orchestrated by the Argentine military dictatorship, created the conditions for the papal mediation and the negotiations that led to the political compromise of 1984. The political agreement somehow improved Argentina's position in relation to what was stipulated by the arbitration of 1977. At the same time, the Peace Treaty of 1984 encompassed the basics of the arbitration award by recognizing Chilean sovereignty over the disputed islands.

Conditions for the Impact of Norms

In normative terms, while the Argentine unilateral rejection of the 1977 award can be considered a legal failure, the negotiations concluded by Argentine President Raúl Alfonsín and Chile's dictator Augusto Pinochet in 1984 were a political success for both parties.

Salience of domestic actors who mobilize norms; role of leaders.   It is clear that both General Augusto Pinochet, the military dictator of Chile between 1973 and 1989, and Raúl Alfonsín, the democratically elected Argentine president (1983–1989), had a common interest in ending the Beagle dispute by peaceful means. As the status quo party, Chile had no interest in prolonging or escalating the dispute. Conversely, when President Alfonsín assumed power in December 1983, he made resolution of the Beagle Channel question his top priority in foreign affairs. After the ignominious defeat in the Falklands/Malvinas War, Alfonsín looked for ways to improve the international image of Argentina. He even had a personal stake in resolving the conflict, by submitting the draft peace treaty to a referendum (see Garrett 1985, 85; Morris 1989, 97).

Type of political regime and peaceful conditions within the countries.   The militarization of the dispute in 1977–1978 could be linked to the military dictatorship in Argentina, which was at the same time fighting a civil war (*guerra sucia*) against its own citizens. Although the Argentine military government initiated negotiations in 1979 with its Chilean military counterpart, the Argentine transition to democracy in 1983 facilitated and accelerated them. The new democratic government in Argentina could accept the principle of peaceful settlement of conflicts in more convincing terms than the previous military *junta*. By contrast, in 1984 the military regime of Pinochet in Chile could be considered sufficiently stable to turn to conflict resolution, given its inherent status quo approach toward the dispute. The peaceful resolution of the dispute could then benefit both countries by improving their respective international images in different ways.

Fitness between the regional normative framework and the given case; degree of institutionalization of the international society. Once the militarized crisis was defused by the intervention of the pope in December of 1978, both parties recognized in the Montevideo Agreement of January 8, 1979, the need to resolve their dispute "in accordance with the spirit of the international norms related to the maintenance of peace" (quoted in CARI 1995, 179–80; my translation). Their mutual commitment to peace was formally reiterated in the Peace Treaty of 1984. From the standpoint of the new democratic government in Argentina, "the signature of the treaty and its ratification will confirm the Argentine traditional policy of Latin American fraternity" (Alfonsín, quoted in Congreso [Argentine Congress] 1988, 80). Furthermore, Alfonsín claimed that the treaty was a broad step toward "peace, integration, and disarmament in Latin America" (Alfonsín, quoted in Morris 1989, 98).

Alternative Explanations

The Beagle Channel dispute was argued in legal and juridical terms, though it was eventually resolved as a political compromise. In juxtaposition to their legal arguments and claims, the two countries sustained serious geopolitical and economic interests in the disputed area. As a rule, geopolitical considerations played a significant role in the foreign policies of both Chile and Argentina in the 1970s and early 1980s, reflecting the strategic priorities of the military dictatorships then in power in both countries (Garrett 1985, 84). The award of 1977 changed the geopolitical situation in the region, opening the door for Chile to get to the Atlantic Ocean. As Malcolm Shaw has rightly pointed out with respect to the Beagle conflict, the Argentine rejection of the 1977 award was a "reflection of the vital interests it sees at brake here, placing the Argentine naval base of Ushuaia in Chilean-controlled waters and affecting Argentine claims to Antarctica and the oil and fish resources of the 200-mile zone south, toward Antarctica" (Shaw, quoted in Puig 1987, 302–3; my translation).

From the Argentine standpoint, there was a stark contradiction between its geopolitical interests and respect for the norms of international law. Coping with the award of 1977, Argentina confronted a particularly difficult normative dilemma: Should it reject the award, and thus violate its honor, reputation, and good name in the Latin American international society? Or should the country accept it, and thus violate what it considered to be its legitimate national interests? By choosing to reject the award in January 1978, Argentina emphasized the political dimension of the conflict, despite that its Declaration of Nullity was formulated in legal (or even legalistic) terms (see Infante Caffi 1984, 34; Paz y Figueroa 1980, xiii).

Furthermore, as in most of the cases reviewed in this chapter, national pride also was at stake in this conflict. To the Argentines, the Beagle Channel Islands were considered as Argentine as the "Malvinas" (Falkland) Islands. Conversely, Chileans feared Argentine nationalism and its expressed vows of expansionism (Garrett 1985, 85).

Against these difficulties and obstacles to reaching a viable solution, the Treaty of Peace of 1984 should be appreciated as a genuine political compromise. It was based on the papal proposal of 1980, which suggested a kind of "sea of peace" that limited the maritime jurisdiction of the parties. This proposal was a kind of delicate political equilibrium between the sovereign rights that Chile sustained and the demands of fairness that Argentina could aspire to. In the final version of the 1984 treaty, however, the definition of the "sea of peace" was abandoned, though the concept of limiting the maritime jurisdiction of the parties remained. Neither side was completely happy with the outcome, but each was content enough to live by its obligations (Millán and Morris 1990, 10; Passarelli 1998, 257). The essence of the political compromise refers then to the provisions about maritime delimitation, as stated in Article 8 of the treaty.[27]

The Treaty of 1984 represented a successful case of peaceful change. Both Argentina and Chile had important incentives to reach an agreement, since each of them was involved in other, perhaps more intractable, international disputes. Argentina faced a continuous conflict with the United Kingdom over the Falklands; Chile still had long-standing disputes with Bolivia and Peru. On the one hand, Argentina recognized Chilean sovereignty over all the disputed islands. Chile thus gained control and recognition over all the islands south of the Beagle Channel, as understood in the 1977 British award. On the other hand, the maritime boundary was drawn from north to south from Cape Horn, thus enabling Argentina to reclaim the bioceanic principle, by restricting Chile's legal maritime jurisdiction to only three miles from the islands in the area. In addition, the provisions of the Treaty included the setting of two binational commissions to promote economic development and cooperation, and to oversee the execution of the agreement (Millán and Morris 1990, 9–10).

Lessons from Norms of Peace in Latin America

In this chapter I have examined the norms of peaceful settlement of international disputes and *uti possidetis* in six territorial disputes that took place in South America in the last 120 years. In terms of the application of norms of peace, the cases can be located in a continnum ranging from a clear peaceful outcome of the dispute (Misiones, 1895) to a political outcome reflecting the results of violence and war (Chaco, 1938). In the gray area between these two extremes, we can find a peaceful resolution following some recourse to violence (Leticia, 1934), a delayed political compromise (Tacna and Arica, 1929), peace negotiations following the rejection of arbitration and a militarized crisis (the Beagle Channel, 1979–1984), and the resolution of a conflict by negotiations after several rounds of war (Oriente/Mainas, 1998).

This continuum of six territorial disputes also reflects a significant movement from legal to political solutions as the dispute becomes more intractable and complex. Thus, we witness an increasing involvement of third parties fulfilling the roles of mediators, conciliators, good offices, guarantors, facilitators, and ad hoc arbitrators in resolving a territorial conflict as it becomes the more significant and difficult for the contending parties to resolve by themselves. In the case of Misiones ("success"), the arbitral award by the United States was accepted by the parties, and they lived almost happily after that. In contrast, in the case of Chaco ("failure") the dispute was decided only by war, while the results of the battlefield were later "legalized" and formalized by a collective decision of the six "neutrals" (Argentina, Brazil, Chile, Uruguay, Peru, and the United States), which decided on the territorial outcome of the Peace Treaty of 1938. Similarly, we find almost the same cast of third-party characters, fulfilling almost an identical role, in the eventual outcome of the Oriente/Mainas dispute between Peru and Ecuador in 1998. At that time, the four guarantors (Argentina, Brazil, Chile, and the United States) decided to resolve the pending "impasses" between the parties in a sort of arbitration/adjudication that fit the Rio Protocol of 1942. In the other three cases we can also trace a regional or international involvement. In the Leticia dispute, Brazil, the United States, and the League of Nations were involved at several levels in conciliation and mediation efforts; in Tacna and Arica the United States exerted considerable pressure on the parties to reach a political compromise through its good offices and mediation; and in the Beagle Channel dispute, the pope's representative, Cardinal Samoré, fulfilled an indispensable role as a mediator and facilitator. The characteristics of the disputes are summarized in Table 4.2.

Table 4.2. Summary of the Territorial Disputes

Dispute	Date resolved	Type/Outcome	Third parties	Arbitration?
Misiones	1895	success (legal type)	U.S.	U.S.
Leticia	1934	eventual success (political); negotiations; conciliation	U.S. Brazil League of Nations	no
Tacna and Arica	1929	delayed success (political); mediation and negotiations; compromise	U.S.	rejected by Peru in 1925
Beagle Channel	1984	legal failure and political success (mediation and negotiations); compromise	Vatican (pope)	rejected by Argentina in 1978
Oriente/Mainas	1998	legal failure, wars, and political success (mediation and negotiations) compromise	ABC U.S.	rejected by Ecuador in 1960
Chaco	1938	legal failure, war, some form of political compromise	ABC U.S. Uruguay Peru	none (directly); Bolivia ignored the 1878 award in favor of Paraguay

In addition to the norm of peaceful settlement of international disputes, the principle of *uti possidetis* has been extremely popular as invoked in several of the disputes, and even sometimes simultaneously by *both* parties. In the Misiones case Argentina argued for *uti possidetis jure* as against Brazil's *uti possidetis facto*. In the Chaco dispute both parties justified their claims in terms of *uti possidetis,* though Paraguay preferred the *de facto* version that favored and upheld its rights of discovery and possession. In the Oriente/Mainas case, Ecuador sustained a coherent stance based on *uti possidetis juris.* As for Peru, at times it supported its own claims based on the same doctrine, while at others it superseded the principle by invoking the norm of self-determination.

Finally, in the Beagle Channel dispute both Argentina and Chile based their claims on the same doctrine, though Chile added since the late nineteenth-century its rights based on colonization and possession of the disputed territory. In the two remaining cases the norms invoked included a clash between sovereign claims and arguments for self-determination. Thus, in the Leticia dispute Colombia regarded the issue as one of defending its sovereignty over a part of its national territory, while Peru argued that self-determination super-seded the Colombian claims. Similarly, Peru disputed Chilean sovereignty over Tacna and Arica based on claims of self-determination. In addition, the revisionist parties usually presented their normative claims in terms of justice and morality, in juxtaposition to legal arguments. Peru in Leticia and Tacna/Arica, Argentina in the Beagle Channel, Ecuador in Oriente, and even Bolivia in the Chaco introduced arguments of "fairness" and "injustice" to justify their defiance of international law. Moreover, they also argued for a "change in conditions" (*rebus sic stantibus*) to justify their violation of the principle of *pacta sunt servanda*. Table 4.3 summarizes the normative claims in the six disputes.

Regarding the recourse to arbitration, this juridical procedure was applied in four of the six cases (the Chaco award of the 1938 neutrals and the arbitration/adjudication of the 1998 guarantors with respect to Peru and Ecuador were more of a political procedure than a legal one). Interestingly enough, only in the case of Misiones (1895) the "loser" party, Argentina, accepted and fulfilled the award. In three other cases the revisionist parties (Peru in 1925, Ecuador in 1960, and Argentina in 1977–1978) rejected arbitration awards and thus violated norms and treaties they had previously adhered to. In the remaining two cases the parties that regarded themselves as revisionist (Peru in relation to Leticia in 1932, Bolivia in relation to the Chaco since 1906) unilaterally rejected international treaties or third-party awards that favored the opposing (status quo) party.

Despite this common failure to comply with international law, it is interesting to notice that all the revisionist or "renegade" states presented their arguments in normative terms. First, they depicted the rejected treaties or awards as a "violation of international norms," in contradiction to the very principles they were supposed to hold up to. Second, they pointed out the ambiguity, contradictions, and indeterminacy in the language and content of treaties and awards. Third, when the rejecting party recognized that it had violated the principle of *pacta sunt servanda,* it justified that in terms of justice, rather than law and order. Fourth, in some cases, such as Ecuador in 1960 and Argentina in 1977–1978, the rejecting parties stated that they preferred consid-

Table 4.3.   Normative Arguments in the Territorial Disputes

Dispute	Status quo	Revisionist
Misiones	**Brazil** *uti possidetis de facto* possession	**Argentina** *uti possidetis de jure*
Leticia	**Colombia** sovereignty territorial integrity	**Peru** self-determination arguments of justice
Tacna/Arica	**Chile** sovereignty *pacta sunt servanda*	**Peru** self-determination *rebus sic stantibus* arguments of justice
Beagle Channel	**Chile** *uti possidetis juris* discovery and possession *pacta sunt servanda*	**Argentina** *uti possidetis juris* arguments of justice *rebus sic stantibus*
Oriente/Mainas	**Peru** *uti possidetis juris* self-determination *pacta sunt servanda* possession	**Ecuador** *uti possidetis juris* arguments of justice *rebus sic stantibus* discovery
Chaco Boreal	**Paraguay** *uti possidetis de facto* right of discovery and possession	**Bolivia** *uti possidetis de jure* arguments of justice

erations of geopolitics and national interest to those of compliance with international norms. Fifth, the noncompliance might be related to a particular type of political regime (authoritarian, nationalistic, militaristic) that misperceives the surrounding normative milieu, so it stands (and remains) "out of sync" with the current norms of the regional or global international society, such as happened with Argentina in 1976–1983 or with contemporary Iraq until 2003.

The arguments presented for noncompliance are then considered legal, normative, and rational justifications. The treaties and awards are themselves presented as distortions of the "true" principles of international law, morality, and justice—which demand a "just" rejection of an "unjust" award or treaty. The legal stalemate reached by the noncompliance with an arbitration award or international treaty might lead to further escalation and even war (as in the Peruvian-Ecuadorian rounds of 1981 and 1995). And yet the closing of a legal solution might be followed eventually by an opening (or return) to political, rather than legal, avenues of mediation, good offices, and direct negotiations. Peace can and might still be achieved, not by semilegal or juridical means but by political mechanisms. Third parties with vested interests and some modicum of political wisdom are then drawn into the search for a diplomatic solution, looking for political and pragmatic compromises. In several cases the outcomes have not been ideal, but the contending parties could live with them quite well, like the peace treaties between Peru and Chile (1929), Bolivia and Paraguay (1938), Argentina and Chile (1984), and Peru and Ecuador (1998).

CHAPTER FIVE

Norms of Security
Arms Control, Confidence-Building Measures, and Common Security

IN THIS CHAPTER I EXAMINE THE RELEVANT NORMS OF SECURITY IN LATIN America in the context of five different cases dating from 1881 to the present: the demilitarization of the Strait of Magellan in 1881 and the Mayo Pacts of 1902, including a naval arms control treaty, between Argentina and Chile; the evolution of the nuclear nonproliferation regional regime of Tlatelolco (the creation of a nuclear-weapons-free zone) since 1967; the security cooperation (essentially in the nuclear realm) between Argentina and Brazil in the 1980s and 1990s; and the peace initiatives of Contadora (1984–1986) and Esquipulas (1987) to resolve the Central American civil wars. In all the five cases I examine the impact of norms on the prospects for conflict management, resolution, maintenance of peace, and cooperation. The relevant norms of security include arms control and disarmament, demilitarization, neutralization, confidence-building measures (CBMs), collective security, and comprehensive and mutual security.

The context of regional security has been the major framework of reference for the management and resolution of territorial disputes among the Latin American states. Although Latin America has been part of the Inter-American system, security concerns have referred first and foremost to the immediate neighborhood rather than to the extraregional, or global, contexts. For instance, within the framework of the Cold War, Latin America, perhaps with the exception of Cuba, has been a region of low strategic preponderance (Hirst 1989, 37).

In a region with a long history of insecurity, mistrust, border disputes, unequal levels of economic development, and broad disparities in the distribution of power, the main security issues have focused on sudden attempts at military resolutions of long-standing border disputes and diplomatic stalemates, as well as the spread of revolution and counter-revolution across borders, at least until the 1980s. Despite the relative absence of interstate wars, especially in South America since 1883, border control, sovereignty, and national security are still relevant symbols that remain part of the rhetorical elements that have guided key political actors, such as the armed forces, in national debates and the formulation of foreign policies. Moreover, threats of the use of military force have consistently been used in the foreign policies of Latin American countries throughout the twentieth century, but without usually escalating into full-fledged wars. Arms races have also characterized the bilateral relations between Argentina and Chile from 1890 until the 1920s, and again in the 1970s, Argentina and Brazil from World War II until the early 1980s, Peru and Ecuador from the 1940s until 1998, and Colombia and Venezuela in the last few decades of the twentieth century (see Mares 1997, 195 and 202; Varas 1985, 84; Millán 1983, 89; Varas 1988).

Yet the Latin American states have been more concerned with their own domestic political problems than with confronting external security threats. Traditionally, the Latin American armed forces took upon themselves paramount domestic political roles since there was less need to defend their nations from outside aggressors (Varas 1985, 1–2; Glick 1965, 179). Moreover, during the periods of harsh military dictatorships in the 1960s and 1970s, the Latin American armies became a threat to many of their own citizens. Since the processes of democratization in the late 1970s and early 1980s, we have witnessed efforts of regional security cooperation toward a better understanding among the countries of the region, a gradual transcendence of perceptions of mutual threat, and a consensual recognition toward the strengthening of confidence-building measures (Velit Granda 1992, 89).[1]

As early as 1826, Simón Bolívar called an international conference (the Panama Congress) to establish machinery for collective security. Since then several attempts have been made to demilitarize borders, reduce and control armaments, abolish certain weapons, prohibit certain methods of war, prevent subversion, prohibit military use of certain geographic regions and space, create a nuclear-free zone, support nonproliferation of nuclear weapons, limit armaments in order to devote resources for economic and social development, and support general and widespread disarmament (Manwaring 1983, 163).

Several of the case studies in this chapter illustrate the adoption of security norms and the movement from a "system" (in which the parties are merely interconnected) to a "society," if not a "community" (sharing common norms and values). An early example were the Mayo Pacts of 1902 between Argentina and Chile, which celebrated one of the first naval agreements on arms control worldwide. In the 1960s the Latin Americans took the initiative for the creation of the first nuclear-weapons-free zone (NWFZ) worldwide in an inhabited area, institutionalized in the Treaty of Tlatelolco of 1967. This was also the first agreement that established a system of international control and permanent supervision, the OPANAL (Agency for the Prohibition of Nuclear Arms in Latin America and the Caribbean). The Treaty was completed with the final accession of Argentina, Chile, and Brazil in 1994, and Cuba in 1995. Since 1979 Argentina and Brazil have embarked on a cooperative joint venture regarding their nuclear plans, leading from nuclear cooperation to economic integration and eventual adherence to the general principle of nuclear nonproliferation. Finally, against the background of the failure of the OAS conflict-management system in Central America and elsewhere, in the early 1980s several Latin American countries initiated the Contadora process that eventually led to the formation of the broader Support and Rio Groups. The Contadora process contributed decisively to the avoidance of the broadening of war in Central America and established the basis for the peaceful resolution of the Central American civil wars by the Central American states themselves, through the Esquipulas process since 1987 (Hirst 1989, 44–45).

Arms Control and Disarmament

Arms control is a normative process that establishes agreements on weapons and their use—types, deployment, characteristics, safety conditions to prevent accidents, and so forth. By contrast, *disarmament* aims to reduce and even eliminate the number of weapons (Russett and Starr 1989, 383). Although these two normative processes are directly related and usually converge, sometimes they might contradict each other. Arms control might be regarded as a distraction from the (less realistic) pursuit of general disarmament. As a corollary of arms control, we might also refer to demilitarization and neutralization of specific territories, regarding the deployment and quantity of certain weapons.

Historically, there have not been many formal regional, multilateral treaties in Latin America dealing with arms control, demilitarization, neutralization, and disarmament. During their long quest for a system of regional security, Latin American countries rarely considered serious proposals for disarmament. After independence in the early nineteenth century, the new nations of Latin America felt obliged to maintain military establishments adequate to defend their newly acquired statehood (U.S. Congress 1957, 21). Later on, civil wars and domestic turbulence, as well as the continuation of border disputes, the rationale of "hypotheses of conflicts" (possible wars), and ephemeral periods of "armed peace" kept the armies busy and the production and import of weapons flourishing. The relatively minor participation of Latin American countries in arms limitation proposals starkly contrasts with the damaging effects of regional arms races, which were widespread in the 1960s and 1970s. Although overall Latin American military spending has been moderate with respect to other developing world regions, such as the Middle East and South Asia, in the Argentine-Brazilian case their military arms race reached the threshold of nuclear weaponry potential in the 1970s (see Varas 1985, 25; Morris and Slann 1983, 121–22).

Even in cases where states did commit themselves to arms control and disarmament, the efforts have been, in general, quite ineffective regarding the military capability of states. This is because verification was usually left to national discretion, without establishing serious machinery for enforcement, and to the perceived irrelevance of these agreements (Manwaring 1983, 163 and 169). In addition, and similarly to the recourse to legal mechanisms for peaceful settlement, we find a remarkable gap between disarmament and arms control agreements on the one hand, and the lack of actual disarmament measures and practices, concomitant to the production of weapons and continuation of arms races on the other (see Varas 1985, 95; Barahona Riera 1987, 289).

We can mention several factors that have acted to hinder or, alternatively, to promote arms control and disarmament in the region. Among the negative factors that have slowed arms control are the security concerns related to territorial questions and ideological threats; the impact of the United States (at least until the 1970s) in stressing collective security within the OAS; the role fulfilled by the national armed forces themselves in opposing arms control; and, finally, considerations of prestige that led countries such as Argentina and Brazil to pursue their nuclear plans. Alternatively, many of these factors could play a more positive role in promoting conventional and nonconventional (especially nuclear) measures of arms control following the democratization wave of the 1980s. For instance, security concerns have promoted the ban of nuclear weapons in the region since 1967; considerations of prestige and reputation have also promoted arms control; and, finally, the same Latin American armed forces acquiesced to the idea, and eventual reality, of non-proliferation of weapons of mass destruction in the region (see Stinson and Cochrane 1971, 13–16).

Confidence-Building Measures (CBMs)

The mechanisms of confidence-building measures (CBMs) are aimed at reducing interstate tensions, focusing on a step-by-step reduction of mistrust and fear in order to develop confidence, and improving the understanding between nations on security and political matters. CBMs deal not only with the material aspects of security, but also, and perhaps more importantly, with the psychological framework of the military and political decision-making cadres, in terms of perceived threats. Related to the norms of arms control and disarmament, they are in a sense broader than the former, since they include a myriad of dimensions and issues, such as nuclear issues, production and export of weapons, the role of military institutions in the state, bilateral territorial disputes, regional and bilateral antagonisms, economic and social development and the cooperation among the member-states, exchange of information and experiences, deepening of mechanisms of consult and cooperation, and the prevention of possible causes of conflict. CBMs received attention worldwide as a result of the relative success they had in Europe in promoting trust between the Eastern and Western blocs and bringing the Cold War to an end (see Millán 1983, 90; San Martín 1987, 125; Morris 1994, 101 and 107; Child 1996, 13; Velit Granda 1992, 90; Acuña Pimentel 1995, 88).

    In Latin America, where the risk level for an armed conflict has not been as high as in Europe during the Cold War, confidence-building measures have not been as urgently needed because the level of distrust and causes of war have been relatively minor. At the same time, the step-by-step reduction of mistrust and fear and the gradual development of confidence among states by agreed-upon rules of military and political behavior could play and indeed have played a positive and significant role at the subregional level, such as in the relations between Argentina and Brazil or Argentina and Chile. With the advent of democratization in the early 1980s, the scene of Latin American security has become more benign and less threatening to the interested parties.

Hence, military and political CBMs have fulfilled an important role in strengthening peace and stability and promoting the institutionalization of military regional and hemispheric cooperation (Morris 1994, 103).

Several regional multilateral agreements and declarations in Latin America (and in the Americas in general), include confidence-building measures and techniques such as the Inter-American Treaty of Reciprocal Assistance (1947), the Charter of the OAS (1948), the Treaty of Tlatelolco (1967), the Declaration of Punta del Este (1967), the Declaration of Ayacucho (1974), the Amazon Pact (1978), the Code of Conduct of Riobamba (1980), the Agreement of Cartagena (1979) establishing the Andean Group, the Contadora Acts (1984–1986), the Esquipulas II Agreement (1987), the Treaty of Asunción (1991) establishing Mercosur, and the Mendoza Declaration (1991) banning chemical and biological weapons (see San Martín 1987, 129; Millán 1983, 92–93; Caro 1994, 193–94).

In the Southern Cone, CBMs have been instrumental in improving the bilateral relations between Argentina and Brazil since 1979 and between Argentina and Chile since 1984. CBMs have strengthened their mutual trust, through military cooperation, integration of border areas, negotiations and agreements on border disputes, exchange of information, permanent communication, periodical meetings, and even joint military maneuvers in the 1990s (Caro 1994, 195). Although there is no single formal bilateral (or multilateral) agreement regarding collective security, the ABC countries have agreed on certain common normative themes, as related to CBMs. These include the defense of democracy, economic integration and regional cooperation, the respect for the territorial integrity and self-determination of peoples, the right to technological innovation, the maintenance of peace, the protection of natural resources, and the banning of nuclear, chemical, and biological weapons (see Diamint 1994, 151; Hirst and Rico 1992, 38–39).

Similarly, in 1989 the countries of the Andean Group—Bolivia, Colombia, Ecuador, Peru, and Venezuela—signed the Andean Cooperation, Security, and Peace Agreement in Galápagos, Ecuador. Known as the Galápagos Declaration, the agreement included the commitment to ratify all the obligations arising from the principles established in the Charter of the UN and the OAS, as well as the resolution to promote the fulfillment of the Treaty of Tlatelolco and the NPT. With the Declaration of Cartagena, signed on December 4, 1991, the Andean Group transformed these commitments into effective steps toward the banning of weapons of mass destruction (Aravena 1994a, 180–81).

In Central America the Final Contadora Act of June 1986 and the Esquipulas II Agreement of 1987 established mechanisms for verification regarding the limitation of weapons and gradual disarmament. The subsequent process of demobilizing the *Contras* in Nicaragua under the Esquipulas peace plan involved frequent applications of a variety of CBMs. By 1992 the norm of CBMs was firmly embedded in Central American thinking regarding disarmament and the lowering of tensions. This diplomatic activity to promote a peaceful settlement of the Central American civil wars has been noteworthy, since the progressive militarization of the various disputes in the subregion had previously hindered the possibility for political resolution. Thus, CBMs were a key element in the Central American peace process (see Child 1996, 17–19; Morris and Millán 1987, 126).

In sum, both Central America and South America prospered in furthering confidence-building measures in the last two decades, following the democratization wave of the 1980s and the end of the Cold War. The increasing economic interdependence and movement toward economic integration have stemmed from the relative success in reducing tensions, promoting trust, and achieving a stable degree of security cooperation that later on spilled over into functionalist and economic issue-areas (see Guedes da Costa 1998, 12–13; Downes 1998, 24).

Collective Security and New Forms of Security

The norm of collective security, by which all members of a given region or group agree to oppose together a threat to the security of any one of them, has been formally applied in Latin America in the broader context of the Inter-American system, since immediately after World War II. Previously, in the 1820s, Bolívar attempted to institutionalize it within the framework of Spanish American Congresses, without success. Most of the Latin American and Caribbean states belong to the hemispheric system of collective security, institutionalized through the Charter of the OAS (1948) and the American Treaty of Reciprocal Assistance (Rio Pact) of 1947. The Rio Pact placed on a permanent basis the prior temporary regional security arrangements adopted during World War II (see Atkins 1997, 270; Millán 1983, 89–90; Patiño Mayer 1996, 2).[2] Between 1948 and 1982 twenty-three cases were considered under the provisions of the Rio Treaty, especially in Central America. Yet Latin Americans tended to approach with reluctance and skepticism what they regarded as U.S. domination of Inter-American security processes. Hence, many territorial disputes were resolved outside of the Rio Treaty.

By the early 1990s the old concept of a continental collective security became somehow obsolete. Although the end of the Cold War facilitated the peaceful resolution of regional conflicts, such as that of Central America, realities and hypotheses of conflict in Latin America did not disappear completely from the political horizon. On the one hand, the majority of the states in the region supported the political and military status quo, as well as the new orthodoxy of democratization and economic neoliberalism. But on the other hand, there remained fluid and dangerous domestic situations, within the context of serious political and economic changes that could generate regional tensions in the 1990s and into the new millennium, especially in Central America and in the Northern Tier of South America (Colombia, Venezuela, Guyana, and Suriname). Hence, there is a need nowadays to transcend the concept of hemispheric collective security and build a stable framework of cooperative security among the Latin American countries, or even at the subregional level (Varas 1995, 27).

Even before the end of the Cold War, the combined impact of the return to democracy and the implications of the debt crisis in Latin America in the 1980s did create new opportunities to redefine regional security approaches. First, civilian and diplomatic participation in security matters became paramount. Second, the extrapolation of a democratic political culture across borders created a favorable climate for peace, stability, and mutual security, especially in the Southern Cone of South America. Third, security cooperation has become concomitant to efforts of economic integration (Hirst and Rico 1992, 35).

New and broader concepts of security, such as "common," "mutual," "comprehensive," "cooperative," and "human" have added a multidimensional character to traditional security relations. A broader concept of security might include, in addition to the obvious military dimension, diplomatic, political, economic, and cultural aspects. The diplomatic dimension is subordinate to the idea of national sovereignty within the context of a regional vision of security. The political aspect refers to the type of political regime; for instance, a threat to democracy is considered a threat to regional security. With the structural economic reforms of the 1980s and 1990s and the plans for economic integration at the regional and subregional levels, the economic dimension has been reincorporated into the general scheme of security. Finally, the cultural dimension refers to the normative dimension of sharing common values within the Latin American international society (see Mares 1995, 9–21).

In addition, with the reduction of the old "conventional" security threats, the countries of the hemisphere are facing new security risks and more diverse threats. By broadening the concept of security we include issues such as increasing unemployment and poverty, marginality of many sectors of the population, drug trafficking, terrorism, organized crime, violations of human rights, and threats to democratic development and economic well-being (Atkins 1997, 273–74; Druetta and Tibiletti 1993, 54).

The adoption of the more complex and ambiguous concept of "common," "cooperative," or "mutual" security both incorporates and transcends the traditional idea of collective security. One important difference between the two is that while collective security tries to harness the force of the community to deal with the potential transgressor, common security attempts to shy away from the use of force at all (Mares 1994, 271–72). A system of cooperative security is based on several elements, such as a defensive configuration of the national armed forces, a myriad of CBMs, the establishment of multilateral forums for the prevention of future conflicts, and a coordinated participation in an organized international response for the prevention or deterrence of aggression (Patiño Mayer 1996, 7). The norms of cooperative and common security overlap with the Latin American initiative of *concertación,* which provided the basis for the Contadora/Esquipulas process and the larger Latin American cooperation on political and security matters since 1986. Security concerns were one of the key matters that gave rise to the Permanent Mechanism for Joint Political Action (*Mecanismo de Consulta y Concertación Política Latinoamericana*), more commonly known as the Rio Group. Regarding security, two main goals have been promoted: "to seek solutions suitable to the problems and conflicts that affect the region," and "to promote initiatives and actions intended to improve, by means of dialogue and cooperation, Inter-American relations" (Rio Group Declaration, December 18, 1986, quoted in Aravena 1994a, 183). In this sense, the concept of common security approximates the ideas of a pluralistic security community and the creation of a Latin American "zone of peace."[3]

Norms of Security and Their Implementation in Latin America

The bulk of this chapter focuses on the impact of norms of security on five distinct, though related, case studies. As in the previous chapter, I analyze not only the overall impact of norms, but also the specific conditions under which norms might make an impact. Though the general impression about the impact of norms on these cases is a positive one, there is an interesting variance among cases that showed an initial failure (like Contadora in 1983, or even Tlatelolco in 1967) and only later evolved into an eventual success (like Esquipulas in 1987 or the ABC accession to the Tlatelolco Treaty in 1994). In the first two cases dealing with Argentine-Chilean relations, the results were successful, but either problematic (the implications of the neutralization of the Magellan Strait for the continuation of the Beagle Channel dispute) or ephemeral (the naval arms control convention within the Mayo Pacts of 1902 lasted for only five years). Perhaps the most interesting case is that of the evolution of the bilateral relations between Argentina and Brazil from 1979 to the present, from nuclear rivalry to nuclear cooperation. For each case I introduce the historical and legal background, followed by the normative arguments of both or some of the parties in terms of legal and moral contention. Unlike the bilateral cases of the previous chapter, two of the cases are multilateral (Tlatelolco since 1967; the Central American peace process), while the remaining three refer to the bilateral relations between Argentina and Chile (Magellan 1881 and Pactos de Mayo 1902), and between Argentina and Brazil.

The Demilitarization of the Magellan Strait (1881) and the Mayo Pacts of 1902

As we discussed in the context of the Beagle Channel dispute, Argentina and Chile have always had to confront the problems of one of the longest borders in the world and a history of territorial disputes and militarized crises. Their strained relations always stopped just short of war on several occasions: in 1878, 1898, 1901, and 1978. We should understand the Treaty of 1881 that stipulated the neutralization of the strategic Strait of Magellan, as well as the naval arms control agreement within the Mayo Pacts of 1902 as part of this long history of territorial rivalries. What was the impact of norms of security on the Treaty of 1881 and the Mayo Pacts of 1902? Considering the fact that the naval pact between Argentina and Chile in May of 1902 was the first of its type in the diplomatic history of the Western world, what were its implications in the short and long terms?

Historical and Legal Background

The competition between Argentina and Chile for their respective spheres of influence at the southern reaches of the American continent dates from the beginning of their national independence in the second decade of the nineteenth century. The question of which country should control the Magellan Strait, which connects the Pacific and Atlantic oceans at the bottom of Tierra del Fuego, affected their bilateral relations since the 1840s. By a preliminary treaty signed on August 30, 1855, both parties recognized the principle of *uti possidetis* as a guide to resolve their contending claims. Moreover, on December 6, 1878, they signed another agreement, providing for an elaborate series of steps, including arbitration, to determine the fate of the disputed territory.

In a further attempt to regulate and even resolve their disputes over Patagonia, Tierra del Fuego, and the Magellan Strait, the two countries signed a Boundary Treaty in 1881 that embodied a political compromise within an agreed-upon legal framework (Morris 1989, 53). According to the treaty, the Strait of Magellan was granted to Chile, though it would be demilitarized and neutralized; Chile gave up its claims over Patagonia; and the island of Tierra del Fuego was partitioned between the two countries. In exchange for the neutralization of the strait, Argentina agreed never to block the Atlantic (eastern) access (see Ruiz Moreno 1961, 229–35; Burr 1965, 154–55; Paz y Figueroa 1980, 40–41).

Yet the Boundary Treaty of 1881 did not resolve the Argentine-Chilean dispute over Tierra del Fuego and especially over the Beagle Channel Islands. Argentina and Chile argued about the interpretation and implementation of the agreement regarding the bioceanic principle. From the Argentine standpoint, the bioceanic principle was implicit in the 1881 settlement, including the clause that barred any Chilean presence in the Atlantic Ocean. In contrast, Chile rejected the principle and maintained that the 1881 compromise allocated the entire Strait of Magellan to Chile, thereby giving it an Atlantic outlet at its eastern mouth (Morris 1989, 78). Paradoxically, while the 1881 agreement resolved the question of ownership over the Strait of Magellan, it exacerbated the contending claims of the parties over the Beagle Channel.

On May 1, 1893, the two countries signed another protocol "of clarification" regarding the implementation of the 1881 Treaty. Still, the lack of resolution of other territorial disputes, regarding their Andean boundary in Patagonia and the failed implementation of the border demarcation through arbitration, led to a serious deterioration in the relations between Argentina and Chile and the possibility of war in 1898. In 1899 the military crisis was defused through a friendly meeting between Presidents Roca of Argentina and Errazuriz of Chile at the Magellan Strait ("the embrace of the straits"), and by the initiation of the arbitration process. Yet relations remained strained because of the continuing arms race and the rhetoric of an "armed peace," which was costly to both countries in political and economic terms.

This is the general background for the *Pactos de Mayo* (May Pacts) of May 28, 1902. This set of treaties included a preliminary act, a general treaty of arbitration, a naval limitation (arms control) treaty, and a call to the British arbiter to implement the award over the Andean boundary. In the Preliminary Act both parties declared that they did not sustain territorial expansionist claims and mutually recognized their sovereignty and territorial integrity, emphasizing as well the corollary of nonintervention. This principle had important geopolitical implications because it limited both Argentine intervention in Pacific affairs and eventual Chilean conquests (see Burr 1965, 252; Ruiz Moreno 1961, 244; Scenna 1981, 125). Furthermore, the general treaty of arbitration bounded Chile and Argentina "to submit to arbitration all controversies of whatever nature which for any reason might arise between them, so long as they do not affect the precepts of either nation's constitution" (quoted in Burr 1965, 253). This was the legal basis for the 1971 *compromis* regarding the arbitration of the Beagle Channel dispute. Finally, the agreement on naval arms control committed the two countries not to take possession of warships under construction or to make further purchases, and to reduce their fleets to a "reasonable parity" under an agreement to be reached within one year (Burr 1965, 253).

Following the May Pacts, on January 9, 1903, the two countries signed a naval disarmament protocol, by which they agreed to sell the ships that each had under construction in Great Britain and Italy. Moreover, Chile agreed to disarm its cruiser *Capitán Prat* and Argentina its *Garibaldi* and the *Pueyrredón* (see Burr 1965, 256; Moraga 1969, 133).

Though the "convention respecting the limitation of naval armaments" of May 28, 1902, could be considered as a success, it was an ephemeral one. Its provisions were limited to an initial five-year period and were not renewed. Moreover, the naval restrictions applied only to Argentina and Chile, so that a Brazilian naval arms buildup could lead to a potential Argentine response. At the same time, Argentina and Chile can boast of having signed one of the first naval arms control agreements in the diplomatic history of the Western world (Morris 1989, 68). The Mayo Pacts in general were regarded as "a great advancement of international law, and as a remarkable example of fraternity between two neighboring countries" (Silva 1946, 231; my translation).

Evidence and Impact of the Normative Framework

The political compromise of 1881 and the naval arms control agreement of 1902 reflected several normative positions sustained by Chile and Argentina in their territorial disputes in the late nineteenth and early twentieth centuries, similarly to those that underpinned the Beagle Channel dispute. Thus, both countries based their respective claims on the principle of *uti possidetis* and historical possession. Argentina argued that it had legal control of the Atlantic seaboard from the Rio de la Plata to the farthest point south of Cape Horn, thus confining Chile to the Pacific. Chile rejected the bioceanic principle and explained the 1881 Treaty as a political, not a legal, compromise. Eventually, in 1977 the arbitration award recognized Chile's rejection of the Argentine arguments as a basis for interpreting the 1881 Treaty (Morris 1989, 55–56).

The normative rationale for the 1881 Treaty and the 1902 Mayo Pacts included the argument, raised by both parties, that Argentina and Chile had made enormous sacrifices because they wanted to avoid war, so that peace was maintained by the good will of both governments (Piñero 1924, 89). In other words, the disposition to neutralize and demilitarize the Magellan Strait, as well as the mutual commitment to implement a significant naval arms control and disarmament pact, were evidence of the peaceful intentions of both parties and their efforts to avoid war. The Argentine negotiators particularly emphasized this pacific (if not pacifist) vocation. For instance, Argentine Foreign Minister Joaquín V. González declared that the Mayo Pacts were "pacts of peace, ending the period of 'armed peace'" (quoted in Silva 1946, 239). In addition, Argentina emphasized the principle of nonintervention as one of the normative bases for the 1902 Treaties, as it would be further elaborated the same year in the Drago Doctrine. The underlying argument was that Argentina did not have any significant political or economic interests in the Pacific, so that Chile did not represent a serious threat to Argentina (see Errazuriz Guilisasti 1968, 79; Paradiso 1996, 22).

Conditions for the Impact of Norms

Salience of domestic actors who mobilize norms, role of leaders.   In both countries there were interest groups and elites who were interested in keeping "order and progress," and those who wanted to benefit from continuing the arms race between the two countries. There were liberals that advocated trade and economic development, and there were hard-nose nationalists that focused the foreign policy of their countries on territorial expansion (Paradiso 1996, 20). In this sense, the 1881 and 1902 agreements represented a triumph of the liberal coalitions, as epitomized by the arguments of the Argentine politician Carlos Pellegrini, who reiterated the "European-Atlantic" option of the Argentine Republic in justifying the Mayo Pacts. In his words, "Our political and economic interests are not in the Pacific. All our future, all our moral and material interests, all our enlargement and progress are related to the peoples of the Atlantic" (quoted in Paradiso 1996, 16; my translation). This position also reflected the paramount commercial interests that Argentina had in Europe and its close relations with the United Kingdom.

Type of political regimes and peaceful conditions within the countries.   Both countries experienced at that time a process of economic growth and development and some form of democratic governance that contributed to their eventual reconciliation. This was particularly true for Argentina, which witnessed a phenomenal economic expansion. Following a liberal logic, the disputes between Argentina and Chile could be reduced to a territorial question that could be honorably settled by the 1902 Treaties. Hence, in Pellegrini's view Argentina "should apply all its energies and resources, today absorbed by the armed obsession, to its progress and enlargement in moral and material terms." Thus, Argentina's path to glory could be realized through economic rather than military means (see Burr 1965, 167; Pellegrini, quoted in Ferrari 1969, 100; my translation).

Presence of a hegemonic power.   Both in 1881 and 1902 the United Kingdom exercised a strong pressure on Argentina and Chile to resolve their territorial disputes by peaceful means. In this period the two countries were still under the aegis of the *Pax Britannica,* so it is not a coincidence that Great Britain was nominated the permanent arbitrator between them (Ferrari 1969, 60).

Fitness between the regional normative framework and the given case(s); degree of institutionalization of the international society.   As with the case of Misiones in 1895, in 1881 and especially in 1902 Argentina (and to some extent Chile as well) could profess its explicit adherence to the norms of peace and security that regulated the Latin American international society. For instance, the Argentine Foreign Minister Luis María Drago referred in May of 1903 to the May 1902 agreements as the "definitive triumph of peace and equity" (quoted in Silva 1946, 247; my translation). Moreover, Pellegrini invoked the regional principle of nonintervention that regulated Latin American relations to justify the 1902 agreements: "Any Argentine engagement in the Pacific affairs would be a violation of that principle" (Pellegrini, quoted in Ferrari 1969, 99; my translation).

Alternative Explanations

Beyond the normative underpinnings of the 1881 and 1902 agreements, one can understand their logic in terms of common and diverging interests. Both Chile and Argentina wanted to push their respective competing claims in their southern border, but neither of them wanted a war, in 1878, 1898, or 1902. The 1881 treaty that neutralized the Strait of Magellan was a political compromise, a trade-off between territories and spheres of influence held in dispute.

Argentina gave up its rights to the Strait of Magellan and a position in the Pacific, while Chile renounced its ambitions over Patagonia and its aspirations for a port in the Atlantic.

Similarly, although the Mayo Pacts of 1902 are usually interpreted as a clear diplomatic triumph for Chile, which got a carte blanche in the Pacific (Burr 1965, 254), they benefited the Argentines as well. The treaties guaranteed the peace and prosperity of both countries and formalized the status quo in the Southern Cone of South America that resulted from the Chilean victory in the Pacific War against Bolivia and Peru. Argentina could focus on its vertiginous economic progress, under the slogan of the second Roca Administration that invoked "peace and administration" instead of "armed peace."

There was a common economic rationale in reaching the agreements, since the "armed peace" involved a serious economic burden for both countries. Their common goal was to avoid an unexpected and unnecessary war, and to reduce the economic costs of the naval arms race. The exorbitant sums spent on that race (200 million pesos by Argentina and 110 million pesos by Chile in 1898) could then be saved for more productive goals (see Palacio 1965, 302–3; Barros van Buren 1970, 577; Errazuriz Guilisasti 1968, 55 and 64). In sum, Argentina and Chile chose to reconcile each other not only out of normative concerns, but as a result of a rational cost-benefit analysis as well.

The Nuclear Nonproliferation Regional Regime of Tlatelolco (since 1967)

The most important Latin American contribution to the implementation of norms of disarmament and nonproliferation has been the establishment of the Latin American Nuclear-Weapons-Free Zone (NWFZ) through the Treaty of Tlatelolco (Treaty for the Prohibition of Nuclear Weapons in Latin America), signed in 1967. The Treaty of Tlatelolco institutionalized a regional regime of nuclear nonproliferation, which has been completed with the final accession of Argentina, Brazil, and Chile in 1994, and Cuba in 1995.

Historical and Legal Background

The initiative to establish a nuclear nonproliferation regime in Latin America was launched in the late 1950s. In 1958 the Costa Rican ambassador to the OAS suggested the establishment of a special disarmament commission within the OAS to elaborate a disarmament project for the Latin American nations, including the issue of nuclear weapons. In 1959 Chilean President Jorge Alessandri raised a similar proposal on nuclear nonproliferation. In 1961 Brazil formally proposed to the United Nations that Latin America should establish a nuclear-free zone in order to avoid the introduction of nuclear weapons in a region where they were nonexistent. These initiatives were reinvigorated by the traumatic experience of the Cuban missile crisis of 1962, which convinced several Latin American states that they should promote the denuclearization of their region to shy away from a potential nuclear hecatomb. The Latin American NWFZ was conceived, in fact, as an effort to prevent further incursions by the nuclear superpowers. Mexico joined Brazil, Bolivia, and Chile, and its deputy foreign minister, Ambassador Alfonso García Robles, took the initiative in translating the emerging normative consensus into a legal reality (see Atkins 1997, 314; Serrano 1992, 11; Husbands 1979, 209–10; Redick 1994, 3; Docampo 1993, 23–24; Mirek 1986, 17).

The campaign for a nuclear-free zone in Latin America began in earnest with the declaration of the presidents of Mexico, Chile, Brazil, Bolivia, and Ecuador in 1963. Submitted to the United Nations in order to get its formal endorsement, eleven Latin American nations began a project that was supposed to be Latin American in its goals and implementation (Husbands 1979, 212). Negotiations took place in the years 1964–1967, with the aim of prohibiting nuclear weapons in Latin America, so that the states of the region would undertake "not to manufacture, store or experiment on nuclear arms and devices to launch them" (quoted in Insulza 1987, 52). The negotiation process disclosed the existence of contentious issues that ultimately shaped the final text of the agreement, including Cuban participation, the geographical definition of the NWFZ, decolonization, the right to peaceful nuclear explosions (PNEs), the transit of nuclear weapons in the region, and the nuclear powers' guarantees (Serrano 1992, 27).

The Treaty for the Prohibition of Nuclear Weapons in Latin America was signed on February 14, 1967, in Tlatelolco, Mexico. The United Nations endorsed the Treaty on December 5, 1967; it entered into force on April 22, 1968. In its first article, the Latin American parties to the agreement undertook "to use exclusively for peaceful purposes the nuclear material and facilities which are under their jurisdiction." They further agreed to prohibit "the testing, use, manufacture, production, or acquisition" of any nuclear weapons, as well as their "receipt, storage, installation, deployment, and any form of possession of any nuclear weapons, directly or indirectly." According to the treaty, the regional regime defines what a nuclear weapon is (Article 5), establishes the area of application (Article 4), regulates and enables the rights of the Latin American states to peaceful nuclear explosions (Article 8), creates a special regional organization to verify the compliance (Articles 7 through 11), and organizes a system of control (Article 13 through 18). Article 28 is particularly important since it states that the Treaty will become valid once all the Latin American countries and those signatories of the additional protocols ratify it. Yet the Treaty leaves open the possibility of waiving it, as many Latin American countries have done, though neither Brazil nor Chile waived this clause until 1994. There is a double safeguards system (modified in 1992), by the IAEA (International Atomic Energy Agency) and the Latin American organization OPANAL. The Treaty was supplemented by two protocols related to extra-regional states, such as colonial powers (the Netherlands, France, the United Kingdom, and the United States) and the five nuclear powers—the United States, the former Soviet Union, the United Kingdom, China, and France. As compared to other disarmament treaties, such as the 1959 Antarctic Treaty or the 1971 Sea-Bed Treaty, the Tlatelolco Treaty is narrower in scope, since it does not refer to other weapons of mass destruction or to the prohibition of nuclear explosions for peaceful purposes (the quotations of Article 1 are from Atkins 1997, 315; see also Carasales 1987, 173; Docampo 1993, 24; Subedi 1996, 164–65).

Eight years after the Treaty had been opened for signature it came into force for seventeen out of the twenty-two parties for whom it was initially open to signature. This meant that those seventeen countries not only signed and ratified it, but also waived the conditions of Article 28. As for the remaining five countries, Cuba did not sign the agreement until 1995; neither Brazil nor Chile waived the requirements of Article 28 until 1994; and Argentina failed to ratify the agreement until 1994 (see Serrano 1992, 46; Redick 1981, 120).

In the first two decades after entering in force Argentina, Brazil, and Chile were reluctant to completely join the regional regime. Although Argentina had signed both the NPT and Tlatelolco, it did not ratify them until 1992. Both Brazil and Chile had ratified Tlatelolco but without giving up their reservations under Article 28. Only after the Treaty was amended following a common Argentine-Brazilian initiative to strengthen the role of the IAEA at the expense of OPANAL were the two countries ready to change their attitudes toward the regime. Thus, on January 18, 1994, Argentina and Chile deposited instruments of ratification to the treaty (including the waiving clause) followed by Brazil in May of the same year. By the year 2000 all the thirty-three Latin American and Caribbean states in the region had signed the Treaty; Cuba signed in 1995 and ratified in 2002.

Evidence and Impact of the Normative Framework

At the formal level, the text of the Treaty of Tlatelolco refers to the norms of peace and security. The parties express their desire for "ending the armaments race, especially in the field of nuclear weapons" and "strengthening a world at peace, based on the sovereign equality of states, mutual respect, and good neighborliness." Moreover, the preamble emphasizes the link between NWFZs and "the maintenance of peace and security in the respective regions." Since its inception, the Treaty has been regarded as a keystone in the struggle against the proliferation of nuclear arms. It was the first treaty to create an NWFZ in inhabited areas where there are states; it was signed and ratified almost immediately by the majority of the parties invited to do so; and its provisions have been fairly adequate and effective (Insulza 1987, 51; see also Blix 1997, 1–2). Moreover, through its mechanisms for control and verification, the Treaty represents a good example, though not an ideal one, of CBMs. The idea behind an NWFZ epitomizes the concepts of collective security and, even more than that, of cooperative, common, and mutual security. Finally, in terms of Latin American international society, the Tlatelolco regime, like the Contadora process, embodies a common Latin American foreign policy based on the norms of sovereignty and nonintervention.

Until the complete inception of Argentina, Brazil, and Chile in the regional nonproliferation regime, it could be argued that the Treaty of Tlatelolco was far from being effective. The almost twenty years during which the ABC countries stood at the margins of the general trend of nuclear nonproliferation in Latin America has to be explained in both normative and political terms. Brazil and Argentina were, after all, former "threshold countries" that had developed substantial nuclear plans with potential military uses. Argentina especially contested the global policy of nonproliferation, arguing that it discriminated against the developing countries. Since 1945 Argentina had called for nuclear disarmament, limitations in the global arms race, and a focus on development through the channeling away of military resources (Russell 1989, 53). The Argentine normative position argued that the nonproliferation programs were intended to preserve the technological dominance of the nuclear powers, allowing vertical proliferation and limiting horizontal proliferation (Guglialmelli 1978, 29). By invoking the norms of sovereignty, nonintervention, and especially "developmentalism" (*desarrollismo*), Argentina maintained its ambiguous stance toward the Tlatelolco regime until the early 1990s. On the one hand, it formally supported the regime since it was a Latin American instrument designed to regulate the relations among Latin American states. On the other hand, Argentina did not want to submit its nuclear plans to the exclusive scrutiny of OPANAL, the Latin American agency for control and verification (Insulza 1987, 55). Its normative change in the 1990s could be attributed, first of all, to the return to democracy in the 1980s and to the positive evolution of its bilateral relations with Brazil since 1979. Moreover, by the early 1990s there was an emergent regional consensus that included a full commitment by the ABC countries to the Tlatelolco Treaty, full-scale IAEA safeguards, and an end to all nuclear testing, including that of peaceful nuclear explosions (PNEs) (Redick 1994, 9). In sum, the concept of a common or cooperative security that incorporates and transcends the old ideas of collective security and arms control became an important factor in the perception of a balance favoring the advantages rather than the costs for a nonnuclear status (Serrano 1992, 78).

Conditions for the Impact of Norms

The impact of the normative framework on the Tlatelolco regime has to be examined in two different time periods, the initial institutionalization of the regime (the Treaty of 1967), and the final incorporation of the ABC countries (in 1994).

Salience of actors who mobilize norms.   Unlike all the other cases we have discussed so far, this is a multilateral one. Hence, instead of referring to domestic actors in bilateral situations, we should refer to the role of specific countries in a regional context. In this sense, Brazil and Mexico were particularly responsible for taking the initiative in establishing the regime from 1964 to 1967, and Argentina and Brazil in completing it from 1992 to 1994.

Types of political regimes.   There seems to be an interesting link between the degree of democratization in the region and the support for the NWFZ. In the mid–1960s many Latin American countries were still governed by democratic regimes; those that had already experienced military coups, like Argentina in 1966 or Brazil in 1964, were reluctant to fully join the Tlatelolco regime. Conversely, once Argentina, Brazil, and Chile returned to democracy they were ready to transcend their qualifications and incorporate themselves into the regional regime.

Fitness between the regional normative framework and the given case; degree of institutionalization of the international society.   The existence of a Latin American international society prior to the initiatives to establish an NWFZ in the region facilitated its inception and institutionalization. The norms of peace and security shared by most, if not all, of the Latin American states were undoubtedly a significant contributing factor to the establishment of a regional nuclear nonproliferation regime. The Latin American tradition of multilateral diplomacy, which gave priority to juridical solutions, in addition to the relative absence of serious interregional conflicts, facilitated the 1964–1967 negotiations (see Redick 1981, 111; Wrobel 1993, 27; Serrano 1992, 42). The amendment process was a joint initiative that responded to twenty-five years of efforts by several member-states and the successive secretaries of OPANAL, aimed at completing the NWFZ. After all, the Treaty of Tlatelolco was and remained a Latin American initiative, which preceded the global approach to the NPT and made the region into a vanguard of a nuclear-weapons-free world community (Blix 1997, 2).

Alternative Explanations

In terms of rational choice and *Realpolitik,* why did Tlatelolco take place? Why did Argentina, Brazil, and Chile change their positions and decide to join the regime?

Several factors favored the creation of a NWFZ in Latin America. First, there was the traumatic shock of the Cuban missile crisis and the profound decision of many Latin American countries to avoid its potential repetition. Second, a nuclear arms race was perceived as a potential threat to the regional security and to the economic goals of the Latin American states as developing countries. Third, a successful creation of a NWFZ could enhance the Latin American reputation. Fourth, the regime was perceived as enabling the Latin American states to somehow set limits to the U.S. nuclear hegemony, by reducing the nuclear danger in the region. Conversely, the ABC countries at that time were reluctant to completely endorse the nonproliferation regime since they still believed that there was a perceived link between acquiring nuclear capabilities and enhancing one's international prestige. Moreover, by limiting nuclear proliferation, the regime indirectly buttressed the virtual nuclear monopoly of the United States in the Western Hemisphere, a fact that was resented by countries like Argentina and Cuba. This also explains the benevolent attitude, if not the active support, of the United States for the formation of the Tlatelolco regime (see Husbands 1979, 212–13; Serrano 1992, 5; Mirek 1986, 25).

As for the more recent developments in the 1990s, several factors explain the change in attitudes of Argentina, Brazil, and Chile with respect to the completion of the regime. First, the nuclear rapprochement between Argentina and Brazil preceded the reform of the Treaty in 1992, and actually led to its development. Once Argentina and Brazil shaped a bilateral regime of nuclear control that satisfied them, they could incorporate themselves into Tlatelolco. The Treaty did not bring them further guarantees and safeguards, but at least it led to political benefits, like being finally "in sync" with the rest of the Latin American international society in terms of prestige and peaceful vocations. In other words, Argentina, and to a lesser extent Brazil and Chile, reached the conclusion in the early 1990s that they could not stay outside of the global nuclear regime of NPT, even if it continued to be discriminatory. Since Tlatelolco was by far a better arrangement than the NPT, it became evident that not joining the regional regime was politically counterproductive, so the incorporation became the most feasible alternative for all of them (see Carasales 1992, 500; Serrano 1992, 67). The decision to renounce the nuclear option was a rational one, based on a cost-benefit analysis and the expectation of political benefits.

The Evolution of the Security Cooperation between Argentina and Brazil

Since 1979 the bilateral relations between Argentina and Brazil moved from conflict to cooperation, leading to a significant rapprochement in the security realm, with special emphasis on nonproliferation and denuclearization, and eventually spilling over into economic integration. Despite the clear potential the two countries had for reaching the nuclear threshold, their nuclear competition evolved into a model of nuclear cooperation.

Historical and Legal Background

Among the South American international disputes of the twentieth century, the Argentine-Brazilian rivalry was one of the longest and the most influenced by geopolitical doctrines (Child 1985, 99–100). It had important reverberations in the domestic and international politics of the region as a whole and a direct impact on the three buffer states of the Southern Cone of Latin America—Uruguay, Paraguay, and Bolivia—in particular. Argentina and Brazil fought a war over Uruguay that ended in 1828, and Brazil was involved in the Argentine Civil War (*la Guerra Grande*) until 1859. Moreover, the possibility of armed conflict ("hypotheses of conflict") remained a tangible element in the military planning of both nations well into the early 1980s.

From the second half of the nineteenth century to the late 1970s, the relationship between the region's two major powers was a complex mixture of conflict and cooperation, as a function of disagreements about their territorial borders (until 1895) and their competing hegemonic ambitions in South America. In the bloody Chaco War of 1932–1935 Argentina and Brazil supported opposing sides. From the early 1920s and especially after World War II, the two countries were often immersed in an arms race that included the development of nuclear technology. Moreover, they adopted diametrically opposed positions regarding the role of the United States in the region and have engaged in a fierce competition over resources such as Paraguayan hydroelectric energy and Bolivian oil and gas. The Argentines regarded Brazil as an expansionary military, economic, and demographic power that threatened areas to its south, west, and southwest. Conversely, the Brazilians regarded their smaller neighbor with suspicion and uneasiness, fearing the kind of volatility and aggressiveness that Argentina demonstrated in its invasion of the Falkland Islands in April 1982 (see Guglialmelli 1979; Selcher 1985, 101–18). At the same time, the Argentine-Brazilian rivalry never escalated into militarized crises such as those between Argentina and Chile in 1878, 1898, and 1978; moreover, their enduring rivalry, unlike that between Peru and Ecuador, did not include opposing claims to a disputed territory after 1895. Thus, the common diplomatic history of Argentina and Brazil has been one of conflict and harmony, war and peace, rivalry and cooperation, and integration. The major periods of rivalry and conflict included 1825–1828 (their only war), 1844, 1870–1876, 1905–1914, and 1960–1980. Conversely, the periods of cooperation were 1864–1870 (the war against Paraguay), 1899–1914 (the ABC concert), and especially since 1979 (Herrera Vegas 1995, 172).

In the late 1970s Brazil initiated a policy of "Latin-Americanization" toward its Spanish-speaking neighbors, including the creation of the Amazon Pact (1978) for joint development of the Amazon Basin, to increase its own economic growth and development. Domestically, the ascendancy of moderate military officers in Brazil and the launching of liberalization contributed to a general climate of openness toward its neighbors. From the Argentine standpoint, the military junta became quite aware of the inferiority of its power compared with Brazil's in economic and conventional military terms— excluding, perhaps, the specific area of nuclear development, in which Brazil was finally catching up to Argentina's lead, making an escalating nuclear arms race a tangible possibility. Moreover, the mounting tensions with Great Britain over the South Atlantic Falkland Islands issue and the deteriorating relations with Chile following the 1977 arbitration award that gave it the Beagle Channel Islands prompted the Argentines to seek an accord with Brazil, against the prospects of an imminent war with Chile and perhaps with the United Kingdom as well (see Hurrell 1998, 235–38; Resende-Santos 1998, 7–22; Segre 1990). These converging motivations led the two countries to resolve in October 1979 a thirteen-year dispute over the hydropower generation of energy along the Paraná River in the tripartite border among Argentina, Paraguay, and Brazil, related to the building of the Itaipú dam. This led to a gradual rapprochement that included economic and military cooperation, especially in the nuclear area.

In 1980 Argentina and Brazil further expanded and improved their relations through presidential visits and a package of ten agreements, including joint arms production and cooperation for the development and implementation of the peaceful use of nuclear energy, covering joint research and the transfer of some nuclear materials. The two nations signed a small but symbolically relevant agreement for nuclear fuel cycle cooperation, which also called for coordination of the nuclear policy of both countries vis-à-vis international forums (see Redick et al. 1995, 111; Martínez-Vidal and Ornstein 1990, 341).

With the return of democracy to Argentina (1983) and Brazil (1985), nuclear cooperation between the two countries further expanded, as the core of a larger, ambitious program of security and economic integration. On November 30, 1985, Presidents Alfonsín of Argentina and Sarney of Brazil met at Foz do Iguaçú to inaugurate a program that took a concrete form on July 31, 1986, with the signing of the Argentine-Brazilian Integration Act and the Integration and Cooperation Program (ABEIP), together with twelve protocols for cooperation in various areas, including nuclear energy. Its significance was primarily political, not economic: setting aside decades of rivalries and competition in order to create the basis for a long-term cooperation. In 1985–1990, nuclear cooperation peaked, as part of a larger effort to bring about economic integration in the region. The new civilian governments in both countries initiated nuclear confidence-building measures that altered well-entrenched perceptions of rivalry. As a result, a full-fledged bilateral regime of cooperation emerged in the nuclear area, aimed at promoting technological development and strengthening mutual trust and transparency, while assuring the international community that neither country intended to develop or acquire nuclear weapons. Both governments sought through these initiatives to improve bilateral relations, and thereby to promote democratic consolidation and economic integration.

Based on the record of nuclear cooperation that had become formalized since 1980, the presidents of Brazil and Argentina, Fernando Collor de Mello and Carlos Menem, adopted the historical Argentine-Brazilian Declaration on Common Nuclear Policy at Foz do Iguaçú on November 28, 1990, which established a binational cooperative organization of nuclear cooperation (the Brazilian-Argentine Agency for the Accounting and Control of Nuclear Materials, or ABCC). The declaration formalized and institutionalized the evolving nuclear regime between the two countries, marking a significant departure from their former approach to nuclear nonproliferation. Beside reconfirming the determination to use nuclear energy exclusively for peaceful purposes, the declaration approved a common accounting and control system to apply to all nuclear activities of both countries and to verify that materials in all nuclear activities of both parties were used exclusively for peaceful purposes. The two presidents also agreed to a verifiable ban on the production of nuclear weapons and peaceful nuclear explosives. Moreover, the declaration called for negotiations with the IAEA for the conclusion of a safeguards agreement ultimately signed at Guadalajara, Mexico, on July 18, 1991. As mentioned before, the conclusion of this bilateral nonproliferation regime opened the way for Argentina and Brazil to finally join the regional regime of Tlatelolco in 1994 and the global regime of the NPT. Argentina and Brazil thus demonstrated that highly nationalistic nuclear programs could be held in check with the implementation of transparency measures and the use of bilateral, regional, and international inspections (see Stanley 1992, 192–95; Redick 1995; Pande 1993, 431–33; Goldemberg and Feiveson 1994, 10–14).

This bilateral nuclear nonproliferation regime, coupled with increased economic integration, has brought about a stable peace between the two countries. Paradoxically, it can be argued that the security and military cooperation were considered as one of the guarantees for the whole process of integration. Thus, the political impact of the successful nuclear rapprochement became a positive counterpoint to the difficulties encountered at the beginning of the process of economic integration (see Cavagnari Filho 1990, 317; Bocco 1989, 26–27). This process was further enlarged and formalized with the establishment of Mercosur, potentially a common market of Argentina, Brazil, Paraguay, and Uruguay, on March 26, 1991.

In the mid- and late 1990s a large number of military exchanges and mutual visits between the two armies, as well as strategic symposia, became commonplace. On April 9, 1996, the two countries signed a presidential document of cooperation in areas of security and defense, including space exploration, nuclear activities, physical and energy integration, and the establishment of a joint working group on strategic issues. This agreement made it possible for the two countries to hold common joint army maneuvers for the first time since 1865. As Thomas A. O'Keefe, president of Mercosur Consulting Group, cogently summarized, "The whole hypothesis of war between Argentina and Brazil has been junked. . . . I don't think that anyone in the Argentine military or in the Brazilian military still sees the other as a potential threat" (quoted in Brooke 1994).

Evidence and Impact of the Normative Framework

The dramatic shift that took place in the bilateral relations between Argentina and Brazil in the 1980s and 1990s materialized in their remarkable security cooperation, especially on nuclear issues. In the security field their improved relations involved the adoption and implementation of the norms of peace and security, such as arms control and disarmament, CBMs and transparency, democratization, and a constructive concept of mutual or cooperative security.

Despite their long rivalry and competition, there has always been a normative compatibility between the two countries, which included a number of common norms and values, such as a "Christian" concept of life; the formal recognition and protection of human rights and individual freedom; the formal adoption of democracy; mutual respect and good neighborhood, with the promotion of nonintervention; the prevention and repression of threats and acts of aggression; and the peaceful settlement of international disputes (Olmos 1986, 122). In the specific context of nuclear agreement, we can add as well the adoption of common paradigms of technological autonomy and developmentalism as common norms and values that moved the two countries toward nuclear cooperation and economic integration.

Argentina and Brazil hold similar attitudes toward the NPT and the Tlatelolco regimes, out of a common normative concern. For decades they had defied the international nuclear nonproliferation regime, refusing to sign the NPT or to grant complete legal standing to the Treaty of Tlatelolco, so they were thought to be moving toward the threshold of nuclear proliferation (Barletta 1997, 2). Their reluctance to fully support nonproliferation until the early 1990s stemmed from their adherence to the norms of sovereignty and juridical equality of states, nonintervention, nationalism, and developmentalism. In both countries the concept of security has been always associated with development, so that their nuclear programs were considered to be a key to achieving technological autonomy, especially during the rule of military dictatorships. Argentina traditionally argued that the constraints put on its nuclear plans were due not so much to fear of the proliferation of nuclear weapons as to the desire to maintain the technological domination and discrimination between the developed and the developing countries. In other words, the NPT gave preferential treatment to the nuclear powers, by calling for the "disarmament of the disarmed" (Carasales 1996). At the same time, Argentina's position on nonproliferation was considered with suspicion as ambiguous, if not hostile (see Carasales 1996, 326; Bocco 1989, 9 and 21; Stanley 1992, 204).

Paradoxically, because of their common normative stance against the global regime of nonproliferation, the two countries developed in the 1980s a particular binational regime of nonproliferation, based on bilateral mechanisms of arms control, disarmament, and CBMs. It was the success of their nuclear relations that facilitated in the early 1990s their adherence to the regional and global regimes of nonproliferation. Moreover, the restoration of democracy was a key development in bringing about their change of attitude regarding the norm of nonproliferation. The nuclear weapons programs left behind by previous military regimes were considered a costly distraction, both in economic and political terms. The new democratic regimes hoped that increased transparency, clear mechanisms of CBMs, and an end to nuclear competition would help them promote peace, stability, and economic development, both within their countries and throughout the region (see Goldemberg and Feiveson 1994, 10–12; Mestre de Sánchez and Mendoza 1988, 31 and 48; Tanzer 1992, 14). With the enlargement of the CBMs in both the nuclear and the conventional realms—including reciprocal visits of politicians and military cadres, measures of transparency and verification, bilateral security accords, and military cooperation—the traditional "hypotheses of conflict" have gradually disappeared (see Diamint 1998). In this way Argentina and Brazil gradually adopted the norm of mutual or cooperative security, hoping to reap potential benefits from reducing tensions generated by their respective nuclear programs (see Redick et al. 1995, 117; De la Balze 1995, 106; Brigagão and Valle 1996, 89).

Conditions for the Impact of Norms

Salience of domestic actors who mobilize the norms.   The bilateral nuclear regime that regulated the relations between Brazil and Argentina had roots in scientific and diplomatic practices dating back to the 1950s. Those practices included scientific and technical research, commerce and industrial development, and the development of an incipient epistemic community of scientists from both countries that argued for bilateral cooperation.

In addition to the role played by these epistemic communities, the internal political changes of 1989–1990 in Argentina and Brazil provided the background for a dramatic improvement in bilateral relations following the elections of Presidents Menem and Collor (Redick et al. 1995, 113–14). President Carlos Menem in particular adopted a pragmatic foreign policy, aligning Argentina closely with the United States and fully incorporating it back into the international community as a respectable member. Thus, presidential leadership and strong foreign ministry support were key to overcoming the resistance of some sectors among the military regarding the transparency of the nuclear regime. A related factor was the civilian leadership's desire to restrain and control some of their armed forces by incorporating the national nuclear programs into a bilateral civilian accounting and control regime.

Type of political regimes and peaceful conditions within the countries. Although the warmer relations between Argentina and Brazil initially took place when the two countries were still ruled by military regimes, it is clear that there is a linear relationship between the democratization of the mid-1980s and the improvement in bilateral relations in general, and in the nuclear issue-area in particular. Democratization provided a crucial impetus to the ongoing nuclear rapprochement and to the evolution of their relationship into the nonproliferation regime (see Stanley 1992, 201; Pande 1993, 430).

Stable distribution of power between the parties. As mentioned above, the fact that by the late 1970s Argentina recognized its uneven distribution of power contrasted with Brazil significantly contributed to the attenuation and eventual end of their enduring rivalry over subparamountcy in Latin America.

Presence of a hegemonic power. Since the mid-1980s and especially after the Cold War, the United States has exercised a certain diplomatic pressure on Brazil and Argentina to give up their autonomous stance on nonproliferation and to join both the NPT and the Tlatelolco regimes. Moreover, evidence of international nuclear arms control progress has provided significant psychological support for the local Argentine-Brazilian nonproliferation initiatives. The end of the Cold War also brought several other countries, including China, France, and South Africa, to join the NPT (Carasales 1996, 331).

Fitness between the regional normative framework and the given case; degree of institutionalization of the international society. As the bilateral nonproliferation regime consolidated in the 1980s, the fitness and congruence between the international and regional regimes on the one hand and the local Argentine-Brazilian nuclear cooperation on the other became more evident. Hence, the norms of nuclear arms control and disarmament, CBMs, and common security sponsored by the Latin American regional society could be incorporated and adhered to by the two potential nuclear powers in the Southern Cone.

Alternative Explanations

The agreement between Argentina and Brazil can be explained, in part, by the impact of norms on their foreign policy behavior. Yet there has also been a strong rationale in terms of cost-benefit analysis and the definition of national interests that led to the convergence and cooperation between the two countries. The immediate causes for the turning point in their relations in 1979 were quite straightforward. For Argentina the near-war crisis with Chile in 1978 and the mounting tensions with Great Britain over the Falkland Islands urged it to seek an accommodation with Brazil. For Brazil the cooperation with Argentina reflected intraorganizational changes and factional politics within the military in the direction of moderation and opening (*abertura*) (Resende-Santos 1998, 2). In addition, we can mention four other explanations for the positive evolution of their relations.

First, and even before signing their agreement in 1979 over the Itaipú dam, the two countries shared similar goals regarding the Tlatelolco regime and the preservation of their autonomy in nuclear matters. The impetus for nuclear cooperation in the 1980s was facilitated by the growing difficulties both countries experienced in gaining access to nuclear supplies and technology, for instance, regarding the restrictions imposed by countries like Canada and West Germany on the transfer of nuclear technology. By establishing a bilateral regime of safeguards and control, the two countries could expect to get easier access to sophisticated technologies. Moreover, the leadership in both countries gradually realized that, whatever their differences, there was not a clear rationale, justification, or need to possess nuclear weapons, and that even the possession of PNEs could disrupt their bilateral relations (see Redick et al. 1995, 111 and 118; Stanley 1992, 201 and 210).

Second, in economic terms there has always been a potential for economic interdependence and integration between Argentina and Brazil that could not be realized due to their historical rivalry, especially in the security and diplomatic realms. Hence, once their security climate improved, the way was open for economic integration as well. Conversely, the mounting economic difficulties and foreign debt crises faced by both countries in the mid-1980s and early 1990s pushed them in the direction of cooperation. Thus, the Argentine-Brazilian security relationship in the 1980s became increasingly embedded in a dense process of economic integration and transactions, organizations, and institutions in the 1990s. Politics, economics, and security have been continually intertwined, reinforcing each other and creating a synergistic effect of a closer (security) community (see Rudman 1990, 3–4; Pande 1993, 433).

Third, in geopolitical and regional terms Argentina and Brazil shared the idea in the 1980s and 1990s of creating an economic pole of high growth in a region without military and strategic conflicts, with political stability and fully inserted into the international political economy. Brazil wanted to consolidate its position in the international system through cooperation, based on democratic stability, economic development, and technological modernization. From the Argentine perspective, the nuclear cooperation and economic integration with Brazil represented one of the inflexion points to accelerate a foreign policy based on openness and cooperation (see Hirst 1988, 6; De la Balze 1995, 15).

The Peace Process in Central America:
From Contadora (1983) to Esquipulas (1987) and Beyond

Revolutionary struggles involving warfare between guerrilla and government forces spread throughout Central America in the 1970s, leading to virulent civil wars in Nicaragua and El Salvador and, to a lesser extent, in Guatemala and Honduras. In Nicaragua the struggle resulted in a victory of the revolutionary Sandinistas in 1979, followed by a civil war between them and the *Contras* insurgency supported by the United States. In Guatemala the government managed to hold guerrillas in check, though the civil war continued until 1996. In El Salvador the war raged at a great cost of life. Against this background, in 1983 a group of Latin American countries initiated a political process at Contadora, Panama, in order to resolve peacefully those conflicts. Though the Contadora initiative ultimately failed, it was replaced and superseded by the Esquipulas process initiated by Oscar Arias Sánchez, the Costa Rican president, in 1987. The Esquipulas II Agreement of August 1987 paved the way for the peaceful resolution of the Central American conflicts. What then explains the (relative) failure of Contadora and the (relative) success of Esquipulas?

Historical and Legal Background

The Contadora process formally began with a two-day meeting involving the foreign ministers of Venezuela, Colombia, Panama, and Mexico, on the Panamanian island of Contadora. The countries involved were concerned about the impact of the armed conflict within and among Central American nations on the political instability of the entire region, as a threat to regional peace and security. They also shared a common distaste for previous unilateral U.S. interventions in the region (see Child 1992, 15; Bagley 1986, 1). Border tensions were common throughout the region, involving El Salvador, Honduras, Nicaragua, and Costa Rica. The goal of the Contadora Group was to mediate among and between their Central American neighbors in order to reach a peaceful solution in the region, against the background of the U.S. intervention in the civil war in El Salvador and its support for the *Contra* insurgency against the Sandinista Marxist regime in Nicaragua. Between 1983 and 1986 the Contadora Group helped to avoid a further escalation of the war, setting the parameters for future peace agreements. In 1985 four democratic countries from South America—Argentina, Brazil, Peru, and Uruguay—formed the Support Group in order to improve the political influence of the Contadora peace initiative. Finally, in 1986 both groups merged into the Rio Group ("Group of Eight"), which later was enlarged to include most of the Latin American countries. The Rio Group has provided since 1986 a mechanism for political dialogue, consultation, and consensus-seeking within the Latin American international society (Frohmann 1994b, 130–31).

On July 17, 1983, the Contadora Group issued a declaration at Cancún calling for renewed efforts to continue the peace process and establishing the principles and recommendations for an eventual peace agreement. Security norms and practices were a major concern of the declaration, including arms control and disarmament, demilitarization, and nonintervention (Child 1992, 18).

On September 3, 1983, the foreign ministers of the five Central American countries, under the sponsorship and mediation of the Contadora group, adopted an initial Document of Objectives at Panama City, Panama. This document specified a common intention to promote democratization and to end the armed conflict in the region, to act in compliance with international law, to revitalize and restore economic development and cooperation in the region, and to negotiate better access to international markets.

One year later, on September 29, 1984, the Contadora group presented the Act for Peace and Cooperation in Central America. The document included a long "laundry list" of commitments to peace, democratization, regional security, and economic cooperation. It further detailed mechanisms for arms control, disarmament, and CBMs, including the provision for regional committees to evaluate and verify compliance with all these commitments. Although the five Central American presidents tentatively approved it, it did not gain the support of the United States since it tacitly recognized the Sandinista regime of Nicaragua.

On January 12, 1986, the Contadora Group and the Support Group presented the Declaration of Caraballeda for peace, security, and democracy in Central America as its final and revised act. It called for the halt of military aid to irregular forces, suspension of military movements, reduction of military bases, national reconciliation, and respect for human rights (Rouquié 1994, 279). On April 7, 1986, the foreign ministers of the Group of Eight— Contadora and Support groups—invited the five Central American governments to Panama to sign the revised and definitive text of the Contadora Act. Verification and CBM mechanisms were even more detailed than in the 1984 draft, continuing the trend of increasing levels of specificity. Yet the U.S. pressure on Costa Rica, Honduras, and El Salvador foiled this effort, and the Contadora mediation effort ran its course. The Latin American members of the Contadora and Support groups did not have enough leverage—economic, military, or diplomatic—to persuade the United States and its Central American allies to accept Contadora's formula for a settlement (Bagley 1986, 76).

While the Contadora group ultimately failed to forge a credible peace formula with the backing of all the relevant governments, it did lay the foundations for such a plan to emerge in subsequent years. In May of 1986 the five Central American presidents met at Esquipulas, Guatemala, and recognized the normative significance and precedent of Contadora as a basis for an eventual peace treaty. A year later, at the second meeting in Esquipulas in August 1987, Oscar Arias Sánchez presented a plan of ten points to reach peace in the region that was eventually accepted and implemented. The Arias Peace Plan differed from the Contadora Act drafts in its emphasis on internal democratization rather than security norms and geopolitical concerns (see Rouquié 1994, 285; McNeill 1988, 30). It referred more specifically to the domestic processes and the political institutions within the different states, imposing demands on issues such as pluralism and freedom and thus compelling a potential regime change for Nicaragua. Moreover, the peace negotiations were supposed to be the product of a common Central American effort rather than a general Latin American one.

The "Procedure for the Establishing of a Firm and Lasting Peace in Central America" (Esquipulas II Agreement) dealt with the issues of national reconciliation; an end to hostilities; democratization; free elections; termination of aid to irregular forces and insurrectionist movements; nonuse of the territory of one state to attack others; negotiations on security, verification, and the control and limitation of weapons; refugees and displaced persons; cooperation, democracy, and freedom for peace and development; international verification and follow-up; and a timetable for the fulfillment of commitments (United Nations 1996, 409; see also Arias 1997, 151).[4] Following Esquipulas II, the presidents of the five Central American nations signed an additional accord in August 1989 to disband the *Contra* rebels, which set in motion the democratization process in Nicaragua and cleared the way for the creation of the UN and OAS mechanisms of verification. The Sandinista regime of Nicaragua fell peacefully after the country's February 1990 elections and the civil war ended in El Salvador in 1992. By the mid-1990s most interstate disputes in the region have been resolved.

Evidence and Impact of the Normative Framework

The peace process of Contadora epitomized one of the few multilateral Latin American initiatives since the Latin American Congress that took place at Santiago de Chile in September of 1856. It represented the resurgence of a Latin American regional identity challenging on normative grounds the U.S. hegemony in Central America and upholding the principles of sovereignty, self-determination, and nonintervention (see Frohmann 1994b, 132; Meyer 1997, 168). The norm of consensus-seeking (*concertación*) stemmed from the Contadora and Support groups, which eventually became institutionalized into the Group of Rio. Since 1986 the Rio Group has provided a mechanism for political dialogue, consultation, and consensus-seeking by gradually learning from the past and establishing mechanisms for mutual trust (Frohmann 1994b, 131; see also Green 1990, 257–59; Aravena 1992, 65–68).

The Contadora process embodied the major norms and principles upheld by the Latin American international society and the international community as a whole. In the "Twenty-one Objectives Document" of September 9, 1983, the five Central American states recognized the relevance of the following norms:

> self-determination of peoples; nonintervention; sovereign equality of states; peaceful settlement of disputes; refraining from the threat or use of force; respect of the territorial integrity of states; pluralism in its various

manifestations; full support for democratic institutions; promotion of social justice; international cooperation for development; respect for and promotion of human rights; prohibition of terrorism and subversion; the desire to reconstruct the Central American homeland through progressive integration of its economic, legal, and social institutions; and the need for economic cooperation among the states of Central America, so as to make a fundamental contribution to the development of their peoples and the strengthening of their independence. (quoted in Child 1992, 174)

As for the norms of security, the Contadora/Esquipulas process included most of them, essentially demilitarization, arms control and gradual disarmament, mechanisms for CBMs and verification, reduction of tensions and national reconciliation, and the concept of mutual or cooperative security, transcending the Inter-American version of collective security.[5] The Contadora process was an important milestone in Central America in that it introduced the norms of CBMs, cooperative security, and the idea of a "zone of peace" for that region (Child 1992, 147). Conversely, a sensible critique of the Contadora process points out its shortcomings and obstacles. The failure of the process resided in its overabundance of details about the minutes and particularities of the required practices to "translate" the agreed-upon norms of security, such as an end to all armed conflict, arms control and reduction of weapons, no foreign military installations, resolution of border conflicts, promotion of a climate of relaxed tensions, mechanisms for control and verification, limitation of military maneuvers and traffic of weapons, and direct communications between governments (see Frohmann 1994b, 132; Durán 1984, 543; Aravena 1994b, 76–77).

In addition, the Arias Plan of 1987 openly linked the norms of peace with those of security by making peace, security, development, and democracy part of the same complex equation (Arias 1997, 151). Thus, Esquipulas II moved the emphasis back from the security dimension to the domestic political one, by linking security arrangements with the need for political accommodation and democratization.

Conditions for the Impact of Norms

Role of actors who mobilize norms. It is evident that the President of Costa Rica, Oscar Arias Sánchez, fulfilled an essential role as a skilled international conciliator in presenting his peace plan in February of 1987, which led to the presidential summits of the five Central American nations at Esquipulas II (August 1987), Alajuela, Costa Rica (January 1988), and Costa del Sol, El Salvador (February 1989).

Presence of a hegemonic power.   As mentioned above, the Contadora initiative challenged the U.S. hegemony in Central America, especially its intervention in El Salvador and Nicaragua (see Díaz Callejas 1985, 150; and Tinoco 1989, 36). While the United States foiled the Contadora process through its pressure on Costa Rica, El Salvador, and Honduras to ignore the Caraballeda Declaration of 1987, its position regarding the Arias Plan was much more encouraging, if not fully supportive.

Fitness between the regional normative framework and the given case; institutionalization of the international society.   Beyond the Contadora initiative stood a group of eight concerned and democratic Latin American states, which created the political incentives for the Central American states to negotiate among themselves in the Esquipulas process of 1986–1987. Moreover, while the Arias Plan (Esquipulas II) of 1987 focused on the peacemaking by and for Central Americans, the mechanisms for verification and implementation included the OAS and the United Nations throughout the 1990s (United Nations 1996, 409).

The Central American peace process has been a multilateral and extra-regional effort since its origins at Contadora in 1983. The normative framework that encouraged and supported the implementation of norms of peace and security included several circles of adherence: the five Central American states themselves, the immediate regional neighbors (the Contadora states and, to a lesser extent, the United States, all of whom supported the Arias Plan), the more distant South American neighbors, and the international community as a whole. As for the Latin American international society, one can conclude that the Central American peace process of the 1980s was rooted in a long history of Latin American multilateral cooperation to resort to peaceful settlement, going back to Bolívar's efforts in the early part of the nineteenth century (Meyer 1997, 170).

Alternative Explanations

The peace process in Central America cannot be attributed only to the significant normative impact of the Contadora, Support, and Rio groups on the five Central American states themselves. In juxtaposition to the normative framework to implement norms of peace and security, there were several factors that favored the resolution of the long civil wars in El Salvador and Nicaragua, and later in Honduras and Guatemala, including the end of the Cold War, the exhaustion of the belligerents, creative peacemaking by countries like Costa Rica and Mexico, and the emergence or reemergence of skilled and credible national conciliators.

It can be argued that the support, if not the benign indifference, of the United States toward Esquipulas, as opposed to its strong opposition to the Contadora process, could be attributed to the end of the Cold War in the late 1980s and the implications of the "Irangate" scandal in the United States. The United States was now ready to change its policy toward Nicaragua and, especially, El Salvador, and to support democratization and reconciliation efforts in the region (Goodfellow and Morrell 1990, 1–2).

Moreover, Esquipulas II managed to generate more local support among the directly concerned Central American states, including Nicaragua, than the previous Contadora process. Its framework for achieving national reconciliation and regional peace was welcomed, in contrast to the much more complicated and comprehensive nature of the Contadora draft treaties, so Esquipulas II was more palatable for the Central American presidents (McKenna 1989, 68).

Oscar Arias Sánchez, the president of Costa Rica and main author of the successful peace initiative, summarized the differences between Contadora and Esquipulas and the reasons for the latter's success as follows:

> Ultimately, the Contadora group was unable to persuade the five countries of the region to sign an agreement. In contrast, the Esquipulas process, which included direct dialogue between the parties, required less than one year to reach important agreements about concrete points relating to the fundamental causes of the problems that it sought to resolve.
>
> In the realm of international law, we can conclude that Contadora was unable to clarify certain basic principles for the parties, namely: the prohibition of the use or threat of force, the principle of nonintervention, and the right of peoples to self-determination. Each party interpreted these principles to suit its own interests. In Esquipulas, on the contrary, we, the presidents, agreed from the start on a similar interpretation of these principles. This consensus was fundamental because the various parties were able to derive common criteria to resolve their conflicts; this ability guided our transactions as we modified our negotiation styles and political objectives. (Arias 1997, 157)

Although the initial process of Contadora failed to reach its objective of finalizing a peace agreement, it succeeded in starting a long-term process of consultation, dialogue, and collaboration among four, and then eight, Latin American countries, in relation to five Central American ones (Frohmann 1994b, 134). Moreover, the Contadora drafts set the normative parameters for the links among security, peace, democratization, and development, which were instrumented since Esquipulas II by the Central American states. The success of Esquipulas, where Contadora failed before, was attributed to a change in emphasis from security and geopolitical concerns (Contadora) to political and domestic conflicts, in an effort to reach national reconciliation rather than resolving external threats (Aravena 1994b, 79). In terms of cost-benefit analysis, Esquipulas could be presented as a "win-win" situation for all the parties concerned, including the Sandinista regime in Nicaragua, which probably did not expect at that time to lose the general elections of 1990.

Lessons from the Norms of Security in Latin America

Table 5.1 shows that the norms of security have been relevant to explain, at least in part, the relative success of the five cases examined in this chapter, when working in unison with other norms that stand at the core of the Latin American international society. As we will analyze in further detail in the next chapter, in all of these cases the impact of the normative framework was enhanced, rather than contradicted, by a series of cost-benefit analysis calculations by the actors themselves. In the multilateral cases, in contrast to the bilateral ones, the normative impact has tended to be more diffused and delayed, due to the larger number of norms and issue-areas invoked and the larger number of participants. Finally, there is a logical link among the norms of security themselves: CBMs are linked to measures of arms control and disarmament, and the broader those practices are, the more the parties move in the direction of common or mutual security.

Table 5.1. Summary of the Cases for Norms of Security

Case	Parties	Norms of Security	Other Norms
Strait of Magellan (1881) Pactos de Mayo (1902)	Argentina and Chile (bilateral)	arms control and disarmament demilitarization neutralization	*uti possidetis* peaceful settlement
Tlatelolco (since 1967)	all the countries of the region (multilateral)	arms control and disarmament nonproliferation CBMs collective security common security cooperative security "zone of peace"	peaceful settlement democratization
nuclear cooperation (since 1979)	Argentina and Brazil (bilateral)	arms control and disarmament CBMs nonproliferation cooperative and mutual security "zone of peace"	sovereignty nonintervention developmentalism
Central America peace process (Contadora and Esquipulas, since 1983)	five Central American states, eight other Latin American states, United States, OAS, and UN	arms control and disarmament demilitarization CBMs common and cooperative security "zone of peace"	peaceful settlement development democratization

CHAPTER SIX

Latin American Norms in a Comparative Perspective

IN THIS FINAL CHAPTER I SUMMARIZE MY EMPIRICAL AND THEORETICAL findings.[1] I infer patterns and draw generalizations about the impact of international norms of peace and security, as reflected in a myriad of successful, failed, and "mixed" cases from Latin America. Have the norms of peace and security made a difference for the international relations of the region? If the answer is positive, what has been their significance? Moreover, under what conditions did these norms have a certain influence? I also briefly compare the impact of norms in Latin America with their effect on other regions of the world. On the theoretical level, I emphasize the relevance of a neo-Grotian approach to the study of international relations, as against other positivist and constructivist approaches. On the policy level, I suggest ways to transcend the false dichotomy between norms and interests.

At the beginning of this book, I stated that international norms could be recognized as a distinctive phenomenon in international relations, separated from the actors' self-interests, at least for analytical purposes, though in practice they might overlap. My working assumption has been that norms do make a difference in the quality of life in international society and, in more specific terms, that international norms of peace and security affect the foreign policy of the member-states of that society. Accordingly, I have formulated three research questions: (1) Where do international norms come from? (2) What is the impact of norms on the domestic and foreign policy behavior of states in a given regional society? and (3) Under what conditions can regional norms affect the foreign policies of states? While I have referred in a cursory fashion to the first question in chapters 2 and 3, I have given a more comprehensive answer to the second and third questions in chapters 3 through 5. Thus, the empirical bulk of the book assessed the impact of norms of peace in six territorial disputes involving relevant South American dyads, as well as the influence of norms of security in five cases involving both bilateral and multilateral relations.

Conditions for the Impact of Norms: How (Much) and When?

How (Much) Do Norms Have an Impact?

As presented in chapter 3, the major norms of the Latin American society include: (1) sovereignty, equality of states, and nonintervention; (2) *uti possidetis* and territorial integrity; (3) peaceful settlement, *convivencia* (peaceful coexistence), and *concertación* (consensus-seeking); (4) arms control, disarmament, CBMs, collective and comprehensive security; and (5) political legalism, democracy, and human rights. Chapter 4 focused on the norms of peaceful settlement of international disputes and of *uti possidetis*. Similarly, chapter 5 dealt with the relevant norms of security. How have all these norms affected the international relations of the region?

The Latin American international society since 1883 provides rich empirical evidence for the potential impact of norms of peace and security across a wide variety of cases ranging from plain successes (Misiones, 1895; Argentina-Brazil, 1980s and 1990s) to serious failures (Chaco War, 1932–1935). We can then build a continuum between these two extremes that could include success but with counterproductive effects in the long run (Magellan, 1881); ephemeral success (Mayo Pacts, 1902); eventual success after protracted conflict (Tacna and Arica, 1929); success because of serendipity (Leticia, 1934); success in the long run (the Tlatelolco regime, 1994); mixed success or success in the long run (Esquipulas as opposed to Contadora); success after initial failure and crisis (Beagle Channel, 1984); and success after failure and recurrent wars (Oriente/Mainas in 1998). The record of the Latin American society is summarized in Table 6.1.

Table 6.1. The Record of the Latin American Society

Case	Result	Normative Justification	Winner	Loser	Details
Misiones	success	yes	Brazil	Argentina	arbitration (accepted)
Tacna–Arica	eventual success (protracted)	yes	Chile and Peru	Bolivia	arbitration (rejected); good offices and negotiations
Chaco	failure	yes	Paraguay	Bolivia	conciliation (attempts); war; after war, adjudication
Leticia	success (but serendipity)	yes	Colombia	Peru	mediation and negotiations
Oriente/ Mainas	success (after failure)	yes	Peru	Ecuador	several wars, then negotiations, good offices, adjudication
Beagle Channel	success (after failure)	yes	Chile	Argentina	arbitration (rejected); military crisis, mediation, negotiations
Magellan Strait	success (counterproductive)	yes	Argentina/Chile		negotiations
Mayo Pacts	success (ephemeral)	yes	Argentina/Chile		negotiations
Tlatelolco	success (in the long run)	yes	all of Latin America		multilateral negotiations
Argentina/ Brazil	success	yes	Argentina/Brazil		negotiations
Contadora/ Esquipulas	mixed success	yes	Latin America and Central America	Nicaragua (Sandinistas)	multilateral negotiations

From this table, we can infer that the impact of the normative framework in Latin America has been relevant at least in three different ways:

> 1. *The maintenance of the long peace in South America, at least since* 1883. This has been evident in the cases of Misiones, Tacna-Arica, Leticia, Beagle Channel, Magellan Strait, Mayo Pacts, Tlatelolco, and Argentina-Brazil. The evidence is less than robust in the cases of Oriente/Mainas before 1995 or Contadora-Esquipulas until 1987.
> 2. *The reshaping of state interests in terms of foreign policies, so that states act according to the regional normative framework.* This was especially relevant in the cases of Misiones, Leticia, Magellan, Mayo Pacts, Tlatelolco, and Argentina-Brazil in the 1980s and 1990s and to a lesser extent in Oriente/Mainas after 1995, Leticia in 1934, and Beagle Channel in 1984.
> 3. *The movement and upgrading of already-existing peaceful relations in Latin America in the direction of a pluralistic security community.* This has been demonstrated in the cases of the Beagle Channel (1984), Tlatelolco (in the mid-1990s), and Argentina-Brazil (since the mid-1980s).

Interestingly, it should be noticed that there has been an overall consensus among the Latin American states in justifying their actions and policies in normative terms, even in cases of unresolved disputes, crises, and wars. Overall, most of the countries involved in the eleven case studies have agreed, at least at the rhetorical level, on the relevance of norms such as peaceful settlement, *uti possidetis,* mutual respect of sovereignty, CBMs, and collective or comprehensive security. The norms invoked in the different cases are summarized in Table 6.2.

Table 6.2. Norms Invoked in the Latin American Society

Case	Both (or All) Parties	Party # 1 (usually status quo)	Party # 2 (usually revisionist)
Misiones	peaceful settlement uti possidetis	**Brazil** uti possidetis facto possession	**Argentina** uti possidetis (juris) pacifism right of succession
Tacna-Arica	moral norms peaceful settlement	**Chile** pacta sunt servanda sovereignty	**Peru** rebus sic stantibus self-determination justice
Chaco	sovereignty uti possidetis	**Paraguay** uti possidetis facto discovery and possession	**Bolivia** uti possidetis (juris) justice

Table 6.2. Norms Invoked in the Latin American Society (*cont.*)

Case	Both (or All) Parties	Party # 1 (usually status quo)	Party # 2 (usually revisionist)
Leticia	peaceful settlement	**Colombia** sovereignty territorial integrity *pacta sunt servanda*	**Peru** self-determination justice *rebus sic stantibus*
Oriente/ Mainas	*uti possidetis juris* peaceful settlement	**Peru** self-determination *pacta sunt servanda* possession	**Ecuador** justice *rebus sic stantibus* discovery
Beagle Channel	*uti possidetis juris* peaceful settlement	**Chile** discovery and possession *pacta sunt servanda*	**Argentina** justice *rebus sic stantibus*
Magellan Strait and Mayo Pacts	*uti possidetis juris* possession peaceful settlement naval arms control	**Chile** neutralization	**Argentina** demilitarization nonintervention pacifism
Tlatelolco	peaceful settlement democratization nuclear nonproliferation arms control common security	**All Latin American countries** (emphasis on ABC in the 1990s)	
Argentina and Brazil	arms control and disarmament CBMs nuclear nonproliferation cooperative/mutual security sovereignty and nonintervention "developmentalism"	**Argentina and Brazil**	
Contadora/ Esquipulas	arms control and disarmament CBMs and demilitarization peaceful settlement democratization common security development	**Central American states and eight other Latin American states**	

Another way of assessing the impact of norms in Latin America is to refer back to the six paths of influence presented in chapter 2. The first path (general shaping of foreign and domestic policies, or at least its structural normative constraining) can be demonstrated in terms of norms as shaping or reshaping state interests (Misiones, Leticia, Magellan, Mayo Pacts, and Tlatelolco). The second path (domestic) is evidenced through the third wave of democratization in the region (see the cases of the Beagle Channel for Argentina, Tlatelolco in the mid-1990s, and Argentina-Brazil since the mid-1980s). The third path (functionalist/rationalistic) has been demonstrated in the multilateral cases of security arrangements, such as Tlatelolco and Contadora/Esquipulas. The fourth path (constructivism) overlaps and translates the effects of norms as shaping interests and identities in most of the cases. The fifth path (Grotian approach) emphasizes multilateral instruments of regional law, institutions of the regional society, and processes of legitimation of behavior. In the Latin American context this has been evident in cases such as Chaco (the final Peace Treaty of 1938), Oriente (the final agreement of 1998), Tlatelolco, and Contadora/Esquipulas (both multilateral). Finally, the sixth path (international law and international ethics) has affected, at least in rhetorical terms, each and all of the eleven case studies. Even those countries that violated the norms of international law justified their actions in terms of justice, morality, and the clause of *rebus sic stantibus*.

As mentioned in chapters 2 and 3, the effect of the regional norms and institutions on Latin American politics can be considered both constitutive and regulative, both shaping interests and identities as well as reflecting them. Moreover, in some cases (especially those associated with democratization and protection of human rights) the origins and effects have had a "double" or combined source, both domestic and international, or what might be called intermestic. Notice that in replying to my second research question, it is difficult, if not impossible, to refer to these paths of influence and the empirical evidence for their impact in terms of independent variables as explaining, in a predetermined or mechanistic way, a certain behavior. In this sense the constructivist approach scores an important insight: norms can lead to, promote, influence, affect, impact, shape, constitute, enable, and regulate behavior, rather than simply "cause" or "explain" it.

Under What Conditions Do Norms Have an Impact?

Conversely, the third research question, "Under what conditions can norms influence the foreign policies of states?" can be dealt with in a more positivist fashion, by suggesting a series of alternative, and sometimes overlapping hypotheses drawn from the domestic and international realms. In chapter 2 I suggested seven hypotheses that could be tested empirically in chapters 4 and 5. On these hypotheses, the degree of influence of international norms is directly related to the

1. salience of the domestic actors who mobilize the norms;
2. openness and liberal-democratic nature of the political regimes;
3. peacefulness of conditions within the countries involved;
4. stability and degree of recognition of the distribution of power between (or among) the parties involved;
5. visibility of the presence of a hegemonic power;
6. degree of institutionalization of the international society;
7. degree of fitness between the preexisting international normative framework and the relevant case.

The results of the testing of these hypotheses in the Latin American context are summarized in Table 6.3.

Table 6.3. Conditions for the Impact of Norms (Testing the Hypotheses)

	H1	H2	H3	H4	H5	H6+ H7
Case	Salience of actors	Open/liberal regimes	Peaceful conditions	Power distribution	Hegemonic power	Society and fitness
Misiones	yes (Argentina)	yes (Argentina)	yes (both)	symmetrical	no	yes (arbitration)
Tacna-Arica	yes (Leguía, Peru; Alessandri, Chile)	no	yes (both)	turning symmetrical	yes	yes (arbitration, good offices)
Chaco	no	no	yes (Paraguay)	symmetrical	not clear (USA, Argentina, Brazil)	not clear (conciliation, normative dissonance)
Leticia	no	yes (Colombia)	yes (Colombia)	symmetrical	yes (USA, Brazil)	yes (third parties)

Table 6.3.   Conditions for the Impact of Norms (Testing the Hypotheses) (*cont.*)

Case	H1 Salience of actors	H2 Open/liberal regimes	H3 Peaceful conditions	H4 Power distribution	H5 Hegemonic power	H6+ H7 Society and fitness
Oriente/ Mainas	yes (Fujimori, Peru; Mahud, Ecuador)	no (until the 1980s)	yes (Ecuador)	turning symmetrical	yes (USA, Brazil)	not clear (arbitration, third parties, normative dissonance)
Beagle Channel	yes (Alfonsín, Argentina; Pinochet, Chile)	yes (Argentina after 1983)	yes (Argentina after 1983)	asymmetrical (Argentina)	no	yes (arbitration, normative dissonance, mediation)
Magellan Strait and Mayo Pacts	yes (Argentina)	yes (both)	yes (both)	symmetrical	no	yes
Tlatelolco	yes (Brazil, Mexico in 1967; ABC in 1994)	yes (most)	yes (most)	multilateral	no	yes
Argentina/ Brazil	yes (epistemic communities; Menem, Argentina; Collor, Brazil)	yes (after 1983)	yes (both)	asymmetrical (Brazil)	no	yes
Contadora/ Esquipulas	yes (Arias, Costa Rica)	yes (Costa Rica only)	no (only Costa Rica)	multilateral	yes (USA in Esquipulas)	yes

This table shows that the "domestic" hypotheses (1 through 3) seem to be less relevant than the "international" ones (4 through 7). For instance, norms have had a significant effect even without open and liberal democracies within the relevant countries, and without favorable conditions of domestic peace. As for the more realist hypotheses (4 and 5), the results are also rather ambiguous. Norms have had an effect mostly in symmetrical cases of power distribution, but also in cases in which the power distribution moved from being unbalanced to being more symmetrical. Likewise, the presence of a hegemonic power has not been crucial to facilitate (or impose) the preferred normative framework. In contrast, the last two hypotheses (6 and 7), which can be catalogued as Grotian, are the more relevant, tracing a clear correlation between normative successes and degree of coherence and fitness with the preexisting international (regional) framework. Likewise, cases of failure are characterized by a normative dissonance regarding the regional society, in which the "renegade" parties present their arguments in terms of justice and morality, as opposed to order and respect for the status quo.

Alternative Explanations for the Impact of Norms

The impact of the Latin American normative framework upon the international relations of the region should be gauged against alternative explanations for the phenomena of the long South American peace and the "upgrading" of the peaceful relations in the Southern Cone and in the region in general. Elsewhere I have pointed to alternative explanations such as balance of power, U.S. or Brazilian regional hegemony, geographic isolation, irrelevance and impotence to fight international wars, third-party threats, economic development and prosperity, dependence and interdependence, and a general satisfaction with the territorial status quo (see Kacowicz 1998).

Turning to the eleven case studies in chapters 4 and 5, I found six alternative explanations that provide a feasible rationale for the outcome of the cases: (1) geopolitical considerations, including third-party threats; (2) cost-benefit analysis and (potential) common interests among or between the parties; (3) the importance of the territory in question; and (4) ad hoc explanations. These explanations are summarized in Table 6.4.

Among these six explanations, geopolitical considerations and cost-benefit analysis in terms of potential economic cooperation stand out. Geopolitical calculations, including consideration or perception of third-party threats, were relevant in seven out of the eleven cases: Misiones, Tacna-Arica, Chaco, Beagle Channel, Tlatelolco, Argentina-Brazil, and Contadora/Esquipulas. Moreover, in all of the cases, perhaps with the exception of resolving the Chaco dispute by peaceful means, all the parties opted (eventually) for the adoption of norms of peace and security, out of economic and cost-benefit calculations. Ad hoc factors, such as misperceptions, virulent nationalism, and national pride, played a role in bringing about normative failures. Conversely, serendipity favored peaceful settlement, such as the assassination of the Peruvian president in 1933 or bad weather that avoided a South Atlantic naval encounter between Chileans and Argentines in December of 1978.

Table 6.4. Alternative Explanations for the Impact of Norms

Case	Geopolitical Considerations And Third-Party Threats	Cost-Benefit Analysis (Economic Reasons)	Ad Hoc	Other/ Territory
Misiones	Chile as a threat (to Argentina)	yes	U.S. bias for Brazil	31,000 sq km
Tacna–Arica	Bolivia as a threat (to Chile)	yes	asymmetrical interests	24,000 sq km
Chaco	geopolitical importance for both resolution of Tacna-Arica (against Bolivia)	no	failure of norms misperceptions nationalism survival (for Paraguay)	384,000 sq km
Leticia	no	yes (need for development)	assassination of Sanchez Cerro	14,000 sq km
Oriente/ Mainas	no	yes (need for development)	power politics misperceptions nationalism	256,000 sq km
Beagle Channel	U.K. as a threat (for Argentina) bioceanic principle gateway to the Atlantic Ocean	yes (potential integration)	national pride nationalism bad weather (avoided war)	few islands, 30,000 sq miles of sea (76,800 sq km)

Table 6.4. Alternative Explanations for the Impact of Norms (cont.)

Case	Geopolitical Considerations And Third-Party Threats	Cost-Benefit Analysis (Economic Reasons)	Ad Hoc	Other/ Territory
Magellan Strait and Mayo Pacts	gateway to the Atlantic Ocean bioceanic principle	yes (costs of arms race)	aversion to war	Magellan Strait naval arms control
Tlatelolco	Cuban missile crisis U.S. interference in Latin America	yes (economic and political costs)	reputation limits to U.S. hegemony	multilateral win–win situation
Argentina/ Brazil	Chile as a threat (for Argentina) U.K. as a threat (for Argentina)	yes (potential economic integration)	democratization position in the international system	nuclear weapons/energy win–win situation
Contadora/ Esquipulas	geopolitical implications for Contadora group	yes (need for development)	end of Cold War ripeness democratization	mutilateral win–win situation

Latin America in a Comparative Perspective

Is the Latin American international society a unique case in comparative terms? As stated in chapter 3, the answer to this question is both positive and negative. In affirmative terms, Latin America is rather unique in its plethora of formally stated norms and declarative intentions of a certain prescriptive behavior, dating back to the beginning of the nineteenth century. Moreover, the contrast between its "civilized" and relatively peaceful international relations and the anarchy, lack of governance, civil wars, and recurrent cycles of authoritarianism until the 1980s within the borders of its member-states is quite peculiar. The paradox of great internal violence and instability contrasted with the relatively nonviolent international relations can be partly explained by a potential trade-off between domestic and international wars. Moreover, Latin America stands out, in terms of its political culture, in the gap ("normative dissonance") between its formal(istic) and rhetorical adherence to norms of legal/judicial procedures in peaceful settlement, democratic governance, and adherence to arms control and disarmament, on the one hand, and its social practices in reality, on the other.

Yet at the same time it is clear that the case of Latin American international society is not unique. There are other regional examples of contemporary international societies that have reached higher levels of institutionalization of their societal and political relations, moving in the direction of pluralistic security communities, such as North America, Western Europe, or Southeast Asia. Within Latin America, perhaps only its Southern Cone—and more specifically Mercosur—might qualify nowadays as an incipient pluralistic security community, with higher degrees of social links and institutionalization, in relative terms.

There are sixteen regions for comparison, including South America, Central America and the Caribbean, North America, Western Europe, Australasia/Oceania, Eastern Europe, Northeast Asia, Southeast Asia, South Asia, Central Asia, West Africa, North Africa, East Africa, Central Africa, Southern Africa, and the Middle East (see appendix 1).

Tables 6.5 and 6.6 trace the impact of norms of peace and security across these sixteen regions (their data is summarized in appendix 2). Table 6.5 summarizes the record of international wars and territorial disputes in the international system from 1945 to the present. The table includes information regarding the number of territorial disputes, major territorial changes as a result of international war or other forms of territorial aggression, and the number of territorial disputes still pending or not resolved (see appendix 2 for details).

Table 6.5. Record of International Wars and Territorial Disputes from 1945 to 2001

Region	International Wars	Territorial Disputes	Violent Territorial Changes
South America	3	17	0
Central America and Caribbean	1	4	0
North America	0	4	0
Western Europe	1	13	1
Australasia/ Oceania	0	0	0
Eastern Europe	5	7	0
Northeast Asia	2	6	1
Southeast Asia	4	6	3
South Asia	4	3	4
Central Asia	3	3	0
West Africa	1	13	1
North Africa	3	9	0
East Africa	5	8	0
Central Africa	1	3	0
Southern Africa	0	5	0
Middle East	8	16	4
TOTAL	41	117	14

Note: The list does not include civil wars or wars of decolonization ("national liberation"). The data was compiled based on Simmons (1999) and Zacher (2001). For a detail of the cases see appendix 2.

Table 6.5 shows that South America and Central America have had a relatively small number of international wars. In the case of South America the three wars correspond to two additional rounds of fighting between Peru and Ecuador in 1981 and again in 1995 (with a relatively small number of casualties), and the Falklands/Malvinas War of 1982. Yet the military conflict between Argentina and the United Kingdom was a North-South, or colonial, war rather than one among Latin American states. In the case of Central America the only significant war was the "Football War" between El Salvador and Honduras in 1969. Compared to other regions of the world, the ratio of territorial disputes proportional to the number of international wars is by far the highest. This means that Latin America in general, and South America in particular, have been characterized by the presence of territorial disputes that have not escalated into war, out of a normative conviction and predilection for peaceful settlement, and/or a preference to keep the status quo. In comparative terms Latin America has shown a consistently conservative attitude toward territorial changes initiated by violence, so that territorial integrity has been regularly kept, probably more than in many other regions of the world.

As far as the norms of security are concerned, with respect to the formalization of arms control and disarmament agreements, regional frameworks of collective security (alliances), and general organizations dealing with peace, security, and cooperation, Latin America is less unique (see Table 6.6). This table demonstrates that there are other regions of the world that exhibit higher degrees of institutionalization and formalization, first and foremost Western Europe and North America. Likewise, the record of arms control, disarmament, and multilateral frameworks of CBMs is not particularly impressive in the Latin American context, perhaps because conventional security problems have not affected the region as they have in other parts of the world. The Organization of American States is considered the only overall regional organization that deals with peace and security. Its members come from three different regions: North America, Central America, and South America. In Latin America (Mexico, Central America, and South America) the Rio Group fulfills relatively minor political roles of regional coordination and consensus-seeking. There is a particular arms control regime, the NFZ Tlatelolco regime of nuclear nonproliferation, which today includes all Central American and South American countries, as well as Mexico.

Table 6.6. Formalization of Regional Norms of Security

Region	Arms Control and Disarmament; CBMs	Collective Security; Common Security	Peace and Security (General)
South America	Inter-American Convention against the Illicit Manufacturing of and Trafficking in Firearms, Ammunition, Explosives, and Other Related Materials (1998) Treaty for the Prohibition of Nuclear Weapons in Latin America (Tlatelolco Treaty) (1967) Agency for the Prohibition of Nuclear Weapons in Latin America and the Caribbean (OPANAL) (1969)	Inter-American Treaty of Reciprocal Assistance (Rio Treaty) (1947)	Organization of American States (1948) Andean Community of Nations (Andean Group) (1966) Rio Group (1986)
Central America and the Caribbean	Inter-American Convention against the Illicit Manufacturing of and Trafficking in Firearms, Ammunition, Explosives, and Other Related Materials (1998) Treaty for the Prohibition of Nuclear Weapons in Latin America (Tlatelolco Treaty) (1967) Agency for the Prohibition of Nuclear Weapons in Latin America and the Caribbean (OPANAL) (1969)	Inter-American Treaty of Reciprocal Assistance (Rio Treaty) (1947)	Organization of American States (1948) Rio Group (1986) Organization of East Caribbean States (OECS) (1981)
North America	Inter-American Convention against the Illicit Manufacturing of and Trafficking in Firearms, Ammunition, Explosives, and Other Related Materials (1998)	Inter-American Treaty of Reciprocal Assistance (Rio Treaty) (1947) North Atlantic Treaty Organization (NATO) (1949) (USA and Canada, with Western Europe)	Organization of American States (1948)

Table 6.6. Formalization of Regional Norms of Security (*cont.*)

Region	Arms Control and Disarmament; CBMs	Collective Security; Common Security	Peace and Security (General)
Western Europe	Treaty on Conventional Armed Forces (1992) Helsinki Final Act on CBMs (1975) Treaty on Open Skies (1992) Vienna Document on CBMs (1999)	NATO (1949) Western European Union (WEU) (1955) Organization for Security and Cooperation in Europe (OSCE) (1990)	European Community/European Union (EU/EC) (1957/1992)
Australasia/ Oceania	South Pacific Nuclear Free Zone Treaty (Rarotonga) (1985)		South Pacific Forum (SPF) (1971)
Eastern Europe	Treaty on Conventional Armed Forces (1992) Helsinki Final Act on CBMs (1975) Treaty on Open Skies (1992)	Warsaw Pact (1955–1991) Organization for Security and Cooperation in Europe (OSCE) (1990) Partnership for Peace (PfP) (1993)	
Northeast Asia	Council for Security Cooperation in the Asia Pacific (CSCAP) (1994)		
Southeast Asia	Treaty on the Southeast Asia Nuclear Weapons-Free Zone (Bangkok Treaty) (1997) Council for Security Cooperation in the Asia Pacific (CSCAP) (1994) ASEAN Regional Forum (ARF) (1994)	Association of Southeast Asian Nations (ASEAN) (1967)	ASEAN (1967)
South Asia			South Asian Association for Regional Cooperation (SAARC) (1991)

Table 6.6. Formalization of Regional Norms of Security (*cont.*)

Region	Arms Control and Disarmament ;CBMs	Collective Security; Common Security	Peace and Security (General)
Central Asia	Conference on Interaction and CBMs in Asia (CICA) (1992)	Organization for Security and Cooperation in Europe (OSCE) (1990)	Commonwealth of Independent States (1992)
West Africa	African Nuclear-Weapons Free Zone Treaty (Pelindaba Treaty) (1996)		Organization of African Unity (OAU) (1963) Economic Community of West African States (ECOWAS) (1975)
North Africa	African Nuclear-Weapons Free Zone Treaty (Pelindaba Treaty) (1996)	Arab League (1945)	Organization of African Unity (OAU) (1963) Arab Maghreb Union (1989)
East Africa	African Nuclear-Weapons Free Zone Treaty (Pelindaba Treaty) (1996)		Organization of African Unity (OAU) (1963)
Central Africa	African Nuclear-Weapons Free Zone Treaty (Pelindaba Treaty) (1996)		Organization of African Unity (OAU) (1963)
Southern Africa	African Nuclear-Weapons Free Zone Treaty (Pelindaba Treaty) (1996)		Organization of African Unity (OAU) (1963) Southern African Development Community (SADC) (1992)
Middle East	Arms Control and Regional Security Working Group (ACRS) (1991) Euro-Mediterranean Initiative (1995)	Arab League (1945) Gulf Cooperation Council (GCC) (1981)	

Theoretical Implications

Review of the Concept of Norms and Different Approaches

In chapter 2 I presented six definitions of international norms. According to Micha Bar, norms are "social constructs of shared expectations of proper modes of behavior in a given society."[2] Since knowing what proper behavior is depends on standards of behavior that are prescriptive/normative in nature, then the different definitions might converge. We can summarize them in a *synthetic* manner, as follows: *International norms are standards of behavior, defined in terms of rights and obligations, that reflect a set of collective expectations regarding the proper behavior of states (and other actors) in a given context or identity. Norms regulate the mutual behavior of states, which are specific subjects of international law.*

As for the classification of norms, they can be moral (ethical) or not, as in the case of norms of peace. In this book I have focused primarily on the nonethical aspect of norms, due to the apparent contradiction between a universal morality and a regional or particular cultural and normative framework. At the same time, many of the norms of peace and security reviewed in this book can be considered in ethical, altruistic terms, like peaceful settlement of international disputes.

Moreover, the distinction among constitutive, regulative, and practical norms is blurred in practice. For instance, in the case of Latin America sovereignty and nonintervention can be considered as constitutive; peaceful settlement and *uti possidetis* as regulative; and norms of security—such as arms control and CBMs—as practical. At the same time, peaceful settlement can be constitutive and practical.

In chapter 2, I presented several approaches for the study of international norms. For neorealists, international norms are epiphenomena, reflecting a given power structure and the underlying material forces, though norms might have an impact as an ancillary mechanism for the normal conduct of international relations. For neoliberals, norms overlap with rational choice calculations and serve the egoistic interests of individual rational actors. Thus, norms are exogenously determined coordinating mechanisms that enable actors to overcome problems of collective action. In sum, for both neorealists and neoliberals norms are largely the product of rational utility calculations on the part of state actors.

In contrast, for constructivists norms are constitutive components of both the international society and of states' interests. Norms shape the identities of the state actors and partially define their interests, beyond merely constraining the state behavior.

Between the positivist and post-positivist approaches we might then locate the Grotian approach. According to it, the importance of norms is paramount, since "normal" international relations can take place only within a framework of normative rules, which are essential for the maintenance of order and justice.

A Plea for the Adoption of a Neo-Grotian Approach

As for the different approaches, all seem to have been relevant for the analysis of the Latin American international society: realism (power); liberalism (egoistic interests); constructivism (knowledge and cognition); and the Grotian approach (international law and society). Among these, I prefer Grotians because of their synthetic location between positivism and post-positivism, realism and liberalism, international law and the empirical evidence on the impact of norms and institutions on the behavior of states. From this perspective, the existence and persistence of international norms assume the reality of an international society, which can be viable within a regional or global framework. These international norms are expressed empirically, through social practices and institutions such as the instruments of international law.

Since norms act in an autonomous fashion, and while international law and practices shape both behavior and interests, one can notice a great overlap between the older Grotian approach and the more recent constructivist approach. Both schools refer to international law in a more serious way than structural realists and rationalist (neoliberal) institutionalists do. Yet, in contrast to constructivism, a neo-Grotian approach has the advantage of testing empirically the propositions about the potential impact of norms through the perusal of legal instruments and the examination of the behavior in practice.

The Grotian approach is a nuanced one, ranging from a pluralist to a solidarist perspective, from an emphasis on human relations and human rights to a focus on state sovereignty and the society of states. This research tradition assumes that: (1) international relations are a branch of human relations at the heart of which are basic norms and values such as independence, security, order, and justice; (2) there is a need to interpret the thoughts and actions of the people involved in international relations; and (3) world politics is an anarchical society, with distinctive norms, rules, and institutions but without a central authority (see Jackson and Sorensen 1999, 139–74). For instance, unlike neorealists and neoliberals, Hedley Bull believed that norms matter in understanding and explaining not just international law, but also other institutions of the international society such as war or the balance of power. Hence, the relationship between law and power is absolutely crucial to the whole international society approach.

Policy Implications

Transcending the False Dichotomy between Norms and Interests

There is a false dichotomy between normative research and rational choice. The two are interrelated: one cannot have a rational choice analysis without a previous normative framework and vice versa. More often than we tend to think, norms and self-interests tend to coincide rather than stand in opposition to each other. They usually move in the same direction, and they might complement each other. Thus, interests might shape norms, but norms also shape interests.

Only when we refer to moral norms is there a clear ontological discrepancy between universal morality and interests or prudent calculations. But when we refer to nonmoral norms, such as prudence, then there is a convergence between the fulfillment of interests and the adherence to a given normative framework. Moreover, in practice normative (in other words, moral) concerns and considerations of interest might lead to the adoption of the same foreign policy, so they might become blurred. For instance, the process of peaceful change by which the United States transferred back the Panama Canal Zone to Panama was motivated by both power politics and *Realpolitik* considerations (Henry Kissinger supported the move), as well as by moral concerns regarding decolonization (the position of President Jimmy Carter). Similarly, one might advocate the creation of a Palestinian state in the Palestinian territories of the West Bank (Judea and Samaria) and the Gaza Strip out of normative (moral) concerns dealing with self-determination and the end of the occupation of the Palestinian people, as well as with considerations of the national interest of Israel (maintaining its identity as a Jewish and democratic state).

Normative Dissonance: The Gap between Rhetorics and Practice

We found in chapters 4 and 5 that in the Latin American region an interesting "normative dissonance" between the legalistic and formal aspects of norms, on the one hand, and their translation into a more open, pragmatic, and "plastic" reality, on the other. For instance, despite their formidable recourse to arbitration in the nineteenth and twentieth centuries, Latin American countries in many instances have preferred to shy away from legalistic/juridical solutions—which tend to be zero sum—in favor of ad hoc, political solutions, that are mixed-motive and lead to a feasible (if not ideal) political compromise. Thus, we can trace a significant movement from legal to political solutions as the dispute becomes more intractable and complex. We witness an increasing involvement of third parties fulfilling roles of mediation, conciliation, good offices, guarantors, facilitators, and ad hoc arbitrators in resolving intractable territorial conflicts the more significant and difficult the dispute becomes for the contending parties to resolve by themselves.

Relevance of Norms and How to Study Them

By the end of the day (and of this book), I might have persuaded some of the agnostic readers that norms indeed do matter, by registering the "oughts" of society and by reflecting what people do or want to do. In the Latin American context norms have made a difference at least in rhetorical and discursive terms in all the cases examined in chapters 4 and 5, including failures such as the Chaco War. Moreover, norms have affected the foreign behavior of states, if not their domestic conduct. Yet, norms tend to be context- and path-dependent. That explains why it is so difficult to study in scientific terms the effects of moral norms, so we focus therefore on social conventions and practices that are not necessarily moral.

How should we study norms, or how should we recognize a norm when we see one? In chapter 1, I suggested three complementary methods to study norms: (1) an analysis of the intersubjective, social reality by the actors themselves, traced through their "discourse" in their language (such as Spanish or Portuguese) (the interpretative method); (2) a qualitative content analysis of the international norms, "translated" into instruments of international law and formal institutions/organizations in a regional context; and (3) an historical, descriptive analysis of the political behavior (essentially the foreign policies) of the states in a certain region of the world over a long period of time, according to the prescribed norms of peace and security.

This methodology is basically "vicarious" or "by proxy": We try to grasp the effects of norms by approximation, through instruments of international law (agreements, treaties, declarations, arbitration awards), by rhetorical declarations by the leaders of the different parties, as well as different narratives and stories. Hence, the impact of norms has to be assessed like a Rashomon story, bringing the version of each of the relevant parties.

In this way, even by adopting a clear neo-Grotian philosophical and theoretical position, we end by being proto-constructivists (even if we do not use their terminology or language) when we deal with the impact of international norms. We should recognize that positivism is ill suited to study norms because of its contradictory metaphysics. Positivism presupposes an "external" world of cause and effect, of independent and dependent variables. Notice, for example, that the seven hypotheses formulated in this book do not deal with the impact of norms per se, but with the conditions under which norms might make a difference. By contrast, constructivism views international relations as socially constructed, in which one cannot separate subjects from objects. The basic constructivist argument that norms constitute and shape reality (both interests and identities) is essentially correct. Therefore, we should give up our (positivist) efforts to present norms as "independent variables" and foreign policy behavior as "dependent variables." The reality is more plastic, open, and complex than that. At the same time, constructivism does not tell us exactly what to do once we reach the positivist dead-end, and here is where international law and the Grotian approach more generally can bridge ontology and epistemology, theory and praxis, metatheory and coping with real problems in the real world.

Ultimately, the statement "norms do matter" should be examined in a relative, not an absolute, perspective. They matter in relation to what? To whom? In which context? In our imperfect world, recognized as such by great political philosophers like Kant and Rousseau, we need to study norms empirically in order to grasp, if not to understand, the complexities of the political phenomena beyond the realities of power politics. At the same time, we should not conceive of international norms as simple "independent variables" in a mechanistic fashion, but rather as reasons, motivations, justifications, and rationale for states and other actors to behave in a certain way. Thus, it is not that norms cause states to behave accordingly, but rather that norms affect (impact, influence) the behavior of states in a certain prescribed, or at least desired, direction.

List of Regions and Countries

South America (12)
Argentina, Bolivia, Brazil, Chile, Colombia, Ecuador, Guyana, Paraguay, Peru, Suriname, Uruguay, and Venezuela.

Central America and the Caribbean (21)
Antigua and Barbuda, Bahamas, Barbados, Belize, Costa Rica, Cuba, Dominica, Dominican Republic, El Salvador, Grenada, Guatemala, Haiti, Honduras, Jamaica, Nicaragua, Panama, St. Christopher, St. Kitts-Nevis, St. Lucia, St. Vincent-Grenadines, and Trinidad and Tobago.

North America (3)
Canada, Mexico, and the United States

Western Europe (19)
Austria, Belgium, Cyprus, Denmark, Finland, France, Germany, Great Britain, Greece, Iceland, Ireland, Italy, Luxembourg, Malta, Netherlands, Norway, Portugal, Spain, Sweden, and Switzerland.

Australasia/Oceania (11)
Australia, Fiji, Kiribati, Naru, New Zealand, Papua New Guinea, Solomon Islands, Tonga, Tuvatu, Vanuatu, and Western Samoa.

Eastern Europe (22)
Albania, Armenia, Azerbaijan, Belarus, Bosnia, Bulgaria, Croatia, Czech Republic, Estonia, Georgia, Hungary, Latvia, Lithuania, Macedonia, Moldova, Montenegro, Poland, Russia, Serbia, Slovakia, Slovenia, and Ukraine.

Northeast Asia (7)
China, Japan, Mongolia, North Korea, Russia, South Korea, and Taiwan.

Southeast Asia (10)
Brunei, Cambodia, Indonesia, Laos, Malaysia, Myanmar, Philippines, Singapore, Thailand, and Vietnam.

South Asia (6)
Bangladesh, Bhutan, India, Nepal, Pakistan, and Sri Lanka.

Central Asia (7)
Afghanistan, Kazakhstan, Kirgizstan, Russia, Tajikistan, Turkmenistan, and Uzbekistan.

West Africa (16)
Benin, Burkina Faso, Cape Verde, Gambia, Ghana, Guinea, Guinea Bissau, Ivory Coast, Liberia, Mali, Mauritania, Niger, Nigeria, Senegal, Sierra Leone, and Togo.

North Africa (5)
Algeria, Chad, Morocco, Libya, and Tunisia.

East Africa (11)
Burundi, Eritrea, Ethiopia, Kenya, Madagascar, Mauritius, Rwanda, Somalia, Sudan, Uganda, and Tanzania.

Central Africa (6)
Cameroon, Central African Republic, Zaire, Equatorial Guinea, Gabonese Republic, and Sao Tome and Principe.

Southern Africa (10)
Angola, Botswana, Lesotho, Malawi, Mozambique, Namibia, South Africa, Swaziland, Zambia, and Zimbabwe.

Middle East (16)
Bahrain, Cyprus, Egypt, Iran, Iraq, Israel, Jordan, Kuwait, Lebanon, Oman, Qatar, Saudi Arabia, Syria, Turkey, United Arab Emirates, and Yemen.

International Wars and Territorial Disputes from 1945 to 2001

INTERNATIONAL WARS

The list does not include civil wars, interventions, and wars of decolonization ("national liberation struggles").

South America (3)
Peru-Ecuador, 1981; Falkland Islands (Argentina and United Kingdom), 1982; Peru-Ecuador, 1995.

Central America and the Caribbean (1)
El Salvador–Honduras War (Football War), 1969.

North America (0)

Western Europe (1)
Greece–Turkey (Turkish Invasion of Cyprus), 1974.

Australasia/Oceania (0)

Eastern Europe (5)
USSR-Hungary, 1956; Armenia-Azerbaijan (Nagorno-Karabakh), 1988–1994; Yugoslavia-Croatia, 1991–1995; Bosnia-Herzegovina War (Bosnia-Herzegovina, Croatia, and Yugoslavia), 1992–1995; Kosovo (NATO and Serbia), 1999.

Northeast Asia (2)
Korean War, 1950–1953; Sino-Soviet Dispute, 1969.

Southeast Asia (4)
Malaysian-Indonesian Confrontation, 1963–1966; Vietnam War, 1964–1973; Vietnam-Kampuchea War, 1978–1979; Sino-Vietnamese War, 1979.

South Asia (4)
Kashmir Dispute (First Indo-Pakistani War), 1947–1949; Sino-Indian War, 1962; Second Indo-Pakistani War, 1965; Third Indo-Pakistani War (Bangladesh War of Independence), 1971.

Central Asia (3)
Soviet-Afghan War, 1979–1989; Armenia-Azerbaijan, 1988–1994; United States and Afghanistan, 2001.

West Africa (1)
Mali–Burkina Faso, 1985.

North Africa (3)
Morocco-Algeria (War of the Sands), 1963; Saharan War, 1975– ; Libya-Chad, 1986–1987.

East Africa (5)
Ethiopia-Somalia, 1964; Kenya-Somalia (Shifta War), 1963–1967; Ogaden War (Ethiopia-Somalia War), 1977–1978; Tanzania-Uganda, 1978–1979; Ethiopia-Eritrea, 1998–2000.

Central Africa (1)
Angola-Zaire (Shaba Wars), 1977–1978.

Southern Africa (0)

Middle East (8)
First Arab-Israeli War, 1948–1949; Suez War (Second Arab-Israeli War), 1956; Six Day War (Third Arab-Israeli War), 1967; October War (Yom Kippur War, Fourth Arab-Israeli War), 1973; Lebanon War, 1976–2000; North Yemen–South Yemen Dispute, 1979; First Gulf War (Iran-Iraq War), 1980–1988; Second Gulf War (Kuwait Crisis), 1990–1991.

SIGNIFICANT TERRITORIAL DISPUTES SINCE 1945

South America (17)
Suriname-Guyana, 1975–1995; Bolivia-Chile, 1945–2001; Argentina–United Kingdom (Falkland Islands), 1945–2001; Argentina-Chile (Beagle Channel), 1945–1984; Argentina, Chile, and United Kingdom (Palmer/Antarctica), 1956–1958; Argentina-Chile (Palena), 1958–1968; Argentina-Uruguay (Rio de la Plata),

1969–1973; Bolivia-Chile (Lauca River), 1962–1964; Brazil-Paraguay (Parana River), 1962–1985; Colombia-Venezuela (Monjes Islands), 1952–1999; Colombia-Nicaragua (Archipiélago de San Andrés), 1979–1999; Peru-Ecuador (Oriente), 1945–1998; Venezuela-British Guyana (Essequibo), 1960–1970; Venezuela-Guyana (Essequibo), 1982–1999; Argentina-Chile (Continental Ice/Campo de Hielo), 1985–1994; Brazil-Uruguay, 1945–1995; Argentina-Chile (Laguna del Desierto), 1945–1994.

Central America and the Caribbean (4)
Belize-Guatemala, 1975–2001; El Salvador-Honduras, 1945–1992; Honduras-Nicaragua, 1957–2001; El Salvador, Nicaragua, and Honduras (maritime boundary), 1981–2001.

North America (4)
Canada–United States (maritime boundary), 1945–2001; Canada–United States (Gulf of Mayne), 1981–1984; Cuba–United States (Guantanamo dispute), 1960–2001; Honduras–United States (Swan Island), 1945–1991.

Western Europe (13)
Gibraltar, United Kingdom, and Spain, 1964–2001; Netherlands–Belgium (border), 1957–1959; Greece-Turkey (Aegean Sea), 1975–1999; Sweden–Denmark (Hesseloe), 1978–1984; West Germany–France (Saarland status), 1950–1957; France–United Kingdom (Minquiers and Ecrehouse), 1951–1953; Netherlands-Germany (border), 1949–1963; East Germany–Denmark, 1969–1988; Sweden–Soviet Union (Eastsee), 1969–1988; Denmark–United Kingdom (fishery dispute), 1961–1964; United Kingdom–Norway (fishery dispute), 1948–1951; Iceland-Norway (fishery dispute), 1993–1999; Iceland–United Kingdom (fishery dispute), 1952–1976.

Australasia/Oceania (0)

Eastern Europe (7)
Czech Republic, Slovakia, and Liechtenstein, 1990–1999; Greece-Albania, 1948–1949; Hungary-Slovakia (power plant Gabchikowo), 1989–1994; Poland–East Germany, 1977–1989; Soviet Union–Romania, 1964–1968; Armenia-Azerbaijan (Nagorno-Karabakh), 1988–1994; Serbia, Bosnia-Herzegovina, and Croatia, 1991–1995.

Northeast Asia (6)
China and Soviet Union/Russia, 1969–1995; China-Taiwan (Quemoy), 1954–2001; Japan and Soviet Union/Russia (Kurile Islands), 1945–2001; China, Vietnam, and Taiwan (Paracel Islands), 2001; North Korea–South Korea, 1953–2001; China–North Korea (Paektu–san Mountain), –2001.

Southeast Asia (6)
Burma-China, 1948–1960; Thailand-Cambodia, 1953–1991; Indonesia-Papua, 1960–1969; Laos-Thailand, 1975–1992; Malaysia-Philippines, 1961–1977; Brunei, China, Malaysia, Philippines, Taiwan, and Vietnam (Spartly Islands), 1974–2001.

South Asia (3)
China-India (Aksai Chin), 1954–1993; China, Pakistan, and India, 1963; India-Pakistan (Kashmir), 1947–2001.

Central Asia (3)
Iran–Soviet Union (Azerbaijan), 1945–1946; China-Kazakhstan, 1990–1993; Azerbaijan, Iran, Kazakhstan, Turkmenistan, and Russia (Caspian Sea boundaries), –2001.

West Africa (13)
Liberia-Guinea (Mount Nimba region), 1958–1960; Mali-Mauritania (Hodh desert and Savannah region), 1958–1963; Ghana–Ivory Coast, 1959–1989; Liberia-Ivory Coast, 1960; Ghana-Togo (Volta region), 1960–1994; Benin-Niger (border), 1963–1965; Upper Volta (Burkina Faso)–Mali (Agacher Strip), 1960–1988; Ghana–Upper Volta, 1964–1966; Mali-Mauritania, 1960–1963; Guinea, Guinea Bissau, and Senegal, 1998; Mauritania-Senegal, 1989–1990; Upper Volta (Burkina Faso)–Niger, 1963–1987; Dahomey-Niger (Island of Lete), 1963.

North Africa (9)
Chad-Libya (Aouzou strip), 1973–1994; Morocco-Mauritania, 1976–1979; Morocco-Algeria (Tindouf), 1963–1970; Tunisia-Algeria (Sahara), 1961–1970; Libya-Malta, 1973–1986; Tunisia-Libya, 1976–1988; Algeria-Libya, –2001; Egypt-Sudan (Hala'ib Triangle), 1945–2001; Egypt-Sudan (Wadi Halfa), 1958–1959.

East Africa (8)
Mauritius, Madagascar, and France (Tromelin), 1976–1999; Eritrea-Djibouti, 1995–1998; Eritrea-Yemen (Hanish Islands), 1995–1998; Ethiopia-Somalia (Haud and Ogaden), 1955–1989; Ethiopia-Kenya (Gadaduma), 1963–1970; Ethiopia-Sudan, 1965–1977; Uganda-Kenya, 1976–1989; Ethiopia-Eritrea, 1998–2001.

Central Africa (3)
Cameroon-Nigeria (Bakassi peninsula), 1961–2001; Zaire-Zambia (Lake Mweru), 1980–1987; Equatorial Guinea–Gabon (Corsico Bay Islands), 1972.

Southern Africa (5)
Angola, Zambia, and Zaire, 1963–1974; Malawi-Zambia, 1981–1986; Malawi-Tanzania, 1967; Mozambique, Zambia, Malawi, and Tanzania, 1966–1974; Namibia-South Africa (Walfishbay), 1977–1994.

Middle East (16)
Bahrain-Qatar (sea borders), 1967–1999; Israel-Egypt (Sinai), 1967–1979; Israel-Syria (Golan Heights), 1967–2001; Iran-Iraq (Schatt-al-Arab), 1969–1999; Iran–United Arab Emirates (Islands dispute), 1970–1999; Iraq-Kuwait, 1961–1994; Egypt, Jordan, Iraq, Syria, Lebanon, and Israel (Israel-Arab states dispute), 1948–2001; Israel-Lebanon, 1974–2000; Israel–Palestinian Authority, 1993–2001; Saudi Arabia–Kuwait (Islands dispute), 1965–1999; Yemen-Oman, 1981–1992; Oman–United Arab Emirates, 1977–1981; Saudi Arabia–Qatar, 1990–1991; Yemen–Saudi Arabia, 1992–1999; Saudi Arabia–Oman (Buraimi), 1949–1975; Turkey–Soviet Union, 1945–1947.

SIGNIFICANT VIOLENT CHANGES OF TERRITORY FROM 1945 TO 2001

As a consequence of wars, conquest, invasion, and other forms of territorial aggression; based on Zacher (2001, 225–28).

South America (0)

Central America and Caribbean (0)

North America (0)

Western Europe (1)
Turkey-Cyprus, 1974–2001 (major change).

Australasia/Oceania (0)

Eastern Europe (0)

Northeast Asia (1)
North Korea–South Korea, 1950–1953 (major change).

Southeast Asia (3)
China-Burma, 1956 (minor change); North Vietnam–South Vietnam, 1962–1975 (major change); China–South Vietnam, 1974 (major change).

South Asia (4)
Pakistan-India, 1947–1948 (major change); China-India, 1962 (major change); Pakistan-India, April 1965 (minor change); India-Pakistan (creation of Bangladesh), 1971 (major change).

Central Asia (0)

West Africa (1)
Mali–Burkina Faso, 1985 (minor change).

North Africa (0)

East Africa (0)

Central Africa (0)

Southern Africa (0)

Middle East (4)
Arab states–Israel, 1948 (major change); Israel–Arab states, 1967 (major change); Egypt and Syria–Israel, 1973 (minor change); Iran–United Arab Emirates, 1971 (major change).

CHAPTER ONE.   THE NORMATIVE DIMENSION OF INTERNATIONAL RELATIONS

1. According to Nicholas Onuf, norms as social and legal conventions are always deontological because agents encounter them in the form of ought-statements (personal correspondence with the author, July 30, 1999).

2. I thank Emanuel Adler for his comments on this issue.

3. I thank Nicholas Onuf for his insights and comments on this issue.

4. That is a useful suggestion made by Michael W. Doyle (personal correspondence, July 16, 1999).

5. See Kacowicz 2000a; Puig 1983; and Ebel, Taras, and Cochrane 1991.

6. This is Micha Bar's wonderful insight, among many others.

CHAPTER TWO.   A FRAMEWORK FOR THE THE STUDY OF
INTERNATIONAL NORMS

1. This definition has been seriously criticized by Onuf, who argues that there is nothing automatically normative about expectations (anticipating the future). In his view, "norms are social, but sharing expectations does not, by itself, make them so" (Onuf 1998, 9).

2. For other references to international norms in terms of international ethics, see Johnson 1991; Beitz 1979; Frost 1996; Hoffmann 1981; McElroy 1992.

3. According to Nicholas Onuf (1989), all norms as rules are always, simultaneously, constitutive and regulative. It is exactly this property that accounts for the co-constitution of structures and agents as a continuous and pervasive process. Moreover, all norms are always practical—they cease to exist if they are never put to use.

4. See especially Adler 1997; Wendt 1992, 1999; and Katzenstein 1996.

5. According to Franck, legitimacy can be defined as a property of a rule or rule-making institution which itself exerts a pull toward compliance on those addressed normatively (Franck 1990, 16). Thus, states comply with international norms and rules because they perceive them as having a high degree of legitimacy.

CHAPTER THREE. LATIN AMERICA AS AN INTERNATIONAL SOCIETY

1. On the "hemispheric" reference to an American international law see, *inter alia,* Alvarez 1922; Fenwick 1963; and Mares 1997, 204–5.

2. According to the Chilean jurist Alejandro Alvarez, cooperation, solidarity, and peaceful settlement were unique features of the Inter-American system, in contrast to other legal regional systems in the world (quoted in Mackenzie 1955, 435).

3. For a comprehensive list of the principles and norms of Bolivarianism, see Mackenzie 1955, 442–49; Mendoza Cubillo 1990, 106–7; and Garaicoa 1959, 50–51. The eight major points emphasized by Bolívar were (1) perpetual neutrality of the confederated states; (2) nonintervention; (3) fixed principles of international law, including peaceful settlement of disputes; (4) abolition of slavery; (5) protection of the national sovereignty and the popular will of the member-states, including the adoption of democratic principles; (6) establishment of compulsory arbitration; (7) periodical meetings of the regional Congress; and (8) the creation of a federal army and navy.

4. The Foreign Minister of Ecuador, I. Robles, appealed in 1895 to the Latin American states in a last attempt to keep Latin Americanism alive in contrast to Panamericanism, following the Bolivarian ideals. See Holguin 1945, 51; Ardao 1986, 157.

5. See especially Rodó's famous book *Ariel,* trans. F. J. Simpson (Boston: Houghton Mifflin Co., 1922).

6. On the issue of U.S. hegemony and the South American peace, see McIntyre 1993, 3–4; Kacowicz 1998, 89–91; R.Pastor 1992, 22–25.

7. On the Latin American "legalistic culture," see Holsti 1996, 171; Karst and Rosenn 1975, 58–65; Ebel and Taras 1990, 195–200; Dealy 1984/1985, 109–11; Eisenstadt 1998, 257; Becker 1997, 5, 16; Eder 1959, 1–5; and De Vries 1972, 2.

8. A more comprehensive list of norms and rules, as general principles of Inter-American (and Latin American) law include the following: (1) mutual respect for sovereignty and independence; (2) equality of states; (3) nonintervention; (4) international law as the standard of conduct; (5) observance of treaties; (6) repudiation of the use of force; (7) peaceful settlement of international disputes; (8) mutual defense; (9) principles of economic, social, and cultural cooperation; (10) recognition of the fundamental human rights; and (11) right of resistance (based on Fenwick 1963, 134–50). Other norms were previously mentioned under the general principles of Bolivarianism.

9. Briefly, the Calvo Doctrine stated that "America as well as Europe is inhabited today by free and independent nations, whose sovereign existence has the right to the same respect, and whose internal public law does not admit of intervention of any sort on the part of foreign peoples, whoever they may be" (Carlos Calvo 1896, 350; quoted in De Vries and Rodríguez-Novas 1965, 99). Similarly, the Drago Doctrine of 1903 stated that "the public debt [of an American state] cannot occasion armed intervention nor even the actual occupation of the territory of American nations by a European power" (quoted in De Vries and Rodríguez-Novas 1965, 102–3).

CHAPTER FOUR. NORMS OF PEACE: PEACEFUL SETTLEMENT AND *UTI POSSIDETIS*

1. For a general analysis of the absence of wars in South America and the reference to South America as a "zone of peace," see Kacowicz 1998, 67–124.

2. See the text of the 1826 Treaty at http://www.mundolatino.org/i/politica/ Tratados/congpana.htm ("Tratado de Unión, Liga y Confederación Perpetua"). The text of the Gondra Treaty is found in Harley 1934, 387–91 ("Treaty to Avoid or Prevent Conflicts between the American States"). As for the Anti-War Treaty of Non-Aggression and Conciliation (Saavedra Lamas Pact), see Harley 1934, 590–94 ("South American Anti-War Treaty Relating to Non-Aggression and Conciliation"). The pact condemned wars of aggression and obliged signatories not to recognize territorial arrangements brought about by force of arms or not obtained by peaceful means.

3. We will continue to see the effects of *uti possidetis* in international law by states that request a convenient solution to their border disputes, such as in the future case of the Israeli-Syrian dispute over the Golan Heights. I thank Moshe Abalo for his suggestions on this point.

4. See the text of this treaty ("Reconocimiento del territorio litigioso con el Brasil y de los cuatro ríos que lo comprenden") in Argentina 1901, 274–81; and in Zeballos 1893, 113–17.

5. See text of the treaty ("Tratado del Arbitraje con el Brasil para solucionar la cuestión de límites") in Argentina 1901, 347–50; and in Zeballos 1893, 119–21.

6. On December 4, 1889, Argentina was the first country that recognized the new Republic of the United States of Brazil. As the Argentine Foreign Minister, Zeballos, stated: "The new Republic was looked upon, in America and in Europe, with reserve. The Argentine government hastened to produce an act which broke such vacillations, initiating, at the same, a transcendental South American policy with regard to the November [Brazilian] revolution" (Zeballos 1893, 730).

7. In his argument Zeballos quoted Dr. Irigoyen as follows: ". . . in reference to states whose titles are derived from international contracts, in which the rivers and points of division have been designated, it seems to me impossible a stipulation founded upon the *uti possidetis,* which is only acceptable when, in the absence of fixed limits, the possession is provisorily or definitively sanctioned" (Zeballos 1893, 665–66).

8. After the award, Zeballos recognized that "Brazil has collected the fruits of its diplomatic tradition." He also added that "there is no reason that the result of the arbitral award will raise popular preoccupations regarding the victor [Brazil]. The award should serve to consolidate the community of [common] political and commercial interests between the parties" (quoted in Silva 1946, 195; my translation). Similarly, Argentine President Uriburu declared to the Congress in 1895 that "the [Argentine] Government has accepted the award, which terminates the conflict. In this way, the lack of understanding has ended in a proper way, according to the culture of both parties, so we can expect the good relations to even improve in favor of the important common interests that link both countries" (quoted in Silva 1946, 196; my translation).

9. Article 3 of the Treaty of Ancón (celebrated at Lima, on October 20, 1883) reads as follows: "The territory of the provinces of Tacna and Arica . . . shall continue in the possession of Chile subject to Chilean laws and authority during a period of ten years, to be reckoned from the date of the ratification of the present treaty of peace. That term expired, a plebiscite will decide by popular vote whether the territory of the above-mentioned provinces is to remain definitively under the dominion and sovereignty of Chile or is to continue to constitute a part of Peru" (quoted in Dennis 1967, 297–98).

10. The Protocol of Submission to Arbitration and Supplementary Agreement of July 20, 1922, stipulated: "It is hereby recorded that the only difficulties arising out of the Treaty of Peace [of 1883] regarding which the two countries have not been able to reach an agreement, are the questions arising out of the unfulfilled stipulations of Article III of said Treaty" (quoted in Dennis 1967, 307).

11. According to Coolidge, "From an examination of the history of the negotiations the Arbitrator is unable to find any proper basis for the conclusion that Chile acted in bad faith. The record fails to show that Chile has ever arbitrarily refused to negotiate with Peru the terms of the plebiscitary protocol. . . . The Arbitrator is far from approving the course of Chilean administration and condoning the acts committed against Peruvians to which reference has been made, but finds no reason to conclude that a fair plebiscite in the present circumstances cannot be held under proper conditions or that a plebiscite should not be held . . ." (Coolidge 1925, 312 and 314).

12. In the presentation of its case to the U.S. arbitration, the Peruvians argued as follows: ". . . the plebiscite was not carried out at the proper time [in 1894], because the Chilean Government evidently found it to its interest not to have the plebiscite held at the time the Treaty provided and interposed obstacles to the timely execution of the Treaty, and has since that time [1894], initiated and pursued measures of oppression and coercion in the occupied territory of Tacna and Arica by driving out numberless Peruvian inhabitants, suppressing all Peruvian influences and subsidizing the introduction of a Chilean population; and that 'the present circumstances' have through Chile's arbitrary action over a period of thirty years and the death of many of the inhabitants of the territories living in 1894, so vastly changed over those of 1894 contemplated by the Treaty, that a plebiscite under the 'present circumstances' prevailing in the territory would be not an execution but a mockery of the Treaty of Ancón" (quoted in Peru 1923, 21).

13. "For the whole of America, the future of her growing nations, there can be no uncertainty; they need the stabilizing influence of a just and moral precedent. The present is not a litigation in which two interests contend with arguments more or less deserving of attention. It is a conflict the solution of which calls for neither compromise nor compensations. On the one hand, we have a wrong effected by physical force; on the other, a right ruthlessly ignored. This is the essence of the case" (Peru 1923, 254).

14. On August 3, 1932, representatives of every nation in the Western Hemisphere, except the two belligerents, signed a document that stated: "The nations of America declare that the dispute in the Chaco is capable of peaceful solution . . . that they will not recognize any territorial arrangements in this controversy that are not obtained by peaceful means, nor the validity of acquisitions obtained by occupation or conquest by force of arms" (quoted in Farcau 1996, 44).

15. This rationale reminds us of the surprise attack of Iraq on Iran in September of 1980 that led to a virulent nine-year war.

16. According to the Peruvian representative to the Council of the League of Nations, "Peru is not the aggressor. The events at Leticia, the expulsion—without bloodshed—of the Colombian authorities, took it by surprise. A group of Peruvians, urged by an excess of patriotism and giving violent expression to public opinion in

the country, which condemned the Salomon-Lozano Treaty, seized a Peruvian town founded by the Peruvians more than a century ago, of which Colombia took possession only two years ago, in 1930" (quoted in Windass 1970, 78).

17. Editorial of *El Comercio* (Lima), March 3, 1933, quoted and translated in Wood 1966, 216.

18. Letter from Alfonso López to President Benavides, May 10, 1933, in López 1936, 22–24; my translation.

19. This position was articulated by Senator Laureano Gómez at the Colombian Congress in a motion presented as follows: "(1) Colombia does not have any pending boundary dispute; (2) By defending the inviolability of public treaties against acts of violence, Colombia sustained the common cause of all the civilized nations on earth. Hence, until the aggression in Leticia is reversed and Colombia regains the exercise of its exclusive sovereignty over the totality of its territory, there is no room for diplomatic negotiations about the revision of treaties; (3) Colombia will never accept, under conditions of peace or war, to lose its Amazonic border, to which the honor and vital interests of the nation are linked" (quoted in Gómez 1934, 37–38; my translation).

20. In his letter to the Foreign Minister of Peru, Stimson argued: ". . . There is no dispute between the two parties regarding the present ownership of Leticia. This was recognized by Peru in the Treaty of 1922 as belonging to Colombia and your Government now affirms again its view that this Treaty is valid. [Yet] your Government now desires a future modification of the frontier line which would transfer Leticia to Peru in return for 'adequate territorial compensations.' As pointed out, that, under Article II of the Briand-Kellogg Pact, can be sought only by pacific means. . . . For if it were conceivable that Peru was seeking to obtain her desire to modify the Treaty of 1922, not by pacific means, but by a forcible and armed support of the illegal occupation of Leticia, would such a position not be entirely contrary to the provisions of Article II of the Kellogg-Briand Pact, which provides that no solution of a controversy shall be sought except by pacific means?" (Text of Secretary Stimson's Note to the Foreign Minister of Peru Regarding the Application of the Pact of Paris to the Dispute between Colombia and Peru concerning Leticia; Washington, DC, January 25, 1933; quoted in Harley 1934, 568–73).

21. Unfortunately, political assassination can fulfill the opposite role of derailing an ongoing peace process, as in the case of the death of Israeli Prime Minister Yitzhak Rabin on November 4, 1995.

22. Letter from López to Benavides, May 2, 1933; letter from Benavides to López, May 8, 1933; quoted in López 1936, 19–22 (my translation). The Bolivarian nations are Peru, Colombia, Venezuela, Ecuador, and Bolivia.

23. For instance, Peru argued, "The fulfillment of international treaties, according to the norms of international law, cannot be subjected to the will of one of the parties" (Luis Alvarado, in Peru 1961, 50; my translation).

24. Article 4 of the Presidential Act of Brasilia states: "They [Peru and Ecuador] recognize the importance of the agreements achieved for the ideals of peace, stability, and prosperity which animate the American Continent. For that reason and in conformity with Article I of the Protocol of Peace, Friendship and Boundaries of Rio de Janeiro of 1942, they solemnly reaffirm the renunciation of threat and the use of

force in relations between Peru and Ecuador, as well as every act which might affect the peace and friendship between the two nations" (quoted in Marcella 1999, 245).

25. The reader should be warned that, unlike the other cases depicted in this chapter and chapter 5, I was a direct participant in this dispute, as a former Argentine conscript soldier in the years 1978–1979. I was mobilized to Junín de los Andes, Neuquén, not far from the Chilean border, as a member of the 10th Infantry Brigade, between November 1978 and January 1979. I am thus particularly thankful to the providence and to the pope for avoiding a futile war that would have cost the lives of thousands of youngsters, perhaps including my own.

26. The Treaty of Limits between Chile and Argentina of July 23, 1881, established in its Article 3 that "Tierra del Fuego will be Chilean in its Western sector and Argentine in its Eastern sector . . . the Islands to the East of Tierra del Fuego [belong] to Argentina; Chile [owns] the Islands to the South of the Beagle Channel and to the West of Tierra del Fuego" (quoted in *Revista Chilena* 1984, 182, my translation).

27. Article 8 states: "The Parties agree that, within the area comprised between Cape Horn and the easternmost portion of Staten Island, the legal effects of the territorial sea shall be restricted, in their mutual relations, to three marine miles, measured from their respective base lines. Within the area indicated above each Party may invoke the maximum breadth of territorial sea allowed by International Law in regard to third-party States" (quoted in Nordquist 1992, 123).

CHAPTER FIVE.   NORMS OF SECURITY: ARMS CONTROL,
CONFIDENCE-BUILDING MEASURES, AND COMMON SECURITY

1. In the words of Cesar Gaviria, the General Secretary of the OAS, "Since 1995 we can point to a series of events: Ecuador and Peru moving in the direction of peace; the signing of a Treaty of Democratic Security in Central America; a treaty on military cooperation signed between Argentina and Brazil, including joint maneuvers; the announcement of Argentina and Chile of joint military exercises. . . . All those events show a tendency in the Hemisphere towards dialogue and peaceful settlement of conflicts; the search for confidence; and the consolidation of important processes of cooperation in the subject of security" (Gaviria 1998, my translation).

2. According to Article 3 of the Rio Pact, "The High Contracting Parties agree that an armed attack by any State against an American State shall be considered as an attack against all the American States and, consequently, each one of the said Contracting Parties undertakes to assist in meeting the attack in the exercise of the inherent right of individual or collective self-defense recognized by Article 51 of the Charter of the UN (quoted in Atkins 1997, 270).

3. On the idea of Latin American as a potential or tangible pluralistic security community, see Kacowicz 1998, 118–21; Kacowicz 2000b. Latin America as a "zone of peace" (ZOP) is analyzed and criticized in, among others, Palma 1992; Varas 1992, 83–85; Mercado Jarrín 1989, 94–97; and Mares 1994, 273. Mares suggests that a ZOP resembles true collective security arrangements, linked to elements of democratization, integration, and common security.

4. The complete list of the issues and procedures "to establish steady and long-standing peace in Central America" include (1) national reconciliation (dialogue, amnesty, and the establishment of national reconciliation committees); (2) exhortation toward a cease-fire; (3) democratization; (4) free elections; (5) cease of aid to irregular forces and to rebels; (6) restriction on the use of the territory of one state to attack other states; (7) negotiations concerning security matters, verification, control and restriction of armaments; (8) refugees and displaced persons; (9) cooperation, democracy, and freedom for peace and development; (10) international verification and f–ollow-up; and (11) schedule for execution of commitments (Arias 1987, 13–18, my translation).

5. The Contadora Act for Peace and Cooperation in Central America (1984) includes in its Preamble the clause that "the achievement of genuine regional stability depends on the adoption of agreements on security and disarmament questions . . ." Moreover, "agreements on regional security must be subject to an effective system for verification and control" (Bagley et al. 1985, 190–91).

CHAPTER SIX.   LATIN AMERICAN NORMS IN A COMPARATIVE PERSPECTIVE

1. I thank Michal Lewin-Epstein for her research assistance and compilation of Tables 6.5 and 6.6., as well as the appendices.

2. Micha Bar, personal correspondence with the author, April 23, 1998.

Acevedo, Domingo E., and Claudio Grossman. 1996. "The Organization of American States and the Protection of Democracy." In *Beyond Sovereignty,* edited by Tom Farer, pp. 133–49. Baltimore, MD: Johns Hopkins University Press.

Acuña Pimentel, Jaime. 1995. "Nuevas Propuestas de Seguridad en América Latina." In *Chile y Brasil,* edited by Francisco Aravena, pp. 85–91. Santiago, Chile: CLADDE-FLACSO.

Adler, Emanuel. 1991. "Cognitive Evolution: A Dynamic Approach for the Study of International Relations and Their Progress." In *Progress in Postwar International Relations,* edited by Emanuel Adler and Beverly Crawford, pp. 43–88. New York: Columbia University Press.

———. 1997. "Seizing the Middle Ground: Constructivism in World Politics." *European Journal of International Relations* 3, no. 3 (September): 319–63.

———, and Michael Barnett, eds. 1998. *Security Communities.* Cambridge: Cambridge University Press.

Alvarez, Alejandro. 1922. *International Law and Related Subjects from the Point of View of the American Continent.* Washington, DC: Carnegie Endowment.

Amescua, Ernesto C. 1986. *La Alternativa Iberoamericana.* Madrid: Ediciones Daimón de México.

Aravena, Francisco Rojas. 1992. "Los Acuerdos de Paz en Centroamérica y los Nuevos Paradigmas de la Cooperación para la Paz." In *Seguridad, Paz, y Desarme,* edited by Augusto Varas, pp. 145–66. Santiago, Chile: CLADDE-FLACSO.

———. 1994a. "Security Regimes in the Western Hemisphere: A View from Latin America." In *Security, Democracy, and Development in US-Latin American Relations,* edited by Lars Schoultz et al., pp. 171–97. Miami: North-South Center.

———. 1994b. "Esquipulas: Un Proceso de Construcción de Confianza." In *Medidas de Confianza Mutua en América Latina,* edited by Augusto Varas and Isaac Caro, pp. 73–99. Santiago, Chile: FLACSO.

Ardao, Arturo. 1986. "Panamericanismo y Latinoamericanismo." In *América Latina en sus Ideas,* edited by Leopoldo Zea, pp. 157–71. Mexico, DF: Siglo XXI Editores.

Arend, Anthony C. 1997. "Legal Rules and International Politics: A Constructivist Approach." Paper presented at the annual meeting of the International Studies Association, Toronto, March 19.

Argentina. 1901. *Tratados, Convenciones, Protocolos y Demás Actos Internacionales Vigentes (Publicación Oficial).* Buenos Aires: Imprenta La Nación.

———, Congreso Nacional. 1988. *Antecedentes: Documentos y Tratados que Versan sobre Cuestiones Limítrofes Argentino-Chilenas, en Particular Acerca de las Suscitadas en la*

Zona Austral y Especialmente en cuanto al Canal de Beagle. Buenos Aires: Biblioteca del Congreso de la Nación, Dirección de Referencia Legislativa.

Arias, Oscar S. 1987. *Procedimiento Para Establecer la Paz Firma y Duradera en Centroamerica.* San José, Costa Rica: Oficina de Apoyo de la Presidencia de la República.

———. 1997. "Esquipulas II: The Management of a Regional Crisis." In *Cultural Variation in Conflict Resolution: Alternatives to Violence,* edited by Douglas P. Fry and Kaj Bjorkqvist, pp. 147–58, Mahwah, NJ: Lawrence Erlbaum Associates.

Atkins, G. Pope. 1995. *Latin America in the International Political System.* 3rd ed. Boulder, CO: Westview Press.

———. 1997. *Encyclopedia of the Inter-American System.* Westport, CT: Greenwood Books.

Axelrod, Robert. 1986. "An Evolutionary Approach to Norms." *American Political Science Review* 80, no. 4 (December): 1095–1111.

Bachler, Samuel Durán. 1975. "La Doctrina Latinoamericana del *Uti Possidetis.*" *Atenea,* no. 432: 261–324.

———. 1976. "La Doctrina Latinoamericana del *Uti Possidetis* (II Parte)." *Atenea,* no. 433: 217–72.

Bagley, Bruce M. 1986. *Contadora: The Limits of Negotiation.* Washington, DC: Johns Hopkins University, Latin American Studies Program, SAIS.

———, Roberto Alvarez, and Katherine J. Hagedorn, eds. 1985. *Contadora and the Central American Process: Selected Documents.* Boulder, CO: Westview Press.

Bailey, Norman A. 1967. *Latin America in World Politics.* New York: Walker.

Barahona Riera, Francisco. 1987. "Situación Actual de los Acuerdos de Limitación de Armamentos y Desarme en América Latina y el Caribe." In *Paz, Desarme, y Desarrollo en América Latina,* edited by Augusto Varas, pp. 289–305. Buenos Aires: Grupo Editor Latinoamericano (GEL).

Barkun, Michael. 1964. "International Norms: An Interdisciplinary Approach." *Background* 8, no. 2 (August): 121–30.

Barletta, Michael. 1997. "The Legitimate Imposition of Transparency: Emergence of an Argentine-Brazilian Nuclear Regime." Paper presented at the annual meeting of the International Studies Association, Toronto, March 20.

Barnett, Michael N. 1997. "Bringing in the New World Order: Liberalism, Legitimacy, and the United Nations." *World Politics* 49, no. 4 (July): 526–51.

Barros, Jayme de. 1938. *Ocho Años de Política Exterior del Brasil.* Rio de Janeiro: DNP.

Barros van Buren, Mario. 1970. *Historia Diplomática de Chile, 1541–1938.* 2nd ed. Santiago, Chile: Editorial Andrés Bello.

Beck, Robert J. 1996. "International Law and International Relations: The Prospects for Interdisciplinary Collaboration." In *International Rules: Approaches from International Law and International Relations,* edited by Robert J. Beck, Anthony C. Arend, and Robert D. Vander Lugt, pp. 3–33. Oxford: Oxford University Press.

Becker, David G. 1997. "The Rule of Law in Latin America: A Framework for Analysis." Paper presented at the 1997 annual meeting of the American Political Science Association, Washington, DC, August 28–31.

Beitz, Charles R. 1979. *Political Theory and International Relations.* Princeton, NJ: Princeton University Press.

Benavídes Correa, Alfonso. 1988. *Una Difícil Vecindad: Los Irrenunciables Derechos del Perú en Arica y los Recursables Acuerdos Peruanos-Chilenos de 1985.* Lima: Universidad Nacional Mayor de San Marcos, Editorial de la Universidad.

Bicchieri, Cristina. 1990. "Norms of Cooperation." *Ethics* 100, no. 4 (July): 838–61.

Blix, Hans. 1997. "Statement by the Director General of the IAEA, on the Occasion of the 30th Anniversary of the Tlatelolco Treaty." http://www.opanal.org/Articles/Aniv-30/blix.htm. Agency for the Prohibition of Nuclear Weapons in Latin America and the Caribbean (OPANAL).

Bocco, Héctor Eduardo. 1989. "La Cooperación Nuclear Argentina-Brasil: Notas Para una Educación Política." *FLACSO—Serie de Documentos e Informes de Investigación,* no. 82 (October).

Brigagão, Clovis, and Marcelo F. Valle. 1996. "Argentina-Brasil: Modelo Regional de Confianza Mutua Para la Seguridad Nuclear." In *Integración Solidaria: América Latina en la Era de la Globalización,* edited by Ana Carrillo, pp. 87–101. Caracas: Instituto de Altos Estudios de América Latina.

Brooke, James. 1994. "The New South Americans: Friends or Partners?" *New York Times,* April 8.

Brown, Chris. 1995. "International Theory and International Society: The Viability of the Middle Way?" *Review of International Studies* 21, no. 2 (April): 183–96.

Bull, Hedley. 1966. "The Grotian Conception of International Society." In *Diplomatic Investigations: Essays in the Theory of International Politics,* edited by Herbert Butterfield and Martin Wight, pp. 51–73. London: George Allen and Unwin.

———. 1977. *The Anarchical Society: A Study of Order in World Politics.* London: Macmillan.

Burley, Anne-Marie. 1992. "Law and the Liberal Paradigm in International Relations Theory." *Proceedings of the 86th Annual Meeting of the American Society of International Law.* Washington, DC, April 1–4, pp. 180–85.

Burr, Robert N. 1965. *By Reason or Force: Chile and the Balancing of Power in South America, 1830–1905.* Berkeley: University of California Press.

Butterworth, Robert L. 1976. *Managing Interstate Conflict, 1945–1974: Data with Synopses.* Pittsburgh: University Center for International Studies, University of Pittsburgh.

Buzan, Barry. 1993. "From International System to International Society: Structural Realism and Regime Theory Meet the English School." *International Organization* 47, no. 3 (Summer): 327–52.

Calvert, Peter. 1983. "Boundary Disputes in Latin America." *Conflict Studies* 146: 3–28.

Carasales, Julio C. 1987. *El Desarme de los Desarmados: Argentina y el Tratado de No Proliferación de Armas Nucleares.* Buenos Aires: Pleamar.

———. 1992. "En el Final de Un Largo Camino: Argentina y Tlatelolco." *America Latina/Internacional* 9, no. 32 (April–June): 497–502.

———. 1996. "A Surprising About-Face: Argentina and the NPT." *Security Dialogue* 27, no. 3 (September): 325–35.

Caro, Isaac. 1994. "Cooperación Pacífica y Medidas de Confianza Mutua en Chile." In *Medidas de Confianza Mutua en América Latina,* edited by Augusto Varas and Isaac Caro, pp. 189–201. Santiago, Chile: FLACSO.

Carr, Edward H. 1964. *The Twenty Years' Crisis, 1919–1939: An Introduction to the Study of International Relations.* 3rd ed. New York: Harper and Row.

Carrasco, German. 1978. *Argentina y el Laudo Arbitral del Canal Beagle*. Santiago, Chile: Editorial Jurídica de Chile.

Carrión Mena, Francisco. 1989. *Política Exterior del Ecuador: Evolución, Teoría, Práctica*. Quito, Ecuador: Editorial Universitaria.

Cavagnari Filho, Gerardo Lesbat. 1990. "Brasil-Argentina: Autonomía Estratégica y Cooperación Militar." In *Argentina-Brazil: Perspectivas Comparativas y Eje de Integración*, edited by Mónica Hirst, pp. 315–38. Buenos Aires: Tesis.

Centeno, Miguel Angel. 2002. *Blood and Debt: War and the Nation-State in Latin America*. University Park: Pennsylvania State University Press.

Checkel, Jeffrey T. 1997. "International Norms and Domestic Politics: Bridging the Rationalist-Constructivist Divide." *European Journal of International Relations* 3, no. 4 (December): 473–95.

———. 1998. "The Constructivist Turn in International Relations Theory: A Review Essay." *World Politics* 50, no. 2 (January): 324–48.

Child, Jack. 1985. *Geopolitics and Conflict within South America: Quarrels among Neighbors*. New York: Praeger.

———. 1992. *The Central American Peace Process, 1983–1991: Sheathing Swords, Building Confidence*. Boulder, CO: Lynne Rienner.

———. 1996. "Peacekeeping, Confidence-Building." In *Beyond Praetorianism: The Latin American Military in Transition*, edited by Richard L. Millett and Michael Gold-Bis, pp. 11–35. Miami: North-South Center.

Chile. 1923. *Tacna-Arica Arbitration: The Case of the Republic of Chile*. Washington, DC: National Capital Press.

Claude, Inis L. 1966. "Collective Legitimization as a Political Function of the United Nations." *International Organization* 20, no. 3 (Summer): 367–79.

Clissold, Stephan, and Alistair Hennesy. 1968. "Territorial Disputes." In *Latin America and the Caribbean*, edited by Claudio Veliz, pp. 403–12. New York: Praeger.

Colombia, Legación en España de. 1933. *Un Gran Triunfo de Colombia*. Madrid: Imprenta de Juan Pueyo.

Consejo Argentino para las Relaciones Internacionales (CARI). 1995. *Las Relaciones Argentino-Chilenas: Política Económica, Exterior y de Defensa*. Buenos Aires: CARI.

Coolidge, Calvin. 1925. *Arbitration Award and Opinion of President Coolidge*. Washington, DC: n.p.

Cortell, Andrew P., and James W. Davis. 1996. "How Do International Institutions Matter? The Domestic Impact of International Rules and Norms." *International Studies Quarterly* 40, no. 4 (December): 451–78.

———. 1997. "Understanding the Domestic Legitimacy of International Norms and Institutions." Paper presented at the annual meeting of the American Political Science Association, Washington, DC, August 28–31.

Cukwurah, A. O. 1967. *The Settlement of Boundary Disputes in International Law*. Manchester, England: Manchester University Press.

Cutler, A. Claire. 1991. "The 'Grotian Tradition' in International Relations." *Review of International Studies* 17, no. 1 (January): 41–65.

Davis, Harold E. 1959. "Latin American Political Experience: An Essay in Interpretation." In *A Symposium on the Law of Latin America*, edited by the Washington Foreign Law Society, pp. 6–21. Washington, DC: Washington Foreign Law Society.

Day, Alan, ed. 1982. *Border and Territorial Disputes*. Harlow, England: Longman.

Dealy, Glen C. 1984/1985. "The Pluralistic Latins." *Foreign Policy* 57 (Winter): 108–27.

———. 1992. *The Latin Americans: Spirit and Ethos*. Boulder, CO: Westview Press.

De la Balze, Felipe M. 1995. "Argentina y Brasil: Enfrentando el Siglo XXI." In *Argentina y Brasil: Enfrentando el Siglo XXI*, edited by Felipe M. de la Balze, pp. 13–130. Buenos Aires: LARI.

Delgado Jara, Diego. 1985. *Problema Territorial: Oligarquía y Pueblo*. Cuenca, Ecuador: Universidad de Cuenca.

Denegri Luna, Félix. 1996. *Perú y Ecuador: Apuntes para la Historia de Una Frontera*. Lima: Bolsa de Valores, Instituto Riva-Agüero, Universidad Pontificia Católica del Perú.

Dennis, William J. 1967. *Tacna and Arica: An Account of the Chile-Peru Boundary Dispute and of the Arbitration by the United States*. Hamden, CT: Archon Books.

De Vries, Henry P. 1972. *Cases and Materials on the Law of the Americas: An Outline of Latin American Law and Society*. New York: Inter-American Law Center, Columbia University.

———, and José Rodríguez-Novas. 1965. *The Law of the Americas: An Introduction to the Legal Systems of the American Republics*. Dobbs Ferry, NY: Oceana Publications.

Diamint, Rut. 1994. "La Seguridad Estratégica Regional y las Medidas de Confianza Mutua Pensadas desde Argentina." In *Medidas de Confianza Mutua en América Latina*, edited by Augusto Varas and Isaac Caro, pp. 141–63. Santiago, Chile: FLACSO.

———. 1998. "Política de Seguridad Argentina, Estabilidad Democrática, y Regímenes Internacionales." Paper presented at the meeting of the Latin American Studies Association, Chicago, September 24–26.

Díaz Callejas, Apolinar. 1985. *Contadora: Desafío al Imperio*. Bogotá: Editorial Oveja Negra.

Docampo, César. 1993. "El Acuerdo Argentino-Brasileño Para el Control Mutuo del Material Nuclear y La Plena Vigencia del Tratado de Tlatelolco." *Serie Documentos de Trabajo EURAL*, no. 147.

Donadio, Alberto. 1995. *La Guerra con el Perú*. Bogotá: Planeta.

Downes, Richard. 1998. "Building New Security Relationships in the Americas: The Critical Next Steps." In *The Role of the Armed Forces in the Americas: Civil-Military Relations for the 21st Century*, edited by Donald E. Schultz, pp. 13–30. Carlisle Barrachs, PA: Strategic Studies Institute.

Druetta, Gustavo, and Luis Tibiletti. 1993. "La Seguridad Estratégica Regional en el Cono Sur." In *Cambios Globales y América Latina*, edited by Isaac Caro, pp. 53–60. Santiago, Chile: CLADDE-FLACSO.

Dunne, Timothy. 1995. "The Social Construction of International Society." *European Journal of International Relations* 1, no. 3 (September): 367–89.

Durán, Esperanza. 1984. "La Solución de Contadora para el Logro de la Paz en Centroamérica." *Estudios Internacionales* 17, no. 6 (October–December): 537–47.

Ebel, Roland H., and Raymond Taras. 1990. "Cultural Style and International Policy-Making: The Latin American Tradition." In *Culture and International Relations*, edited by Jongsuk Chay, pp. 191–206. New York: Praeger.

———, and James D. Cochrane. 1991. *Political Culture and Foreign Policy in Latin America: Case Studies from the Circum-Caribbean*. Albany: State University of New York Press.

Ecuador, Ministerio de Relaciones Exteriores. 1938. *Las Negociaciones Ecuatorianas-Peruanas en Washington, Agosto 1937–Octubre 1938*. Volume 2. Quito, Ecuador: Imprenta del Ministerio de Gobierno.

Eder, Phanor. 1959. "Common and Civil Law Concepts in the Western Hemisphere." In *A Symposium on the Law of Latin America*, pp. 1–5. Washington, DC: Washington Foreign Law Society.

Eisenstadt, Shmuel N. 1998. "The Construction of Collective Identities in Latin America: Beyond the European Nation-State Model." In *Constructing Collective Identities and Shaping Public Spheres: Latin American Paths*, edited by Luis Roniger and Mario Sznajder, pp. 245–63. Brighton, England: Sussex Academic Press.

Elster, Jon. 1989. *The Cement of Society*. New York: Cambridge University Press.

Errázuriz Guilisasti, Octavio. 1968. *Las Relaciones Chileno-Argentinas Durante la Presidencia de Riesco, 1901–1906*. Santiago, Chile: Editorial Andrés Bello.

Espíndola, Roberto. 1998. "Integration or Conflict: Foreign Policy Prospects in Latin America." Paper presented at the 39th annual meeting of the International Studies Association, Minneapolis, March 17–21.

Espinosa Moraga, Oscar. 1969. *El Precio de la Paz Chileno-Argentina, 1810–1969*. Santiago, Chile: Editorial Nascimento.

Etchepareborda, Roberto. 1982. *Zeballos y la Política Exterior Argentina*. Buenos Aires: Pleamar.

Farcau, Bruce W. 1996. *The Chaco War: Bolivia and Paraguay, 1932–1935*. Westpoint, CT: Praeger.

Fenwick, Charles G. 1963. *The Organization of American States: The Inter-American Regional System*. Washington, DC: Kaufmann Printing.

Ferrari, Gustavo. 1969. *Conflicto y Paz con Chile, 1898–1903*. Buenos Aires: Eudeba.

Finnemore, Martha. 1996. *National Interests in International Society*. Ithaca, NY: Cornell University Press.

———, and Kathryn Sikkink. 1998. "International Norms, Dynamics, and Political Change." *International Organization* 50, no. 2 (Autumn): 887–917.

Florini, Ann. 1996. "The Evolution of International Norms." *International Studies Quarterly* 40, no. 3 (September): 363–89.

Franck, Thomas M. 1990. *The Power of Legitimacy among Nations*. Oxford: Oxford University Press.

———. 1995. *Fairness in International Law and Institutions*. Oxford: Clarendon Press.

Frohmann, Alicia. 1990. *Puentes sobre la Turbulencia: La Concertación Política Latinoamericana en los Ochenta*. Santiago, Chile: FLACSO.

———. 1994a. "Consenso Político y Diplomacia Colectiva: De Contadora al Grupo de Río." In *Cambio de Paradigmas en América Latina: Nuevos Impulsos, Nuevos Temores*, edited by H. Mols et al., pp. 141–52. Caracas: Nueva Sociedad.

———. 1994b. "Regional Initiatives for Peace and Democracy: The Collective Diplomacy of the Rio Group." In *Collective Responses to Regional Problems: The Case of Latin America and the Caribbean*, edited by Carl Kaysen, Robert A. Pastor, and Laura W. Reed, pp. 129–41. Cambridge, MA: American Academy of Arts and Science.

Frost, Mervyn. 1996. *Ethics in International Relations: A Constitutive Theory*. Cambridge: Cambridge University Press.

Garaicoa, Teodoro Alvarado. 1959. "El Derecho Bolivariano." In *Latinoamérica y el Derecho Internacional Americano,* edited by Secretaría General de la Undécima Conferencia Interamericana, pp. 45–59. Quito, Ecuador: Editorial La Unión Católica.

García-Amador, F. V., ed. 1983. *The Inter-American System: Treaties, Conventions, and Other Documents.* New York: Oceana Publications.

Garner, William R. 1966. *The Chaco Dispute: A Study of Prestige Diplomacy.* Washington, DC: Public Affairs Press.

Garrett, James L. 1985. "The Beagle Channel Dispute: Confrontation and Negotiation in the Southern Cone." *Journal of Interamerican Studies and World Affairs* 27, no. 3 (Fall): 81–109.

Gaviria, César. 1998. "Tercera Conferencia de Ministros de Defensa de las Americas." In Organization of American States. http://www.oas.org/EN/PINFO/SG/113098.htm. Cartagena, November 30. Accessed on May 22, 2001.

Gilpin, Robert. 1981. *War and Change in World Politics.* Cambridge: Cambridge University Press.

Glick, Edward B. 1965. "The Non-Military Use of the Latin American Military." In *Latin America,* edited by Norman Bailey, pp. 179–91. New York: Praeger.

Goertz, Gary. 1994. *Contexts of International Politics.* Cambridge: Cambridge University Press.

——— , and Paul Diehl. 1992. "Toward a Theory of International Norms: Some Conceptual and Measurement Issues." *Journal of Conflict Resolution* 36, no. 4 (December): 634–64.

——— . 1994. "International Norms and Power Politics." In *Reconstructing Realpolitik,* edited by Frank W. Wayman and Paul F. Diehl, pp. 101–22. Ann Arbor: University of Michigan Press.

Golbert, Albert S., and Yenny Nun. 1982. *Latin American Laws and Institutions.* New York: Praeger.

Goldemberg, José, and Harold A. Feiveson. 1994. "Denuclearization in Argentina and Brazil." *Arms Control Today* 24, no. 2 (March): 10–14.

Goldstein, Erik. 1992. *Wars and Peace Treaties, 1816–1991.* London: Routledge.

Goldstein, Judith, and Robert O. Keohane. 1993. "Ideas and Foreign Policy: An Analytical Framework." In *Ideas and Foreign Policy: Beliefs, Institutions, and Political Change,* edited by Judith Goldstein and Robert O. Keohane, pp. 3–30. Ithaca, NY: Cornell University Press.

Gómez, Laureano. 1934. *Para la Historia: El Conflicto con el Perú en el Parlamento.* Bogotá: Santa Fé.

Goodfellow, William, and James Morrell. 1990. "The Esquipulas Process." *International Policy Report* (December): 1–10.

Grader, Sheila. 1988. "The English School of International Relations: Evidence and Evaluation." *Review of International Studies* 14: 29–44.

Green, Rosario. 1990. "Nuevas Formas de Concertación Regional en América Latina: El Grupo de los Ocho." In *El Sistema Internacional y América Latina,* edited by Luciano Tomassini, pp. 257–75. Buenos Aires: GEL.

Guedes da Costa, Thomaz. 1998. "International Security and Institutions in the Americas: Fundamental Questions and Impasses for New Approaches." Paper presented at the meeting of the Latin American Studies Association, Chicago, September 24–26.

Guglialmelli, Juan E. 1978. "Argentina Ratifica el Tratado de Tlatelolco, Mientras las Superpotencias Condicionan su Adhesión al Segundo Protocolo Adicional." *Estrategia* 52/53 (March–June): 5–29.

———. 1979. *Geopolítica del Cono Sur.* Buenos Aires: El Cid Editor.

Harley, John E. 1934. *Documentary Textbooks on International Relations: A Text and Reference Study Emphasizing Official Documents and Materials Relating to World Peace and International Cooperation.* Los Angeles: Suttonhouse.

Henkin, Louis. 1995. *International Law: Politics and Values.* Dordrecht: Martinus Nijhoff Publishers.

Herrera Vegas, Jorge Hugo. 1995. "Las Políticas Exteriores de la Argentina y de Brasil: Divergencias y Convergencias." In *Argentina y Brasil: Enfrentando el Siglo XXI,* edited by Felipe A. M. de la Balze, pp. 171–215. Buenos Aires: LARI.

Hirst, Mónica. 1988. "El Programa de Integración Argentina-Brasil: De la Formulación a la Implementación." *FLACSO: Serie de Documentos e Informes de Investigación,* no. 67 (July): 1–27.

———. 1989. "Las Iniciativas Latinoamericanas en Materia de Desarme." In *Desarme y Desarrollo: Condiciones Internacionales y Perspectivas,* edited by Fundación Arturo Illía, pp. 37–52. Buenos Aires: GEL.

———, and Carlos Rico. 1992. "Regional Security Perceptions in Latin America." *Serie de Documentos e Informes de Investigación: FLACSO Buenos Aires,* no. 129, May.

Hoffmann, Stanley. 1981. *Duties beyond Borders: On the Limits and Possibilities of Ethical International Politics.* Syracuse, NY: Syracuse University Press.

Holguin, Alfredo. 1945. *Itinerario Internacional de Latinoamérica.* Bogotá: Kelly.

Holguín Pelaez, Hernando. 1980. *El Caso del Canal Beagle: Proceso Histórico-Jurídico.* Bogotá: Bloque Editorial Andino Ltd.

Holsti, Kalevi J. 1993. "Armed Conflicts in the Third World: Assessing Analytical Approaches and Anomalies." Paper presented at the annual meeting of the International Studies Association, Acapulco, Mexico, March.

———. 1996. *The State, War, and the State of War.* Cambridge: Cambridge University Press.

Hopf, Ted. 1998. "The Promise of Constructivism in International Relations Theory." *International Security* 23, no. 1 (Summer): 171–200.

Hudson, Manley O. 1933. *The Verdict of the League: Colombia and Peru at Leticia.* Boston: World Peace Foundation.

Hughes, Charles E. 1929. *Pan-American Peace Plans.* New Haven, CT: Yale University Press.

Huntington, Samuel P. 1991. *The Third Wave: Democratization in the Late Twentieth Century.* Norman: University of Oklahoma Press.

Hurrell, Andrew. 1998. "An Emerging Security Community in South America?" In *Security Communities,* edited by Emanuel Adler and Michael Barnett, pp. 228–64. Cambridge: Cambridge University Press.

Husbands, Jo L. 1979. "Nuclear Proliferation and the Inter-American System." In *The Future of the Inter-American System,* edited by Tom J. Farer, pp. 204–31. New York: Praeger.

Ibarra, José María Velasco. 1961. *Democracia Jurídica Interamericana*. Quito, Ecuador: Unión Interamericana de Periodistas para la XI Conferencia de Quito.

Infante Caffi, María Teresa. 1984. "Argentina y Chile: Percepciones del Conflicto de la Zona del Beagle." *Estudios Internacionales* 17, no. 67 (July–September): 337–58.

Insulza, José Miguel. 1987. "The Nuclearization of Latin America after Tlatelolco." *Politica Internazionale* 6, no. 1 (Spring): 51–59.

Ireland, Gordon. 1938. *Boundaries, Possessions, and Conflicts in South America*. Cambridge, MA: Harvard University Press.

Jackson, Robert H. 1990. *Quasi-states: Sovereignty, International Relations, and the Third World*. Cambridge: Cambridge University Press.

————. 1993. "The Weight of Ideas in Decolonization: Normative Change in International Relations." In *Ideas and Foreign Policy*, edited by Judith Goldstein and Robert O. Keohane, pp. 11–38. Ithaca, NY: Cornell University Press.

————, and Georg Sørensen. 1999. *Introduction to International Relations*. Oxford: Oxford University Press.

————, and Mark W. Zacher. 1996. "Westphalian Liberalism and the International Territorial Order." Paper presented at the ISA-JAIR Joint Convention, Makuhari, Japan, September 20–22.

Jacobini, H. B. 1954. *A Study of the Philosophy of International Law as Seen in Works of Latin American Writers*. The Hague: Martinus Nijhoff.

Jepperson, Ronald L., Alexander Wendt, and Peter J. Katzenstein. 1996. "Norms, Identity, and Culture in National Security." In *The Culture of National Security*, edited by Peter J. Katzenstein, pp. 33–75. New York: Columbia University Press.

Johnson, James Turner. 1991. "International Norms and the Regulation of War." In *The Long Postwar Peace: Contending Explanations and Projections*, edited by Charles W. Kegley, pp. 290–303. New York: HarperCollins.

Jones, Dorothy V. 1989. *Code of Peace: Ethics and Security in the World of the Warlord States*. Chicago: University of Chicago Press.

————. 1992. "The Declaratory Tradition in Modern International Law." In *Traditions of International Ethics*, edited by Terry Nardin and David R. Mapel, pp. 42–61. Cambridge: Cambridge University Press.

Kacowicz, Arie M. 1994. *Peaceful Territorial Change*. Columbia: University of South Carolina Press.

————. 1998. *Zones of Peace in the Third World: South America and West Africa in Comparative Perspective*. Albany: State University of New York Press.

————. 2000a. "Latin America as an International Society." *International Politics* 37, no. 2 (June): 143–62.

————. 2000b. "Stable Peace in South America: The ABC Triangle, 1979–1999." In *Stable Peace among Nations*, edited by Arie M. Kacowicz, Yaacov Bar-Siman-Tov, Ole Egström, and Magnus Jerneck, pp. 200–219. Lanham, MD: Rowman and Littlefield.

————, and Yaacov Bar-Siman-Tov. 2000. "Stable Peace: A Conceptual Framework." In *Stable Peace among Nations*, edited by Arie M. Kacowicz et al., pp. 11–35. Lanham, MD: Rowman and Littlefield.

Karst, Kenneth L., and Keith S. Rosenn. 1975. *Law and Development in Latin America: A Case Book*. Berkeley: University of California Press.

Katzenstein, Peter J., ed. 1996. *The Culture of National Security: Norms and Identity in World Politics.* New York: Columbia University Press.

Keck, Margaret E., and Kathryn Sikkink. 1998. *Activists beyond Borders: Advocacy Networks in International Politics.* Ithaca, NY: Cornell University Press.

Kegley, Charles W., and Gregory A. Raymond. 1986. "Normative Constraints on the Use of Force Short of War." *Journal of Peace Research* 23, no. 3 (September): 213–27.

———. 1990. *When Trust Breaks Down: Alliance Norms and World Politics.* Columbia: University of South Carolina Press.

Kelsen, Hans. 1942. *Law and Peace in International Relations.* Cambridge, MA: Harvard University Press.

———. 1968. "The Essence of International Law." In *The Relevance of International Law,* edited by Karl W. Deutsch and Stanley Hoffmann, pp. 85–92. Cambridge, MA: Schenkman Publishing Co.

Klotz, Audie. 1995. *Norms in International Relations: The Struggle against Apartheid.* Ithaca, NY: Cornell University Press.

Knight, Franklin W. 1992. "The State of Sovereignty and the Sovereignty of States." In *Americas: New Interpretive Essays,* edited by Alfred Stepan, pp. 11–29. New York: Oxford University Press.

Kocs, Stephen A. 1994. "Explaining the Strategic Behavior of States: International Law as System Structure." *International Studies Quarterly* 38, no. 4 (December): 535–56.

Kowert, Paul, and Jeffrey W. Legro. 1996. "Norms, Identity, and Their Limits: A Theoretical Reprise." In *The Culture of National Security,* edited by Peter J. Katzenstein, pp. 451–97. Ithaca, NY: Cornell University Press.

Krasner, Stephen D. 1982. "Structural Causes and Regime Consequences: Regimes as Intervening Variables." *International Organization* 36, no. 2 (Spring): 185–205.

Kratochwil, Friedrich. 1984. "Thrasymmachos Revisited: On the Relevance of Norms and the Study of Law for International Relations." *Journal of International Affairs* 37, no. 2 (Winter): 343–56.

———. 1987. "Norms and Values: Rethinking the Domestic Analogy." *Ethics and International Affairs* 1: 135–59.

———. 1989. *Rules, Norms, and Decisions: On the Conditions of Practical and Legal Reasoning in International Relations and Domestic Affairs.* Cambridge: Cambridge University Press.

Lagos, Gustavo. 1987. "Autopreservación y Autoexpansión del Estado-Nación y Experiencias de Cooperación Regional en América Latina." In *La Cooperación Regional en América Latina,* edited by Heraldo Muñoz and Francisco Orrego Vicuña, pp. 103–25. Mexico, DF: El Colegio de Mexico.

Lagos Carmona, Guillermo. 1966. *Historia de las Fronteras de Chile: Los Tratados de Límites con Perú.* Santiago, Chile: Editorial Andrés Bello.

Lanús, Juan A. 1984. *De Chapultepec al Beagle: Política Exterior Argentina, 1945–1980.* Buenos Aires: Emecé.

Latorre, Julio Corredor. 1932. *Información sobre el Actual Conflicto entre Colombia y el Perú.* Mexico, DF: A. Mijares y Hno.

Legro, Jeffrey W. 1997. "Which Norms Matter? Revisiting the 'Failure' of Internationalism." *International Organization* 51, no. 1 (Winter): 31–63.

Linz, Juan J., and Alfred Stepan. 1978. *The Breakdown of Democratic Regimes: Crisis, Breakdown, and Reequilibration.* Baltimore, MD: Johns Hopkins University Press.

Little, Walter. 1986/1987. "International Conflict in Latin America." *International Affairs* 63, no. 4: 589–603.

Lobo, Hélio. 1952. *Rio Branco e o Arbitramento com a Argentina.* Rio de Janeiro: Livraria José Olympio.

López, Alfonso. 1936. *La Política Internacional.* Bogotá: Imprenta Nacional.

Mackenzie, Mauricio. 1955. *Los Ideales de Bolívar en el Derecho Internacional Americano.* Bogotá: Imprenta Nacional.

Mahuad, Jamil. 1998. "Statement by Dr. Jamil Mahuad, President of Ecuador, on the Occasion of the Peace Signing Ceremony in Brasilia." Typescript, October 26.

Manwaring, Max G. 1983. "Monitoring Latin American Arms Control Agreements." In *Controlling Latin American Conflicts,* edited by Michael A. Morris and Victor Millán, pp. 163–84. Boulder, CO: Westview Press.

Marcella, Gabriel. 1999. "The Peace of October 1998." In *Security Cooperation in the Western Hemisphere: Resolving the Ecuador-Peru Conflict,* edited by Gabriel Marcella and Richard Downes, pp. 231–35. Miami: North-South Center.

———, and Richard Downes. 1999. "Introduction." In *Security Cooperation in the Western Hemisphere: Resolving the Ecuador-Peru Conflict,* edited by Gabriel Marcella and Richard Downes, pp. 1–19. Miami: North-South Center.

Mares, David R. 1994. "Inter-American Security Communities: Concepts and Challenges." In *Security, Democracy, and Development in US-Latin American Relations,* edited by Lars Schoultz et al., pp. 265–80. Miami: North-South Center.

———. 1995. "Esquema de Seguridad Regional: Una Perspectiva Comparada." In *Chile y Brasil,* edited by Francisco R. Aravena, pp. 9–24. Santiago, Chile: CLADDE-FLACSO.

———. 1997. "Regional Conflict Management in Latin America: Power Complemented by Diplomacy." In *Regional Orders,* edited by David A. Lake and Patrick M. Morgan, pp. 195–218. University Park: Pennsylvania State University Press.

———. 1999. "Political-Military Coordination in the Conflict Resolution Process: The Challenge for Ecuador." In *Security Cooperation in the Western Hemisphere: Resolving the Ecuador-Peru Conflict,* edited by Gabriel Marcella and Richard Downes, pp. 173–94. Miami: North-South Center.

Mariategui, Juan, ed. 1996. *El Conflicto Perú-Ecuador según Fuentes Peruanas.* Lima: Juan Mariategui.

Martínez-Vidal, Carlos, and Roberto M. Ornstein. 1990. "La Cooperación Argentino-Brasileña en el Campo de los Usos Pacíficos de la Energía Nuclear." In *Argentina-Brazil: Perspectivas Comparativas y Eje de Integración,* edited by Mónica Hirst, pp. 339–49. Buenos Aires: Tesis.

Maurtua, Víctor Manuel. 1919. *La Cuestión del Pacífico.* Lima.

McElroy, Robert W. 1992. *Morality and American Foreign Policy.* Princeton, NJ: Princeton University Press.

McIntyre, David. 1993. "'La Paz Larga': Why Are There So Few Interstate Wars in South America?" Typescript, Department of Political Science, University of Chicago.

McKenna, Peter. 1989. "Nicaragua and the Esquipulas II Accord: Setting a Record Straight." *Canadian Journal of Latin American and Caribbean Studies* 14, no. 27: 61–84.

McNeil, Franck. 1988. *War and Peace in Central America.* New York: Charles Scribner's Sons.

Mendoza Cubillo, Margarita I. 1990. *El Pensamiento Confederativo de Bolívar en las Naciones Unidas.* Guayaquil, Equador: Editorial Universitaria de Guayaquil.

Mercado Jarrín, Edgardo. 1989. *Un Sistema de Seguridad y Defensa Sudamericano.* Lima: Centro Peruano de Estudios Internacionales.

Mestre de Sánchez, Teresa, and Oscar Armando Mendoza. 1988. *El Proceso de Cooperación e Integración Argentino-Brasileño desde la Perspectiva Histórica de las Relaciones Bilaterales.* San Juan, Argentina: Universidad Nacional de San Juan, Centro de Estudios para la Integración Latinoamericana.

Meyer, Mary K. 1997. "Cooperation in Conflict: The Latin American Diplomatic Style of Cooperation in the Face of Foreign Threats." In *Cultural Variation in Conflict Resolution: Alternatives to Violence,* edited by Douglas P. Fry and Kaj Bjorkqvist, pp. 159–71. Mahwah, NJ: Lawrence Erlbaum Associates.

Millán, Victor. 1983. "Regional Confidence-Building in the Military Field: The Case of Latin America." In *Controlling Latin American Conflicts,* edited by Michael A. Morris and Victor Millán, pp. 89–97. Boulder, CO: Westview Press.

———, and Michael A. Morris. 1990. "Conflicts in Latin America: Democratic Alternatives in the 1990s." *Conflict Studies* 230 (April).

Mirek, Holger. 1986. "El Tratado de Tlatelolco: Limitaciones y Resultados." *Nueva Sociedad* 84: 16–27.

Moneta, Carlos J. 1988. "El Acercamiento Argentina-Brasil: De la Tensión y el Conflicto a la Competencia Cooperativa." *Documento de Trabajo—Prospel,* no. 11 (January).

Montes, Oscar Antonio. 1978. "Mensaje Declarando la Nulidad del Laudo Arbitral sobre la Cuestión del Beagle." *Estrategia,* no. 50 (January–February): 87–96.

Morgenthau, Hans. 1934. *La Realité des Normes: En Particulier des Norms du Droit International.* Paris: Librairie Felix Alcan.

———, and Kenneth W. Thompson. 1985. *Politics among Nations: The Struggle for Power and Peace.* 6th ed. New York: Alfred A. Knopf.

Morris, Michael A. 1983. "Naval Arms Control in Latin America." In *Controlling Latin American Conflicts,* edited by Michael A. Morris and Victor Millán, pp. 147–61. Boulder, CO: Westview Press.

———. 1989. *The Strait of Magellan.* Dordrecht: Martinus Nijhoff.

———. 1994. "Medidas de Confianza Mutua en Sudamerica." In *Medidas de Confianza Mutua en América Latina,* edited by Augusto Varas and Isaac Caro, pp. 101–32. Santiago, Chile: FLACSO.

———, and Victor Millán. 1983. "Introduction." In *Controlling Latin American Conflicts,* edited by Michael A. Morris and Victor Millán, pp. 1–10. Boulder, CO: Westview Press.

———. 1987. "Confidence-Building Measures in Comparative Perspective: The Case of Latin America." In *Confidence-Building Measures in International Security,* edited by R. B. Byers, F. Stephen Larrabee, and Allen Lynch, pp. 125–42. New York: Institute for East-West Security Studies.

Morris, Michael A., and Martin Slann. 1983. "Proliferation of Weaponry and Technology." In *Controlling Latin American Conflicts*, edited by Michael A. Morris and Victor Millán, pp. 117–46. Boulder, CO: Westview Press.

Mosquera, Carlos Julio. 1994. *La Conciencia Territorial Argentina y el Tratado con Chile de 1881/1893*. Buenos Aires: Círculo Militar.

Müller, Harald. 1993. "The Internalization of Principles, Norms, and Rules by Governments." In *Regime Theory and International Relations*, edited by Volker Rittberger, pp. 361–88. Oxford: Clarendon Press.

Muñoz, Heraldo. 1994. "A New OAS for the New Times." In *Latin America in a New World*, edited by Abraham F. Lowenthal and Gregory F. Treverton, pp. 191–202. Boulder, CO: Westview Press.

Nadelman, Ethan A. 1990. "Global Prohibition Regimes: The Evolution of Norms in International Society." *International Organization* 44, no. 4 (Fall): 479–526.

Nardin, Terry. 1983. *Law, Morality, and the Relations of States*. Princeton, NJ: Princeton University Press.

———. 1992. "Ethical Traditions in International Affairs." In *Traditions of International Ethics*, edited by Terry Nardin and David R. Mapel, pp. 1–22. Cambridge: Cambridge University Press.

Nordquist, Kjell-Åke. 1992. "Peace after War: On Conditions for Durable Inter-State Boundary Agreements." Ph.D. diss., Uppsala University, Sweden.

O'Donnell, Guillermo, and Philippe C. Schmitter. 1986. *Transitions from Authoritarian Rule: Tentative Conclusions about Uncertain Democracies*. Baltimore, MD: Johns Hopkins University Press.

Olmos, Mario E. 1986. *La Cooperación Argentina-Brasil: Nucleo Impulsor de la Integración Latinoamericana*. Buenos Aires: Instituto de Publicaciones Navales.

Onuf, Nicholas Greenwood. 1989. *World of Our Making: Rules and Rule in Social Theory and International Relations*. Columbia: University of South Carolina Press.

———. 1998. "How Things Get Normative." Unpublished manuscript.

Palacio, Ernesto. 1905. *Historia de la Argentina. Vol. 2: 1835–1943*. Buenos Aires: A. Peña Lillo.

Palma, Hugo. 1992. "Zonas de Paz, Posibilidades y Perspectivas en América Latina." In *Seguridad, Paz, y Desarme*, edited by Augusto Varas, pp. 59–79. Santiago, Chile: CLADDE-FLACSO.

Palomar, Jorge. 1996. "Chile: Una Invasión Pacífica." *La Nación Online*, October 13. http://www.lanacion.com.ar.

Pande, Savita. 1993. "Argentina-Brazil Nuclear Accord: Competition to Cooperation." *Strategic Analysis* 16, no. 4 (July): 425–37.

Paradiso, José. 1996. "El Poder de la Norma y la Política del Poder, 1880–1916." In *La Política Exterior Argentina y sus Protagonistas, 1880–1995*, edited by Silvia Ruth Jalabe, pp. 13–25. Buenos Aires: GEL.

Passarelli, Bruno. 1998. *El Delirio Armado. Argentina-Chile: La Guerra que Evitó el Papa*. Buenos Aires: Editorial Sudamericana.

Pastor, Carlos W. 1996. "Chile: La Guerra o la Paz, 1978–1981." In *La Política Exterior Argentina y sus Protagonistas, 1880–1995*, edited by Silvia Ruth Jalabe, pp. 259–308. Buenos Aires: GEL.

Pastor, Robert A. 1992. *Whirlpool: U.S. Foreign Policy toward Latin America and the Caribbean*. Princeton, NJ: Princeton University Press.

Patiño Mayer, Hernan. 1996. "The Future of Cooperative Hemispheric Security in the Americas." In *Beyond Praetorianism: The Latin American Military in Transition*, edited by Richard L. Millet and Michael Gold-Biss, pp. 1–10. Miami: North-South Center.

Patrick, Stewart McLellan. 1997. "The Evolution of International Norms: Adaptation, Learning, Socialization, and Hegemony." Paper presented at the annual meeting of the International Studies Association, Toronto, March 18–22.

Paz y Figueroa, Ricardo Alberto. 1980. *El Conflicto Pendiente*. Buenos Aires: EUDEBA.

Perera, Srilal. 1985. "The OAS and the Interamerican System: History, Law, and Diplomacy." In *The Falklands War: Lessons for Strategy, Diplomacy, and International Law*, edited by Alberto R. Coll and Anthony C. Arend, pp. 132–55. Boston: George Allen and Unwin.

Pérez Canto, Julio. 1918. *El Conflicto Después de la Victoria*. 2nd ed. Santiago, Chile: Zig Zag.

Peru. 1923. *Arbitration between Peru and Chile: The Case of Peru*. Washington, DC: National Capital Press.

———. 1924. *Arbitration between Peru and Chile: The Counter Case of Peru in the Matter of the Controversy Arising Out of the Question of the Pacific*. Washington, DC: National Capital Press.

———. 1961. *Documentos Básicos sobre el Protocolo de Rio de Janeiro de 1942 y su Ejecución*. 3rd ed. Lima: Ministerio de Relaciones Exteriores.

———. 1996. *Frontera Peruano-Ecuatoriana: Selección de Memoranda e Informe Final de George McBride, Asesor Técnico Norteamericano para la Comisión Mixta Demarcadora de Límites*. Lima: Ministerio de Relaciones Exteriores.

Petrocelli, Héctor B. 1995. *Las Misiones Orientales: Parte del Precio Que Pagó Urquiza para Derrocar a Rosas*. Buenos Aires: Instituto de Investigaciones Históricas Juan Manuel de Rosas.

Pettit, Philip. 1990. "*Virtus Normativa*: Rational Choice Perspective." *Ethics* 100, no. 4 (July): 725–55.

Piñero, Norberto. 1924. *La Política Internacional Argentina*. Buenos Aires: J. Menendez e Hijo.

Porcelli, Luis A. 1991. *Argentina y la Guerra por el Chaco Boreal*. Buenos Aires: Centro Editor de América Latina.

Proceedings of the Commission of Inquiry and Conciliation, Bolivia and Paraguay. 1929. Washington, DC, March 13–September 13.

Puig, Juan Carlos. 1983. "Controlling Latin American Conflicts: Current Juridical Trends and Perspectives for the Future." In *Controlling Latin American Conflicts*, edited by Michael A. Morris and Victor Millán, pp. 11–39. Boulder, CO: Westview Press.

———. 1985. *Solución Pacífica de Conflictos en América Latina y Crítica de los Procedimientos Existentes*. Santiago, Chile: FLACSO.

———. 1987. *Integración Latinoamericana y Régimen Internacional*. Caracas: Universidad Simón Bolívar, Instituto de Altos Estudios de América Latina.

Raymond, Gregory A. 1997. "Problems and Prospects in the Study of International Norms." *Mershon International Studies Review* 41, no. 2 (November): 205–45.

Redick, John R. 1981. "The Tlatelolco Regime and Nonproliferation in Latin America." *International Organization* 35, no. 1 (Winter): 103–34.

———. 1994. "Latin America's Emerging Non-Proliferation Consensus." *Arms Control Today* 24, no. 2 (March): 3–9.

———. 1995. "Iniciativas de No Proliferación Nuclear de Argentina y Brasil." *Revista Occidental* 12, no. 3: 341–59.

———, Julio C. Carasales, and Paulo S. Wiebel. 1995. "Nuclear Rapprochement: Argentina, Brazil, and the Nonproliferation Regime." *Washington Quarterly* 18, no. 1 (Winter): 107–23.

Resende-Santos, João. 1998. "From Enduring Rivalry to Cooperation in South America." Paper presented at the annual meeting of the Latin American Studies Association, Chicago, September 24–26.

Revista Chilena de Historia y Geografía. 1984. "El Problema de Límites con Argentina: Cuatro Documentos Fundamentales." 152: 179–217.

Rio Branco, Barão do. 1894 [reprint 1945]. *Questão de Limites entre o Brasil ea República Argentina.* Rio de Janeiro: Ministerio des Relações Exteriores.

Ríos Gallardo, Conrado. 1959. *Chile y Perú: Los Pactos de 1929.* Santiago, Chile: Editorial Nascimento.

Risse-Kappen, Thomas. 1995. "Democratic Peace—Warlike Democracies? A Social Constructivist Interpretation of the Liberal Argument." *European Journal of International Relations* 1, no. 4 (December): 491–517.

Rodó, José Enrique. 1922. *Ariel.* Translated by F. J. Simpson. Boston: Houghton Mifflin Co.

Roniger, Luis, and Mario Sznajder. 1998. "Introduction: Examining Collective Identities and Public Spheres in Latin America." In *Constructing Collective Identities and Shaping Public Spheres: Latin American Paths,* edited by Luis Roniger and Mario Sznajder, pp. 1–10. Brighton, England: Sussex Academic Press.

Ronning, C. Neale. 1963. *Law and Politics in Inter-American Diplomacy.* New York: John Wiley and Sons.

Rouquié, Alain. 1994. *Guerras y Paz en America Central.* Mexico, DF: Fondo de Cultura Económica.

Rout, Leslie B. 1970. *Politics of the Chaco Peace Conference, 1935–1939.* Austin: Institute of Latin American Studies, University of Texas Press.

Roy, Dean A. 1997. "*Uti Possidetis*: The Basis for Peaceful Territorial Resolution and Change in Latin America." Typescript, Department of Government, University of Notre Dame, December.

Rudman, Andrew I. 1990. "Argentine-Brazilian Integration: A Brief Historical Overview." Working Papers, Latin American Program, Washington, DC. The Woodrow Wilson Center, no. 181: 1–13.

Ruggie, John G. 1998. *Constructing the World Polity: Essays on International Institutionalization.* London: Routledge.

Ruiz Moreno, Isidoro. 1961. *Historia de las Relaciones Exteriores Argentinas: 1810–1955.* Buenos Aires: Editorial Perrot.

Russell, Roberto. 1989. "La Posición de Argentina Frente al Desarme, la No Proliferación y el Uso Pacífico de la Energía." In *Desarme y Desarrollo: Condiciones Internacionales y Perspectivas,* edited by Fundación Arturo Illía, pp. 53–82. Buenos Aires: GEL.

Russett, Bruce. 1993. *Grasping the Democratic Peace: Principles for a Post-Cold War World.* Princeton, NJ: Princeton University Press.

Russett, Bruce, and Harvey Starr. 1989. *World Politics: The Menu for Choice.* 4th ed. New York: W. H. Freeman.

Saavedra Lamas, Carlos. 1937. *Por la Paz de las Americas.* Buenos Aires: M. Gleizer.

San Martín, Alejandro. 1987. "Confidence-Building Measures and the Arms Limitations Process." In *Regional Cooperation for Development and the Peaceful Settlement of Disputes in Latin America,* edited by Jack Child, pp. 123–34. New York: Martinus Nijhoff Publishers.

Scenna, Miguel Angel. 1975. *Argentina-Brasil: Cuatro Siglos de Rivalidad.* Buenos Aires: Editorial La Bastilla.

——. 1981. *Argentina-Chile: Una Frontera Caliente.* Buenos Aires: Editorial Universidad de Belgrano.

Scott Palmer, David. 1999. "The Search for Conflict Resolution: The Guarantors and the Peace Process in the Ecuador-Peru Dispute." In *Security Cooperation in the Western Hemisphere: Resolving the Ecuador-Peru Conflict,* edited by Gabriel Marcella and Richard Downes, pp. 21–44. Miami: North-South Center.

Segre, Magdalena. 1990. "La Cuestión Itaipú-Corpus: El Punto de Inflexión en las Relaciones Argentino-Brasileñas." *FLACSO—Serie Documentos e Informes de Investigación,* no. 97 (September): 1–39.

Selcher, Wayne. 1985. "Recent Strategic Developments in South America's Southern Cone." In *Latin American Nations in World Politics,* edited by Heraldo Muñoz and Joseph S. Tulchin, pp. 87–120. Boulder, CO: Westview Press.

Serrano, Mónica. 1992. "Common Security in Latin America: The 1967 Treaty of Tlatelolco." Manuscript, University of London, Institute of Latin American Studies, no. 30.

Sikkink, Kathryn. 1996. "Reconceptualizing Sovereignty in the Americas: Historical Precursors and Current Practices." Paper presented at the conference "The Role of International Law in the Americas: Rethinking Sovereignty in an Age of Regional Integration," Mexico City, June 6–7.

Silva, Carlos Alberto. 1946. *La Política Internacional de la Nación Argentina.* Buenos Aires: Imprenta de la Cámara de Diputados.

Simmons, Beth A. 1999. *Territorial Disputes and Their Resolution: The Case of Ecuador and Peru.* Peaceworks 27. Washington, DC: United States Institute of Peace.

Soares, Teixeira. 1973. *Historia da Formaçaõ das Fronteiras do Brasil.* Rio de Janeiro: Biblioteca do Exercito.

Sørensen, Georg. 1998. "Sovereignty at the Millenium: Change and Continuity in a Fundamental Institution." Paper presented at the Third Pan-European International Relations Conference, Vienna, September 16–19.

Stanley, Ruth. 1992. "Co-operation and Control: The New Approach to Nuclear Non-Proliferation in Argentina and Brazil." *Arms Control* 13, no. 2 (September): 191–213.

Steiner, Kristian. 1998. "Norms and Regional Conflicts in a Post-Westphalian System." Paper presented at the Third Pan-European International Relations Conference, Vienna, September 16–19.

Stinson, Hugh B., and James D. Cochrane. 1971. "The Movement for Regional Arms Control in Latin America." *Journal of Inter-American Studies* 13 (January): 1–17.

St. John, Ronald Bruce. 1976. "The End of Innocence: Peruvian Foreign Policy and the United States, 1919–1942." *Journal of Latin American Studies* 8, no. 2 (November): 325–44.

———. 1994. *The Boundary between Ecuador and Peru.* Durham, England: International Boundaries Research Unit, Department of Geography, University of Durham.

Subedi, Surya P. 1996. *Land and Maritime Zones of Peace in International Law.* Oxford: Clarendon Press.

Tannenwald, Nina. 1992. "Dogs That Don't Bark: The United States, the Role of Norms, and the Non-Use of Nuclear Weapons in the Post WWII Era." Ph.D. diss., Department of Government, Cornell University.

Tanzer, Sharon. 1992. "Reporteur's Summary." In *Averting a Latin American Nuclear Arms Race: New Prospects and Challenges for Argentine-Brazilian Nuclear Cooperation,* edited by Paul L. Leventhal and Sharon Tanzer, pp. 9–46. London: Macmillan.

Thomson, Janice E. 1993. "Norms in International Relations: A Conceptual Analysis." *International Journal of Group Tensions* 23, no. 1: 67–83.

Tinoco, Víctor Hugo. 1989. *Conflicto y Paz: El Proceso Negociador Centroamericano.* Mexico, DF: Editorial Mestica.

Torres Armas, William. 2001. "Bolivia-Paraguay: El Reencuentro de Dos Voluntades." In *Bolivia: País de Contactos: Un Análisis de la Política Vecinal Contemporánea,* edited by Ramiro Orias Arredondo, Alfredo Seoane Flores, and William Torres Armas, pp. 219–70. La Paz, Bolivia: Fundenos.

Treverton, Gregory F. 1984. "Inter-state Conflicts in Latin America." Working Papers, Latin American Program, The Woodrow Wilson Center, no. 154. Washington, DC.

Ullmann-Margalit, Edna. 1977. *The Emergence of Norms.* Oxford: Clarendon Press.

———. 1990. "Revision of Norms." *Ethics* 100, no. 4 (July): 756–67.

United Nations. 1996. *The Blue Helmets: A Review of UN Peace-Keeping.* New York: U.N. Department of Public Information.

United States Congress, Subcommittee on Disarmament of the Committee on Foreign Relations, U.S. Senate. 1957. "Disarmament and Security in Latin America." *Staff Study,* no. 7, May 12.

Varas, Augusto. 1983. "Controlling Conflict in South America: National Approaches." In *Controlling Latin American Conflicts,* edited by Michael A. Morris and Victor Millán, pp. 71–87. Boulder, CO: Westview Press.

———. 1985. *Militarization and the International Arms Race in Latin America.* Boulder, CO: Westview Press.

———. 1988. *La Política de las Armas en América Latina.* Santiago, Chile: FLACSO.

———. 1992. "Zonas de Paz en América Latina: Una Propuesta Factible?" In *Seguridad, Paz, y Desarme,* edited by Augusto Varas, pp. 81–87. Santiago, Chile: CLADDE-FLACSO.

————. 1995. "La Seguridad Hemisférica Cooperativa de Post-Guerra Fría." In *Chile y Brasil*, edited by María Cristina de los Ríosm, pp. 25–634. Santiago, Chile: CLADDE-FLACSO.

Vasquez, John A. 1992. "A Territorial Explanation of War." Paper presented at the annual meeting of the International Studies Association, Atlanta, April.

————. 1993. *The War Puzzle*. Cambridge: Cambridge University Press.

————. 1994. "Building Peace in the Post-Cold War Era." In *From Rivalry to Cooperation: Russian and American Perspectives on the Post-Cold War Era,* edited by Manus I. Midlarsky, John A Vasquez, and Peter V. Gladkov, pp. 207–18. New York: HarperCollins.

Väyrynen, Raimo. 1997. "Norms, Compliance, and Enforcement in Global Governance: Theories and Policies." Paper presented at the Canadian-U.S. Conference on Global Governance, Kroc Institute, University of Notre Dame, May 8–10.

Vázquez Cobo, Alfredo. 1985. *Pro Patria: La Expedición Militar al Amazonas en el Conflicto de Leticia*. Bogotá: Banco de la República, Departamento Editorial.

Velit Granda, Juan. 1992. "Cooperación Para la Paz: Perspectiva del Perú." In *Seguridad, Paz, y Desarme,* edited by Augusto Varas, pp. 89–103. Santiago, Chile: CLADDE-FLACSO.

Waalkes, Scott. 1997. "How International Law Constructs State Interests and Identities: Practical Lessons from the Persian Gulf." Paper presented at the annual meeting of the International Studies Association. Toronto, Canada. March 18–22.

Wallensteen, Peter. 1984. "Universalism vs. Particularism: On the Limits of Major Power Order." *Journal of Peace Research* 21 (August): 243–57.

Watson, Adam. 1992. *The Evolution of International Society*. London: Routledge.

Wendt, Alexander. 1992. "Anarchy Is What States Make of It: The Social Construction of Power Politics." *International Organization* 46, no. 2 (Spring): 391–425.

————. 1995. "Constructing International Politics." *International Security* 20, no. 1 (Summer): 71–81.

————. 1999. *Social Theory of International Politics*. Cambridge: Cambridge University Press.

Whitehead, Lawrence. 1991. "The Imposition of Democracy." In *Exporting Democracy: The United States and Latin America,* edited by Abraham F. Lowenthal, pp. 216–42. Baltimore, MD: Johns Hopkins University Press.

Wiarda, Howard J. 1995. *Democracy and Its Discontents: Development, Interdependence, and U.S. Policy in Latin America*. Lanham, MD: Rowman and Littlefield.

Wight, Martin. 1966. "Western Values in International Relations." In *Diplomatic Investigations,* edited by Herbert Butterfield and Martin Wight, pp. 89–131. London: George Allen and Unwin.

Willis, Barley, ed. 1918. *'Rose Book' of Chile: Communication Exchanged between the Chancelleries of Chile and of Peru Regarding the Question of Tacna and Arica, 1905–1908*. Washington, DC: Government Printing Office.

Wilson, Joe F. 1979. *The United States, Chile, and Peru in the Tacna and Arica Plebiscite*. Washington, DC: University Press of America.

Wilson, Peter. 1989. "The English School of International Relations: A Reply to Sheila Grader." *Review of International Studies* 15: 49–58.

Windass, Stan. 1970. "The League and Territorial Disputes." In *The International Regulation of Frontier Disputes,* edited by Evan Luard, pp. 31–85. New York: Praeger.

Wood, Bryce. 1966. *The United States and Latin American Wars, 1932–1942.* New York: Columbia University Press.

————. 1978. *Aggression and History: The Case of Ecuador and Peru.* New York: Columbia University Press.

Wrobel, Paulo S. 1993. "A Diplomacia Nuclear Brasileira: A Não Proliferação Nuclear e o Tratado de Tlatelolco." *Contexto Internacional* 15, no. 1 (January–June): 27–56.

Zacher, Mark W. 2001. "The Territorial Integrity Norm: International Boundaries and the Use of Force." *International Organization* 55, no. 2 (Spring): 215–50.

Zea, Leopoldo. 1990. *Descubrimiento e Identidad Latinoamericana.* Mexico, DF: Universidad Nacional Autónoma de Mexico.

Zeballos, Estanislao S. 1893. *Arbitration upon a Part of the National Territory of Misiones Disputed by the United States of Brazil; Argentine Evidence Laid before the President of the United States of America.* New York: S. Figueroa.

————. 1894. *Argument for the Argentine Republic upon the Question with Brazil in Regard to the Territory of the Misiones.* Washington, DC: Gibson Brothers.

Zook, David H. 1964. *Zarumilla-Marañón: The Ecuador-Peru Dispute.* New York: Bookman Associates.

ARIE M. KACOWICZ is senior lecturer in international relations at the Hebrew University of Jerusalem.